KOREA: ECONOMIC, POLITICAL AND SOCIAL ISSUES

Korea: Economic, Political and Social Issues

Paul H. Elwood and Jeremy B. Albertus
Editors

Nova Science Publishers, Inc.
New York

For permission to use material from this book please contact us:
Telephone 631-231-7269; Fax 631-231-8175
Web Site: http://www.novapublishers.com

LIBRARY OF CONGRESS CATALOGING-IN-PUBLICATION DATA

Korea:economic,political and social issues/Paul H. Elwood and Jeremy B. Albertus(editors).
p.cm.
Includes bibliographical references and index.
ISBN 978-1-60456-513-3(hardcover:alk.paper)
1. Korea(South) — Economic conditions — 1988-2.Korea(South)—Social conditions — 1988-3. Korea(South) — Politics and government — 1988-2002.4.Korea(South) — Politics and government — 2002-5.Monetary police — Korea(South)6.Teenagers — Substance use — Korea(South)7.Korea(North) — Foreign relations — China.8.China — Foreign relations — Korea(North) I.Elwood, Paul H. II.Albertus, Jeremy B.
HC467.96.K662 2008
330.95195—dc22

2008012144

Published by Nova Science Publishers, Inc. ≈ New York

CONTENTS

PREFACE

Korea is known as the "land of the morning calm", an expression that comes from the ancient Korean dynasty of Koryo (918-1392). Koryo means "high" and "clear", thus symbolizing the clear blue skies of Korea. Thus the beautiful nature of Korea is expressed through its ancient name.

The Korean Peninsula adjoins China in the north-west, while Japan lies to the southeast. Throughout history, this geopolitical location has led to much hardship for Korea, including Japan's colonial rule (1910-1945), the tragic division into South and North Korea at the end of Word War II, and the devastating Korean War (1950-1953). Nevertheless, thanks to the successful implementation of a growth-oriented economic policy from the 1960s, Korea has enjoyed remarkable economic development, which has become known as the "Miracle on the Han-gang River".

With the international exposure of the 24th Summer Olympics which were hosted in Seoul in 1988, Korea's economic achievements and the richness of its unique culture were revealed to the world. More recently, Korea's continued economic advancement was evidenced by its membership in the OECD and WTO in 1996. And while Korea was hit hard by the Asian financial crisis in late 1997, it is now well on the road to recovery as a result of the new administration's effective leadership and the indefatigable spirit of the Korean people.

Korea is striving to emerge as an exemplary member of the global community by actively opening its markets and welcoming foreign investment into the country. Moreover, considerable efforts are being exerted to attract wider attention to its traditional culture and arts, which uniquely reflect Korea's history of several thousand years.

This new book focuses on economic, political and social issues.

Chapter 1 - There exists a large volume of literature on Korean success in economic development. However, Korea has experienced several economic crises in the development process. While the financial crisis in 1997 has received a substantial amount of attention in the mass media and in the academic as well, Korea had not been immune to economic crisis prior to the 1997 financial crisis. This chapter reviews the experiences of economic crises and their resolutions in Korea since the 1960s. The chapter examines each crisis and finds out that the factors that caused one previous crisis later brought about another crisis repeatedly. This indicates that the measures to resolve the previous crises were ultimately ineffective in the sense that the fundamental causes for the economic crisis had remained unresolved and, as a result, recurrence of the crisis has not been prevented. Most of the past crisis resolution measures were focused on disposing of the losses incurred by firms and banks through such instruments as bail-out loans. Stabilization measures were adopted just when the economy had begun to stagnate after a long period of boom, and seldom contributed to preventing recurrence of crisis; they rather amplified the intensity of the crisis. These results contain lessons for the current and future structural adjustment policy, to be adopted as a means to prevent recurrence of economic crisis. First, it should be designed in such a way as to encourage private agents to take initiative, with the government abstaining from direct intervention such as bail-out loans. This would eventually strengthen private sector capacities to overcome adverse shocks. Second, stabilization policies should be implemented in such a preemptive manner that they can prevent an exceptional boom or wide-spread speculation.

Chapter 2 - This paper is concerned with the conduct of monetary and exchange rate policy in Korea. It inquires into the best way of characterizing central bank policy since the financial crisis of 1997-1998, asking specifically whether the Bank of Korea should be portrayed as an open-economy inflation targeter. National officials will insist that the answer is yes – that the Bank of Korea has pursued inflation targeting since at least 2000 and that it no longer targets the exchange rate, either explicitly or implicitly. The central bank has adopted much of the apparatus of inflation targeting, complete with a band for target inflation and a Monetary Policy Report to the National Assembly. The 2004 version, the most recent edition available at the time of writing, stipulates an annual target of 3 per cent plus or minus 1 per cent, along with a medium-term (longer than one year) inflation target of 2.5-3.5 per cent; it makes little mention of the exchange rate. Trends in the dollar/won exchange rate are mentioned in passing, but no implications are drawn for the conduct of monetary policy. From this it would appear that the exchange rate plays little role in monetary policy in Korea.

In a sense it would be surprising were this the case, for in an economy as open and sensitive to foreign trade and investment as Korea, movements in the exchange rate will contain information useful for forecasting movements in inflation and the output gap, the two arguments of the standard objective function of a central bank that engages in flexible inflation targeting. Movements in the exchange rate determine movements in import prices, which are passed through into the prices of domestic substitutes and thereby affect the prospects for inflation. Movements in the exchange rate also affect the short-to-medium-term evolution of the output gap, whether through changes in competitiveness (owing to incomplete passthrough) or balance-sheet effects (if a country's external assets and liabilities are dollarized). They may have implications for other valid concerns of the central bank such as the stability of the financial system. Hence, even if the central bank does not attach utility to the exchange rate itself (even if the value of the currency is not itself an argument of the authorities' objective function), the exchange rate can still be an important intermediate target for monetary policy. This in fact is the conclusion of virtually all recent analytical work on the conduct of inflation targeting in open economies.

In addition, there is the conclusion of authors like McKinnon and Schnabl (2003) that when exchange rate changes are measured at high frequencies the day-to-day volatility of the dollar exchange rates of the principal East Asian countries, including Korea, is not significantly greater than before the crisis. To be sure, other authors have reached different conclusions: Oh (2004a) computes various measures of exchange rate volatility before and after the crisis (the percentage change in the absolute value of the end of day price between successive days, the difference between the highest and lowest price during the day as a percentage of the intra-daily average exchange rate) and finds more than a doubling of both measures between 1 March 1995-31 October 1997 and 1 April 1998-30 September 2003. The same conclusion comes through even more strongly in Eichengreen (2003) when the standard deviation of the exchange rate is normalized by the standard deviation of reserves. Be this as it may, a number of authors have expressed surprise that the won exchange rate has not displayed more variability at high frequencies in the last six years and asked whether the Bank of Korea is not in fact a covert exchange rate targeter.

In this paper the author, therefore, revisits the question of how to characterize the conduct of monetary and exchange rate policy in Korea. Should the Bank of Korea be portrayed as a flexible inflation targeter? Does it use its monetary policy instrument – the overnight call rate – to target inflation and other variables potentially of concern (the output gap, the stability of the financial system) to while allowing the exchange rate to passively adjust to that interest rate setting, which is what would seem to be suggested by the Monetary Policy Report? Or does it attach independent importance to the exchange rate and modify its monetary policy stance when a putative setting for the overnight call right implies an uncomfortably large change in the exchange rate?

The author's answer to the first question is yes: a standard Taylor-type inflation targeting rule is a useful way of characterizing the Bank of Korea's policy. At the same time, movements in the exchange rate are too important for the objectives of central bank policy to effectively be disregarded, as they are in large, less open de facto inflation targeters like the United States. It is not surprising in this light that his analysis suggests that when setting the overnight call rate the Bank of Korea in fact responds to not just expected inflation and the output gap but also to movements in the won/dollar exchange rate. The author thus prefer to think of its monetary regime not as a free float backed by inflation targeting but as a managed float accompanied by modified inflation targeting.

Having provided a characterization of Korean monetary policy, the author next considers some special issues that arise in context of inflation targeting in a relatively advanced emerging market such as Korea. He asks whether the controversy over the role that the exchange rate has actually played in the conduct of monetary policy suggests that Korean policy has been insufficiently transparent. In addition, previously authors (like McKinnon and Schnabl) having asked whether Korea has to follow the United States, Japan and Euroland when formulating its monetary and exchange rate policies, he inquires into the implications of the emergence of China. Finally, he asks how the development of the Korean economy and its financial markets should influence the conduct of monetary and exchange rate policies going forward.

Chapter 3 - Since the Korean government enacted the 'Technology Transfer Promotion Act' in the year 2000 to enhance technology transfer and technology commercialization, the trends of university R&D in Korea have been drastically changed. One of the most dramatic changes was focusing on the entrepreneurial aspects of R&D, such as technology transfer and technology commercialization. And as a result, universities in Korea have enjoyed increased number of transfers and handsome revenues from their technology transfer activities. This paper aimed to identify the major factors related to the amount of revenues from the sales of research outcomes. Utilizing the panel data from Korea Association of University technology managers, accumulated from 2000 to 2004, the authors identified the influential factors to the revenues of universities, as the number of patents, the type and amount of subsidies from the government, the reputation of the universities and the location of Technology Licensing Offices (TLOs). The results emphasized the importance of the effective management of the

TLOs in the early stage of commercialization and productive implementation of government and university policies.

Chapter 4 - The TFT-LCD industry started in Japan, where during 1992-1994 companies invested in eight 2~2.5 generation TFT-LCD production lines. At the time, the main application was in notebook panels. Once Korean firms entered the fray against their large Japanese competitors, the market became overly competitive and supply exceeded demand, leading to repaid price drops. During 1995-1996, the three largest Korean firms Samsung, LG. Philips and Hydis set up four 3~3.5- generation TFT-LCD production lines within the period of one year, following which switched their LCD focus from notebook computers to the monitor product market. Yet fluctuations in international economic trends led to the 1997 Asian economic meltdown, which seriously harmed Japanese and Korean firms. Taiwanese firms were less seriously affected, and although they lacked the large dimension panel production experience of their Japanese and Korean counterparts, Taiwan firms had their advantages. They had the capital, and the downstream industries to support the development of the notebook and monitor industries. Taiwan firms engaged in technology partnerships with Japanese firms and in 1998-1999 established seven 3~3.5-generation TFT-LCD production lines. This was their formal entry into the TFT-LCD arena.

Before 2000, Japan was the dominant producer in the large size TFT-LCD industry, holding 49.5% of the global market, with Korea second with 36.8%. Taiwan only had 13.7%. Yet Taiwanese and Korean firms invested more aggressively in new factories while Japanese firms remained more conservative, which allowed Korea to overtake Japan in the large size TFT-LCD industry in 2001, with a 40.5% share internationally. Japan fell to 33.5% while Taiwan enjoyed 26.1%. As Japanese firms were withdrawing from production of large size TFT-LCD panels and switching to high resolution and low power consumption LTPS (low temperature poly-silicon) display development, Taiwanese firms wrestled 38% of the world market in the first quarter of 2004, while Korea still holding over 45%.

In light of the fact that the three main producers in the large size TFT-LCD product market are Taiwan, Japan, and Korea, the commercial behavior of firms in these countries will intimately influence the development of this industry. Moreover, Taiwan and Korea occupy a process technology niche position in the large size TFT-LCD industry; both nations focus on panel manufacturing. Japan, on the other hand, has a system specification niche position and has emphasized technology R&D, thus taking control of the development of components and manufacturing equipment. This allows Japanese firms to avoid the price slashing competition with Taiwan and Korea and to increase their production technology royalty earnings. Taiwan and Korea firms are Japan's largest technology transfer customers, and the strategic alliances between Japanese and Taiwanese firms are very close. Therefore, there is now more cooperation than competition between Japan and Taiwan.

This study focuses on the large size TFT-LCD industry in Taiwan and Korea, investigating the structures these two countries possess in the industry and the differences in their manufacturing strategies. Future development suggestions for Taiwanese firms will also be presented.

Chapter 5 - Following the trend started in the 1980s and became quite distinctive during the 1990s, the financial systems of the center and the periphery converged towards the Anglo-Saxon market-based model. Let it be so: *prima facie* reason for all evils in the age of the so-called globalization is the unstable character of capital accumulation in the central economies, especially in a world with no limitations to finance capital. For the sake of its own profitability, global finance capital has always been seeking to overcome the devaluation of capital by penetrating into developing and underdeveloped countries. Along with the hegemony of neo-liberal policies and *laissez-faire* ideology, these countries, which are now called "emerging markets" in neoliberal parlance, liberalized capital movements across borders and reduced or totally eliminated foreign exchange controls. This paved the way for deregulation of the domestic financial markets. Thus, offered high arbitrage incomes brought about the large scale short-term capital inflows to such countries, especially in form of "*hot money*". Consequently, the hot money inflows themselves became the cause of instability with high and growing volatility which finally resulted in serious financial crises. Meanwhile, the advocates of neo-liberal policies anticipated that liberalization policies would inevitably remove inequalities between countries and result in convergence. As a matter of fact, convergence has taken place, but not in the way as anticipated by the neo-classical approaches. The "trinity" of financial liberalization, deregulation and integration with international markets has made many countries converged in financial crises; in line with that, instead of reducing intra-national and international income disparities, it has sharpened them.

Triggered by such instability, repeatedly were observed the financial crises, some major of which outburst in Turkey in 1994 and 2000-2001, in Mexico during the years 1994-95, again in 1995 and later in 2001 in Argentina, in 1997 in Southeast Asia, in Russia in 1998, in Brazil in 1999 and 2002. Financial instability as a global fact, on the one hand, is experienced as a very geographical peculiarity; it is, on the other, with abraded border of the "nation", experienced with common features. Thus, from a point of view centered on above mentioned phenomena, not only the detection of similarities but also of differences enables us to elaborate on the present condition of the world and her future, at least it gives us the clues to understand. Turkey, of course, from the geographical standpoint should have been focused on; since the introspection is possible with the case. So, this study aims to make a comparative analysis of the financial crises of Turkey in 1994 and 2001, Mexico in 1994-1995, and South Korea in 1997.

Mexican and South Korean financial crises were selected for a comparison due to two reasons: Firstly, before the 1997 Asian crisis, two regions were distinguished on how they were affected by financial circumstances in developed countries, and on the impact of their own financial policies. These were Latin Americas where financial liberalization policies were implemented rapidly (*big bang* with the sole objective of international market integration) and East Asia where financial policies were designed in order to serve the objectives of economic development. In this context, Mexico can be considered as a typical country in the first category, while South Korea emerges as an important country in the second one. Therefore, the South Korean and the Mexican experiences have been selected for a comparison with Turkey with which they have some similarities. Secondly, fundamental macroeconomic indicators of these two countries can allow the exposition of the hot money flows resulted in instability and financial crushes. When the pre-crisis macroeconomic indicators are taken into consideration, as will be made explicit later, although Mexico and South Korea, unlike Turkey, had quite fiscal balances, they could not avoid the financial crises. Over and above, even the South Korea's incompatible industrial strategy and her proper economic indicators could not preclude the crisis. That is, why the selection of Mexico and South Korea as somewhat reagents provides us with the chance of searching out the reasons Turkish crises. In spite of exhaustive analysis of both Mexican and Korean cases (and recent ones on Turkish case), there will be some methodological and empirical novelties in this study: (i) a detailed analysis of the balance of payments data utilizing a useful and functional conceptual framework will enable us to distinguish arbitrage-seeking ("hot") capital movements from other inflows/outflows; (ii) a decomposition of inflows/outflows into the resident and non-resident components will generate a framework by means of which parallel (pro-cyclical) and diverging (counter-cyclical) behavior of residents/non-residents can be distinguished; (iii) although it is usually possible to find out the destination of resident outflows, non-resident "hot" inflows can, in some countries, be decomposed into the types of asset in which they are invested. Such decompositions can provide the basis for further causal or policy-based analysis.

There is another vital conceptual point to be mentioned: It is the term *new cycle*. A number of economists critical of the neo-liberal policy recipes have emphasized the role and importance of capital movements (and particularly their "hot" components) and their reversal in generating a new type of cycle which, in some cases, incorporates a financial crisis. The large increase in capital inflows leading to a boom and the reversal of it, accompanied, in some cases, by banking and/or currency crises is the typical pattern that explains our *cycle*. Residents may aggravate or dampen the cycle. Although the composition of inflows to developing countries and their maturity has varied over time and by countries, and such variation has affected the overall volatility of the flows, the common feature during the 1990s has been a rapid expansion of private short-term capital flows into and out of developing countries. Accordingly *the new cycle* guides us to the very simple understanding (by empirical means) of our three cases.

The following section compares the financial systems and the process of financial liberalization and deregulation in each country prior to the crises and overviews the path financial crises have followed in each economy. Section three undertakes to set forth the method of calculation of the magnitudes of capital flows and examines the empirical data. A general assessment in the light of the findings of previous sections, in section four, urges us to conclude.

Chapter 6 - In this chapter our primary starting point is the conviction that the post-modern turn in social theory unlocked and valorised the potential of the creative arts and humanities for the sociological imagination. This legitimised a broader rejection than hitherto of those kinds of 'scientifically' based analyses which flattened out the rich complexity of social life. Post-modernism played a highly fruitful and productive role in the social sciences in valorising or re-valorising a long list of dimensions whose legitimacy had been in question. After postmodernism it has been far more difficult to simply dismiss the relevance and powers of, *inter alia*, phenomenology, hermeneutics and interpretation, emotionality, sensuality, a sense of place, social bonds, aesthetics, textuality, narrative and story-telling, a consciousness of time and history, nostalgia, values, and morality. In addition to its role in liberating these many rich dimensions of being, of ontology and the ontic, which had been secreted away and ignored or left underdeveloped, postmodernism also embodied a healthy scepticism towards claims to objective knowledge. The latter, in retrospect, was closely linked to the former. It was inevitable that postmodernism's sensitivity to the greater complexity of being – which included the complicated relationship between being human and such things as meaning, embodiment, emotion and memory – would be mirrored by a greater sensitivity to the embeddedness of knowledge in this complexity, and thus to the ensuing partial and corrigible nature of all kinds of knowledge.

Chapter 7 - In this review of the literature on substance use, juvenile delinquency and criminal behavior, three specific themes are addressed: 1) the prevalence of substance use among Korean adolescents; 2) the risk factors associated with substance use; and 3) the relationship between substance use and delinquency. Studies have shown that the prevalence of substance use/abuse is steadily increasing among Korean adolescents and elsewhere in the world, and the types of frequently used substance have diversified. Familial, intrapersonal, social, and cultural factors all appear to contribute to a given individual's risk for substance use/abuse, and the preponderance of evidence indicates that substance (i.e. alcohol) use could play a causal role for delinquent and violent behavior. However, the relationship between substance use and violence is interactional and multi-factorial, and differs depending on the type of drug.

Chapter 8 - As a result of the economic crisis that rocketed through Asia in 1997-1998 several countries went through political transitions. In South Korea and Thailand, democratic elections resulted in opposition parties coming to power. In Indonesia, President Suharto was forced out of office after more than 30 years in power. In Malaysia, Prime Minister Mahathir's ruling coalition won only 56% of the popular vote (down from 70% in 1995) in 1999 elections, and, for a brief window (from 1997-2001), there was mounting political opposition to Mahathir's regime. This paper asks what the connection is between civil society and political change, and, how might we understand the variation in political transformations that occurred. Research for this project shows that several independent variables are useful in explaining the variation in political transitions: IMF involvement, popular protests, the nature of opposition groups and civil society, and elite coalition formation/dissolution at the highest levels of government.

Chapter 9 - The current relationship between the People's Republic of China (PRC) and the Democratic People's Republic of Korea (DPRK) is more than friendly, but it can hardly be called an alliance relationship. The two countries signed the Treaty of Friendship, Cooperation and Mutual Assistance in July 1961, and the "treaty cannot be revised or abrogated without prior mutual agreement (Article 7)". However, despite the treaty, after the death of Kim Il Sung in 1994, China has not been able to exert strong influence upon North Korea. The leader of DPRK, Kim Jong Il, has been pursuing adventurous and brinkmanship activities independently for the national interests of North Korea, irrespective of the perceptions and national policies of China. Beijing always aspires to have a stable and peaceful security environment, so as to concentrate her efforts towards the modernization of the country. Paradoxically, China does never explicitly express her dissatisfaction of the misbehaviour of her neighbour, though by all means she is very much annoyed by those adventurous activities of North Korea that eventually drag the other powers, including Russia and Japan, into this crucial adjacent area of China. The alliance relationship could not be maintained as it was during the Kim Il Sung period, when Beijing was able to master the external behaviour of Kim, while also serving as a kind of intermediary in North Korea's relationship with the West. A hypothetical scenario could further test the so-called alliance relationship. If North Korea were attacked by the United States, would China assist in rescuing the North Korean regime and nation by sending army, similar to the Korean War in early fifties? Nobody would think that this is a possible scenario, and no serious scholars would also consider that the PRC would send an army to rescue her neighbour.

This paper aims at investigating the dilemmas that China has to face in formulating and elaborating her policies vis-à-vis North Korea, especially after the September 11th incident in

New York which causes a serious dislocation of power constellation in the international political order. Washington has been trying very hard, and not without success, to construct a worldwide "united front" in order to counter-attack terrorism. Beijing supports anti-terrorism, since it is burdened with fighting against the terrorist activities caused by the Xinjiang separtists who seek to establish the so-called East Turkistan. China aspires to establish a peaceful and stable external environment, especially in Northeast Asia, Central Asia, as well as South Asia, so that she could concentrate her energies on Taiwan problem and the South China Sea issues. The brinkmanship activities of North Korea have long been a matter of serious concern among Chinese leaders and analysts. Hopefully, with the "sunshine policy" of President Kim Dae Jung of South Korea which resulted in his visit in Pyongyang in June 2000, and the apparent amelioration of relationship between Pyongyang and Washington in the same year, it seems that China could feel secure and stable regarding her northeast border. However, with the advent of power of President Bush in 2001, who characterizes North Korea as a member of "axis of evil" after Iraq and Iran, Kim Jong Il gain uses the nuclear instrument in exchange for concrete benefits from the United States. He has especially sought for the guarantee of not attacking North Korea, through the establishment of a pact of non-aggression with the United States. Through the vicissitudes of Pyongyang's actions against the Bush administration since 2001, China has to face a series of dilemmas. It is aimed in this paper to reveal these dilemma and to analyze what efforts China has to make in order to resolve the problems caused by these dilemmas.

In: Korea: Economic, Political and Social Issues
Editors: P. H. Elwood, J. B. Albertus
ISBN: 978-1-60456-513-3

Chapter 1

WHY HAS KOREA EXPERIENCED SO MANY ECONOMIC CRISES? THE POLITICAL ECONOMY OF RECURRING ECONOMIC CRISIS IN KOREA

Jong Kyu Lee[1,*] and Sanghack Lee[2,†]
[1]Institute for Monetary and Economic Research, The Bank of Korea
[2]School of Economics, Kookmin University

ABSTRACT

There exists a large volume of literature on Korean success in economic development. However, Korea has experienced several economic crises in the development process. While the financial crisis in 1997 has received a substantial amount of attention in the mass media and in the academic as well, Korea had not been immune to economic crisis prior to the 1997 financial crisis. This chapter reviews the experiences of economic crises and their resolutions in Korea since the 1960s. The chapter examines each crisis and finds out that the factors that caused one previous crisis later brought about another crisis repeatedly. This indicates that the measures to resolve the previous crises were ultimately ineffective in the sense that the fundamental causes for the economic crisis had remained unresolved and, as a result, recurrence of the crisis has not been prevented. Most of the past crisis resolution measures were focused on disposing of the losses incurred by firms and banks through such instruments as bail-out loans. Stabilization measures were adopted just when the economy had begun to stagnate after a long period of boom, and seldom contributed to preventing recurrence of crisis; they rather amplified the intensity of the crisis. These results contain lessons for the current and future structural adjustment policy, to be adopted as a means to prevent recurrence of economic crisis. First, it should be designed in such a way as to encourage private agents to take initiative, with the government abstaining from direct intervention such as bail-out

* Tel: +82-2-759-5412, Fax: +82-2-759-5410, e-mail: jonglee@bok.or.kr
† Corresponding author. Address: School of Economics, Kookmin University, Seoul 136-702, South Korea. Tel.: +82-2-910-4546, Fax: +82-2-910-4519, e-mail: slee@kookmin.ac.kr

loans. This would eventually strengthen private sector capacities to overcome adverse shocks. Second, stabilization policies should be implemented in such a preemptive manner that they can prevent an exceptional boom or wide-spread speculation.

Keywords: Korea, Economic Crisis, Crisis Resolution, Structural Adjustment, Macroeconomic Policy, Economic History of Korea

I. Introduction

There exists a large volume of literature on Korean[1] success in economic development. However, it should be noted that Korea has also experienced several economic crises in the development process. While the financial crisis in 1997 has received huge amount of attention in the mass media and in the academic as well, Korea was not immune to economic crisis prior to 1997 financial crisis. This neglect of past economic crisis of Korea is partly attributable to spectacular performance of the Korean economy. It should, however, be noted that Korean economy had also experienced several economic crises before the 1997 crisis.

The Korean government adopted various policies or institutional devices to prevent recurrence of economic crisis since 1997. Commonly known as 'restructuring policy' or 'structural adjustment policy,' these policies aimed at preventing crisis by improving the structural efficiency of the Korean economy.

Whether such restructuring policies are on the right track, however, has been heavily disputed[2]. In light of a wide variety of criticism from various points of view, this chapter tries to reinterpret Korean experiences of economic crises in the past from a new viewpoint, and also tries to extract lessons for structural adjustment policies.

Most of the discussions and research on structural adjustment, now being extensively studied around the world, draw their arguments from experiences in the process of economic development, rather than from a general theoretical framework. The concept of structural adjustment was introduced by the World Bank; the World Bank came to use the term structural adjustment as it recognized, after many trials and errors, the importance of improving the efficiency of an economic system as a whole in achieving sustained growth. Since, it is practically impossible to design an ideal economic system *a priori*, any country that wants to improve the efficiency of its economic system will need to learn from its own experience, or from other countries' experiences in similar situations.

Foreign experience has only limited usefulness as a reference, however, because there are many factors specific to a country that make its experience difficult to apply to another country's structural adjustment process. In this respect, deriving lessons for a country from its own experience of structural adjustment would be more useful. Perhaps this is why, in the U.S.A., the Great Depression of 1929 is still a popular topic of research. Also, it is quite

---

[1] Korea refers to South Korea.

[2] The set of methods for assessing the effectiveness of restructuring policy includes: 1) comparing performances before and after reforms are introduced, 2) comparing actual performance with reform objectives, 3) comparing the economic performance of the reforming country with those of non-reforming countries, 4) comparing the economic performances of cases of reforming and cases of not reforming through counterfactual simulation (Schandler et al., 1995).

natural for one who wants to resolve a present problem to seek lessons from the past successes and failures.

Despite all the past restructuring, Korea is not immune to future economic crisis. The purpose of this research is to find out ways to enhance the effectiveness of measures for possible future economic crisis in Korea, by making use of the lessons extracted from the past economic crises Korea experienced since the launch of industrialization policy in the 1960s, and their resolutions. Even though Korea's history of economic development is relatively short, it contains several episodes of crisis worthy of thorough analysis. In particular, the experience of overcoming several crises in the past can be a valuable source of lessons useful in resolving the future crisis. Korean experience in crisis resolution as well as economic development can be a valuable asset to other countries seeking to emulate Korean economic success.

This chapter will look into the specifics and backgrounds of, and the policy measures undertaken to deal with four crises in Korea, and analyze the effectiveness of those policy measures. Besides the period since 1997, Korea has had several occasions of severe economic difficulties – including the period from the late 1960s to the early 1970s, that around 1980, and that from the late 1980s to the early 1990s. By comparing the specifics of each crisis, we are able to better understand the nature of the economic crises in Korea. Further, by assessing the effects of policies to resolve the former crises, we may be better able to derive some important policy agenda for overcoming the future crisis.

The discussion will proceed keeping an eye on the causal aspects of each economic crisis: formation of bubbles, deterioration of profitability in the corporate sector, weaknesses in financial structure, maturity mismatches, and policy mistakes. This will provide a basis for comparing crises whose actual causes differed from each other in kind and in specifics.

It should also be mentioned that this chapter reviews critically the past experience in coping with crises. This criticism stems from the observation that the same factors that had caused a previous crisis later brought about another crisis repeatedly. For example, the factors behind the 1997 crisis were similar to those behind the past crises. This implies that the measures taken to resolve the previous crises were ultimately limited and/or ineffective.

The remainder of this paper is organized as follows. Section II starts with general discussion on the definition and causes of economic crisis. Section II then describes and analyzes the details, backgrounds, and policy responses by government to the four Korean episodes of economic crises[3]. In Section III the crisis resolution measures are assessed in terms of their effectiveness. On the basis of this, derivation of effective crisis resolution measures will be considered. In Section IV, the characteristics of the 1997 economic crisis are summarized, and the structural adjustment policy implemented afterwards is compared with those implemented in past cases. Finally, in the Concluding Remarks, the usefulness and limitations of this research are discussed and new research directions are suggested.

[3] The main contents of Section II and Section III are excerpted from Lee (2000). Those who are interested in details are advised to refer to Lee (2000).

II. KOREAN EXPERIENCE IN RESOLVING ECONOMIC CRISES

1. Four Economic Crises of Korea

An economic crisis is a situation of extreme economic difficulties, such as firms and banks going out of business one after another, the prices of goods, exchange rates, or interest rates fluctuating very rapidly, or production decreasing sharply with the unemployment rate increasing. Thus, it is sometimes treated as being equivalent to a severe recession.

This concept, however, does not give any information about the economic crisis, and is not so much helpful to theoretically grasping its systematic aspects. It is thus preferable to define an economic crisis as a situation in which exceptional responses of economic agents to unexpected economic events hamper the proper functioning of major parts of the economic system, and in extreme cases cause the whole system to collapse. In short, an economic crisis refers to a situation in which part or all of the economic system does not function normally, causing economic difficulties.

An economic system comprises various components. When all of the components combine organically and harmoniously, it works properly. When the various components do not combine harmoniously, it malfunctions. In this sense, an economic crisis is a kind of coordination failure – one especially severe in nature.

Table 1. Factors Behind Economic Crises

<table>
<tr><th colspan="2">Theory</th><th>Causes</th></tr>
<tr><td colspan="2">Business Cycles</td><td>– macroeconomic disequilibrium: over-investment, under-consumption
– discrepancy between monetary and natural(real) interest rates
– misperception or incorrect forecast
– changes in profit rate</td></tr>
<tr><td colspan="2">Monetarist</td><td>– banking panic</td></tr>
<tr><td colspan="2">Financial Instability Hypothesis</td><td>– bubbles: speculative mania</td></tr>
<tr><td rowspan="2">Micro-finance Theory</td><td>Intrinsic Factors</td><td>– imperfect information
– information asymmetry
– nature of debt contracts
– asset specificity
– herd behavior
– "me-first" tendency</td></tr>
<tr><td>Immediate Causes</td><td>– deterioration of profitability
– financial fragility
– maturity mismatches
– bubbles</td></tr>
<tr><td colspan="2">Others</td><td>– policy failures
– failures in internal risk control</td></tr>
</table>

The term "economic crisis" carries a strong negative connotation since the phenomenon itself brings economic suffering to many people. It also has a positive aspect, however, because economic problems which need to be addressed reveal themselves in a crisis. For instance, economic crisis tends to occur when an economy suffers from difficulties in adapting itself to a changed environment; once it occurs, the part of the economic system which has been unable to adapt is revealed. Therefore, an economic crisis also plays the positive role of informing policy makers and the general public of what the fundamental weaknesses of the system are, thus providing an opportunity for an economy to correct them and prosper again.

In the course of economic development, an economy faces significant changes in its economic environment. Sometimes, it adapts itself to them successfully. Sometimes, it fails. In the latter case, a crisis or a crisis-like situation takes place. In this sense, economic crisis represents the adaptive failure of an economy. Finally, an economic crisis, though it is exceptional and unique, is a universal phenomenon that can happen to any economy in any phase of development.

The factors leading to economic crises, as identified in the literature, are summarized in Table 1. This list is not intended to be exhaustive; there are many unknown causes, as is revealed by the fact that a crisis usually comes by surprise.

There are two kinds of theories for explaining the factors behind an economic crisis[4]. One pertains to the causes for an economic crisis and the other to the propagation mechanism of an economic crisis. Business cycle theories, monetarists' views, the financial instability hypothesis, and microeconomic finance theories are examples of the former. The views that attribute an economic crisis to policy failures, or to failure in internal risk control, also belong to this type of theory. On the other hand, contagion effects among sectors and countries, the effect of rumor, and the crisis-hit economy's loss of ability to restore equilibrium are the main building blocks of the latter type of theory. Therefore, it would be reasonable to mention two different sets of causes of economic crisis, in accordance with the two theories. Nevertheless, Table 1 lists the causes of economic crisis drawn from the first type of theory alone, since these causes seem to be applicable in case of economic crisis propagation as well.

Table 1 does not include shocks external to an economy as a cause of economic crises. The reason is mainly because this chapter aims at *deriving lessons* from the experience discussed; in other words, recognition of external shocks as the cause of a crisis does not lead to a meaningful answer to the question: what should we do to prevent another crisis? Therefore, it is preferred here to recognize internal vulnerabilities as the main cause of crisis. On the basis of this approach, the table focuses on causes of economic fragility[5].

Among various factors listed, the table refers to intrinsic factors behind an economic crisis, including imperfect information, herd behavior, and so on. These are hard to eliminate since they are intrinsic to human nature or the capitalist economic system. Thus, in cases where these factors are the main cause of a crisis, it would be hard to cure that crisis fundamentally. This is why herd behavior, though frequently blamed as the culprit, is seldom studied in depth. Unlike the case with external shocks, research on intrinsic factors can

---

[4] One of the reasons why there are few studies of economic crisis is that the mainstream economics have considered it too exceptional or abnormal a phenomenon to fit into their equilibrium model framework.

[5] In what follows are arguments that attribute the past economic crises in Korea to worsening world economic environments. However, this is not so much to identify the external shocks as the causes of the crisis as to represent the economic recession or deterioration of profits indirectly by it.

provide significant clues to understanding the process of economic development since the history of economic development can be said to have been a process of overcoming the limits imposed by these factors. Thus, a systematic study of an economic crisis will show the ways to long-term economic development as well as crisis resolution. This theme, however, is beyond the scope of this paper. This chapter will focus on the immediate causes of economic crisis, such as deterioration of profitability, financial fragility, maturity mismatches, and bubbles.

Based on the general understanding of the causes for an economic crisis and the measures for coping with it, we can identify four economic crises in Korea. There have been four crises[6], or similar situations, since the year 1962, when the first five-year economic development plan began. The first economic crisis took place during the period from the late 1960s to the early 1970s; it was characterized by high inflation, large and expanding current account deficits in the wake of the late 1960s economic boom, snowballing foreign debts, decreasing business profits, deteriorating financial soundness of firms, and impending large scale business failures in the early 1970s. The second crisis, around 1980, came about in the wake of the second global oil shock, soaring international interest rates, political unrest, and a bad harvest. Production literally decreased, and the foreign debt situation was so bad that the country could not repay some of them. The third crisis, during the period from the late 1980s to the early 1990s, was called a "critical situation on the whole." It followed deterioration in the international competitiveness of domestic firms, over-consumption and speculative bubbles on assets such as real estate. The fourth crisis, finally, happened in 1997. It was accompanied by serial bankruptcy of large business firms and increases in non-performing loans at financial institutions. Figure 1 depicts the growth rates of GDP since the 1960s and the economic crises in Korea.

2. The 1972 Economic Crisis

A. Unfolding of the Crisis[7]

The Korean economy faced a crisis in the early 1970s after an investment boom in the late 1960s, corresponding to the first half period of the second 5-year economic development plan. Investment stagnated three years in a row, from 1970 on (refer to table 2). Apparently, economic growth rates were not so bad. However, capital formation plummeted, casting doubt on future growth potential. Current account also deteriorated. It seems that not only the government's economic stabilization policy, which began around the end of 1969, but also the worsening of the firms' debt-servicing burdens contributed to the stagnation of business investment; firms could not expand their production capacity since they were under strong pressure to repay debts that had accumulated to very risky levels during the previous boom period. The stagnation of investment was a critical obstacle to the government's ambitious economic development plan to develop the heavy and chemical industries.

[6] Here, an economic crisis is seen simply as a severe economic difficulty or economically critical situation.

[7] This explanation of the 1972 economic crisis is largely based on Kim (1990).

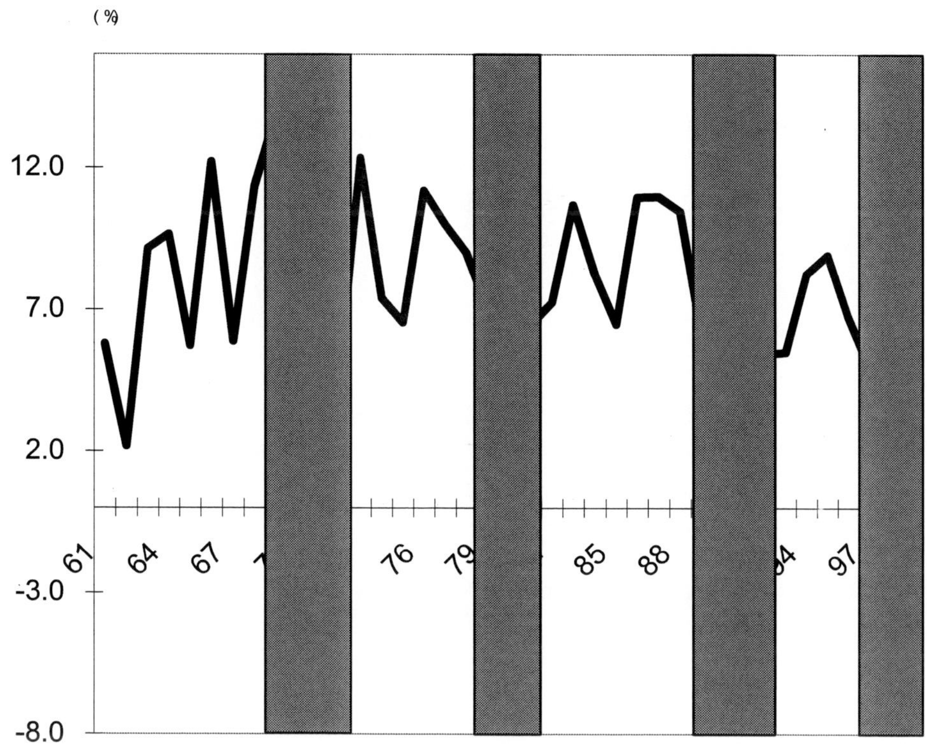

Note: The shaded areas indicate the periods of economic crises.
Source: The Bank of Korea, *Economic Statistics Yearbook*, various issues.

Figure 1. Growth Rates of GDP: Four Crisis Periods.

Table 2. Trends of Major Economic Indicators up to 1972

	1967	1968	1969	1970	1971	1972
Economic Growth[1](%)	5.9	11.3	13.8	8.8	8.6	4.9
(manufacturing)	21.6	27.2	21.6	19.9	18.5	14.3
Consumption	8.3	9.6	9.4	9.5	8.2	4.6
Capital formation	22.6	37.4	24.8	1.0	3.0	1.2
Exports	32.7	39.5	36.1	19.6	21.5	37.5
Imports	30.8	43.6	26.6	8.0	19.2	0.7
Current Account (100mil.USD)	-1.9	-4.4	-5.5	-6.2	-8.5	-3.7
WPI(rate of change, %)	6.5	8.1	6.9	9.4	8.6	13.8
CPI(rate of change, %)	10.9	10.8	12.8	15.5	13.5	11.7
M_2(end of year, rate of change, %)	61.7	72.0	61.4	27.4	20.8	33.8
Budget Balance[2]/GDP(%)	-2.57	-1.83	-3.10	-1.88	-1.70	-5.01

[1] Growth rates of GDP are on the basis of 1975 prices up to 1970 and thereafter on the basis of 1995 prices.

[2] Only the budget of central government is included.

Source: The Bank of Korea, *Economic Statistics Yearbook*, various issues.

Moreover, the number of delinquent firms had increased since the economic recession that began around 1969; many firms could not repay their foreign loans, which were guaranteed by domestic banks. The third-party banks' repayments of the foreign debt amounted to 0.5 billion Won in March 1970, and increased to 2.3 billion Won in August 1971[8]. The increase in business delinquencies might have been affected by the worsening profitability of firms due to the downturn of the business cycle. But the most important factor was the huge debt-servicing burden. The foreign loans that had been raised in large amounts in the late 1960s were reaching maturity. The burden had been further exacerbated by the Won depreciation, from 271.20 Won to 304.35 Won per US dollar in November 1969, and again to 370.80 won in June 1971.

By 1969, the government had recognized the seriousness of the situation and launched an operation to liquidate insolvent firms, by establishing an insolvent-firm liquidation unit under direct control of the president. In May 1969, this unit designated 30 foreign debt laden firms and 56 firms under bank control as insolvent[9].

The government was eventually forced to resort to an emergency decree on August 3rd, 1972, in consideration of the several factors as follows. First, the government perceived it difficult to let many delinquent firms go bankrupt because they were too big to fail and they were also greatly indebted to foreign banks, and their bankruptcies would have triggered a rush by international lenders to collect loans, and at the same time made them unwilling to provide new loans. Once this happened, the Korean economy would have faced severe difficulties in financing its economic development plan for the heavy and chemical industries since domestic savings were very limited in those days.

Second, policy makers began to worry that the firms' weak financial positions might bring about a disaster for firms and banks; the increase in the number of delinquent firms posed a potential threat to the banking system due to the increase in non-performing loans. Moreover, since the government had just started its campaign for heavy and chemical industrialization, the weak financial structures of the major firms were also perceived as a threat to the government's vision of economic development through active investment in those industries.

Finally, the booming curb money market was suspected as one of the main culprits behind the increasing number of corporate insolvency. Curb market lenders collected their loans whenever the borrowers were known to have difficulties in debt-servicing, ignoring the implicit maturities of the loans. The curb markets were thought to have other adverse effects on the economy as well, such as providing tax loopholes and disturbing the orderly operation of the financial system. On these grounds, the government issued the August 3rd Decree, aiming at improving corporate financial structure.

Thus, the early 1970s economic crisis was a corporate crisis in nature; that is, the primary source of the crisis was corporate insolvencies. Such factors as foreign debts, a slowdown in economic growth, and inflation were only secondary.

[8] The size of M_1 was about 300 billion won, and that of M_2 was about 900 billion won at the end of 1970.

[9] The unit was later succeeded by the corporation rationalization commission which took over the job of liquidation of troubled firms.

B. Background of the Crisis

(1) A Boom Financed by High Leverage – Rent Seeking through Financial Regulation

In the background of the worsening corporate financial positions lay the investment boom in the late 1960s, which was financed by ever-increasing leverage. Following the interest rate liberalization measures in September 30, 1965, monetary aggregates expanded rapidly (refer to Table 2). Together with this, the economy began to grow at more than 10 percent a year, with business investment growth averaging 28.3 percent a year during the period from 1967 to 1969. Lacking internal funds, however, domestic firms had to rely on external funds, especially bank loans. This implied that the faster the economy grew, the larger the borrowings of the firms, and the more vulnerable the firms would be to external shocks. This was what happened to Korean firms in the late 1960s. The debt-equity ratio of Korean manufacturing increased from 93.7 percent in 1965 to 394.2 percent in 1971. The financial expenses-to-sales ratio increased, accordingly, from 3.91 to 9.86 percent during the same period.

The high rate of return on investment in real assets, along with rapid economic growth, augmented corporations' ever-increasing demand for borrowing. A development boom raised the prices of real estate in several regions, and speculative investments boosted them further to extremely high levels. This produced a situation in which the gap between the rate of return in the real sector and that in the financial sector never narrowed. Even though the sum of the growth rates of GDP and the consumer price index, which was 22.3 percent on average during the period from 1967 to 1971, was lower than the lending rate for general funds, at 24.2 percent a year, the rate of return in the real sector is believed to have exceeded that in the financial sector because the levels of prices of many products were under strong government control. Moreover, considering the lending rates for policy loans such as equipment funds, the borrowing costs of firms seem to have been no more than half of their rates of return on investment.

(2) Underdevelopment of the Financial System

As a further background cause of the crisis, it can be pointed out that the financial system then was so backward that bank loans were almost the only source of external funds for most firms. The financial markets were segmented into a formal one and an informal one. Securities markets were in such an inactive state that they could be said to have been almost non-existent. There were several reasons for this. Firstly, the stock market was sluggish after a scandalous boom and bust in the early 1960s; secondly, expectation of inflation remained at a high level, which discouraged long-term investments in securities. Also, with most firms in their early stages of development and thus not proven to be creditworthy, fund raising through new issues of equity in the capital market was an unrealistic option. Thus, the increased demand for funds was mostly met by bank loans, and the excess demand for bank loans was spilled over to the curb markets.

Table 3. Financial Indicators of Korean Manufacturing Industry (%)

	1965	1966	1967	1968	1969	1970	1971	1972
Debt-equity ratio	93.7	117.7	151.2	201.3	270.0	328.4	394.2	313.4
Financial expenses-sales ratio	3.91	5.65	5.19	5.90	7.81	9.15	9.86	7.08
Net income-assets ratio	7.9	7.8	6.7	5.4	3.6	0.9	0.9	3.8

Source: The Bank of Korea, *Financial Statements Analysis,* various issues.

Table 4. Interest Rates and Related Indices (%)

	1965	1966	1967	1968	1969	1970	1971	1972
Interest rate on commercial bill discounts[1]	24.0	24.0	24.0	26.0	24.6	24.0	22.0	15.5
Interest rate on equipment funds[2]	11.5	11.5	11.5	11.5	12.0	12.0	12.0	10.0
Economic growth rate(A)	5.7	12.2	5.9	11.3	13.8	8.8	8.6	4.9
Rate of change in CPI [3](B)	13.5	11.2	10.9	10.8	12.8	15.5	13.5	11.7
A+B	19.2	23.4	16.7	21.7	26.7	24.4	22.1	16.4

[1] Offered by deposit monetary banks as of the end of year.
[2] Offered by the Industrial Bank of Korea as of the end of year.
[3] The figure in 1965 is for the Seoul district, and figures in 1966 and thereafter for all cities.
Source: The Bank of Korea, *Economic Statistics Yearbook*, various issues.

The distortion in financial parameters, a side-effect of the measures liberalizing interest rates in 1965, encouraged firms to borrow excessively and thus led them to suffer from excessive debt service burdens. As a result of the policy of keeping interest rates on policy loans at lower-than-the-market level, the loan-deposit interest rate spread became negative. This created excessive speculative demand for funds, thus distorting orderly operation of the financial system, and eventually resulting in the underdevelopment of the Korean financial system.[10]

(3) Adverse Effects of Economic Stabilization Policy

In the latter half of the 1960s, various signs of an overheating economy such as widening current account deficits and soaring prices emerged. The government, therefore, executed a comprehensive stabilization policy in November 1969[11]. However, this aggravated the difficulties of most firms, which had weakness in their financial structure. The main contents of the stabilization policy were regulation of private borrowing from abroad, tightening of government expenditures, control of the money supply, and so on (The Bank of Korea 2000, pp. 166). In particular, the Bank of Korea changed the monetary policy regime, from indirect monetary targeting to direct control of the domestic credits of financial institutions from 1970 on. In the meantime, as the economy cooled down, the Bank of Korea lowered the interest rates, which had been at excessively high levels since the interest rate rationalization in 1965.

[10] Lee and Cheong (2007) offer an empirical and theoretical analysis for the political economy of financial structure of Korean firms. They argue that financial markets are repressed to create rent, which were shared by politicians and business sectors. Kang (2002) also provides a related research on this issue.
[11] This measure was encouraged in part by the IMF.

The firms over-laden with large debts and their debt-servicing costs went to the curb market for funds when their access to financial institutions and foreign loans were limited. Because the interest rate in the curb market then climbed to and maintained levels higher than 3~4 percent a month (over 40 percent a year), the firms' financial burdens increased all the more. Furthermore, the risks of bankruptcy of firms increased as the economy marched into recession.

(4) Worsened World Economic Situation

Economic stagnation in advanced countries, in the wake of the breakdown of the old international monetary system (the Bretton-Woods system), also aggravated the difficulties of Korean firms, along with the domestic business slowdown. The United States found it difficult to maintain a fixed exchange rate for the dollar with its increasing current account and fiscal deficits. Thus, the U.S. suspended the convertibility of the dollar to gold and devalued it in 1971. As major industrial economies also adopted floating exchange rate systems, international financial markets became more volatile and the world economy subsequently began to stagnate. Influenced by this, the growth rate of Korean exports slowed down and, accordingly, profitability of the firms decreased. As a result, the firms' burdens of debt servicing worsened.

C. Crisis Resolution Measures

As the economy began to stagnate in early 1971, the government adopted a loose monetary policy stance, reversing the 1969 stabilization policy by lowering the interest rate and devaluing the Won on June 28th, 1971. In addition, a series of policy measures to boost the economy were adopted in February 1972. In spite of these policy measures, the firms continued to suffer, and the government finally promulgated the 'Emergency Decree for Economic Stability and Growth' on August 2nd, 1972, to come into effect on the following day.

The substance of the August 3rd Emergency Decree included above all rescheduling of the loans borrowed from the curb market as well as the banks (including the conversion of debts into capital) and promotion of policies boosting the economy. With a view to alleviating the debt-servicing burdens of firms, all reported curb-market borrowings were mandated to be converted to a new debt contract, with a three-year grace period followed by repayment in five annual installments at the interest rate of 1.35 percent a month or 16.2 percent a year. In addition, 30 percent of the outstanding short-term bank loans were rescheduled as long-term loans. A portion of the losses to financial institutions incurred by this was compensated for by support from the Bank of Korea. At the same time, the Bank of Korea lowered banks' lending and deposit rates to levels similar to those as before the interest rate liberalization in 1965. Meanwhile, the government provided tax benefits by allowing a higher depreciation ratio for fixed assets and larger corporate income tax deductions, with the purpose of stimulating investment. After the August 3rd Emergency Decree, the government promulgated three acts to attract curb-market funds into formal financial markets - the 'Short-term Financing and Banking Act,' 'the Mutual Savings and Finance Company Act,' and the 'Credit Union Act.'

3. The 1980 Economic Crisis

A. Unfolding of the Crisis

In the period around 1980, economic difficulties arose which were more severe than other difficulties a few years earlier, such as the 1972 recession and the first oil shock in 1973~1974. After a boom period from 1976 to 1978, the gross domestic product decreased, while inflation pressure emerged, in 1980, for the first time since the beginning of the 5-year economic development plans (refer to Table 5). The principal reasons for the decline of GDP were mainly external shocks such as the soaring oil price, political and social unrest, and a bad harvest. The probability of defaults on foreign debt increased as the current account deficit widened, mainly due to the increase in expenses for oil imports. Over-investment in the heavy and chemical industries, meanwhile, was another factor driving firms and banks to become insolvent.

The 1980 crisis unfolded in the following manner. Entering the year 1979, structural problems of the Korean economy began to surface. For example, exports decreased in volume terms in 1979. This decrease in exports reflected the surge in inflation in the latter half of the 1970s, which resulted in deterioration of the export competitiveness and profitability of domestic products (The Bank of Korea, *The 1979 Annual Report*). In addition, the direct control over the exports of some products, which was intended to stabilize domestic prices, also contributed to the decrease in exports. Thus, the decrease in export volume at that time may have resulted from the structural problems of the economy, even though it was affected as well by the world recession, the second oil shock, and neo-protectionism of advanced countries.

In particular, inflation began to soar in 1979. This was mainly due to the adjustment of controlled prices to more realistic levels as well as to the increases in import prices, e.g., of crude oil. The government had been setting the maximum prices of major products since it enacted the 'Act on Price Stability' on March 12th, 1973. During the late-1970s boom, however, numerous ways to circumvent the price controls were devised, such as setting dual prices, underground transactions, refusing to sell, cornering the markets for agricultural products, and so on. As a result, the price controls became ineffective and provoked such adverse effects as distortion of resource allocation and disruption of economic order. In light of this, the government rationalized or liberalized the prices of products and fees for public utilities.

In addition to soaring inflation, the economy suffered from a severe recession in 1980 as a result of a series of external shocks such as the sudden rise in oil prices and domestic political unrest. Private investment in equipment decreased rapidly as economic uncertainty increased in the midst of low capacity utilization following excessive investment in the 1970s. Domestic demand shrank as real income decreased due to inflation and a contraction of consumer confidence. In addition, production shrank because of a poor rice harvest. As a result of this, the economic growth rate became negative and unemployment rate increased, from 3.8% in 1979 to 5.2% in 1980. The ratio of dishonored bills also increased from 0.10% in 1979 to 0.18% in 1980.

Table 5. Trends of Major Economic Indicators circa 1980

	1975	1976	1977	1978	1979	1980	1981
Economic growth[1](%)	6.5	11.2	10.0	9.0	7.1	-2.1	6.5
(manufacturing)	12.9	23.1	14.4	20.8	9.5	-0.9	9.5
Consumption	5.6	6.8	5.2	8.1	6.3	1.1	4.7
Capital formation	7.7	21.0	28.6	34.4	9.7	-10.7	-3.7
Exports	19.3	39.1	20.9	13.8	1.0	8.6	15.7
Imports	1.9	24.7	20.9	28.0	11.8	-5.3	6.6
Current account (100mil.USD)	-18.9	-3.1	0.1	-10.9	-41.5	-53.2	-45.5
WPI(rate of change, %)	26.5	12.1	9.0	11.7	18.8	33.9	20.4
CPI(rate of change, %)	25.3	15.3	10.2	14.4	18.3	28.7	21.3
M_2(end of year, rate of change, %)	27.0	29.2	37.0	39.3	26.8	25.8	27.4
Budget balance[2]/GDP(%)	-3.29	-1.13	-0.83	-0.21	0.38	-1.55	-2.22

[1] Growth rates of GDP at 1995 prices

[2] Only the central government budget is included.

Source: The Bank of Korea, *Economic Statistics Yearbook*, various issues.

Table 6. International Oil Prices, Interest Rates, and Total Foreign Debt

	1978	79	80	81	82
Oil Prices [a]	12.95	29.22	36.68	35.27	32.45
Interest Rate[b]	8.85	12.09	14.19	16.87	13.29
Total Foreign Debt[c]	148.2	202.9	271.7	324.3	370.8
(Net Foreign Debt)[c]	(99.0)	(139.9)	(196.3)	(244.7)	(283.0)

[a] Average crude price (USD/Barrel): U.K. Brent (light), Dubai (medium), and Alaska North Slope (heavy), equally weighted.

[b] Libor 3-month, %.

[c] In 100 million US Dollars.

Sources: IMF, *International Financial Statistics Yearbook* (1997).

National Statistics Office, *Major Statistics of Korean Economy*, various issues.

The current account, which had been in balance and once showed a surplus in 1977, turned into a large deficit in 1979 (refer to Table 6). The deficit reflected, to some degree, the structural problems in energy consumption as well as the increase in oil imports after the oil price hike.

Demand for foreign exchange began far exceeding supply as the current account was in increasingly large deficit. Meanwhile, foreign confidence in the Korean economy deteriorated as a result of the political and social unrest and the economic recession. Foreign debt turned out to be about 15 billion dollars at the end of 1978, and interest payments on this debt amounted to 0.9 billion dollars (Economic Planning Board 1985, p. 6); this was a substantial interest burden, considering the fact that the total exports of the nation were only 12 billion dollars then. Due to the large current account deficit since 1979, the country was in need of additional inflow of foreign funds. It faced difficulties in raising funds in international financial markets, however, because those markets were also in unstable situations with soaring interest rates. The country could hardly have avoided default on its foreign debt but for its drawings from the IMF funds[12]. Foreign debt continued to accumulate, however, up to 37 billion dollars at the end of 1982.

At the same time, adverse effects from the government's promotion of heavy and chemical industries began to appear. Ambitious investments in the heavy and chemical industries during the 1970s had led to duplication of investment in some industries. Domestic markets for heavy and chemical products were small, while the international competitiveness of those firms remained low. Thus, the firms that entered these industries performed poorly in terms of profitability, and it was worried that most of them would go bankrupt in the long run. Even those firms which were highly competitive could not perform well because of the world-wide economic stagnation. Moreover, it had become practically impossible to continue to channel funds to those industries, since their demand for funds was too large. For example, the demand for funds by about 40 firms in the heavy and chemical industries amounted to 80 percent of the increments in money supply that year (Economic Planning Board 1979, p. 1185). Similarly, the overseas construction companies and shipping companies, which also absorbed large investments in the latter half of the 1970s, were accumulating bad assets as well.

In short, the nature of the 1980 economic crisis was a combination of several kinds of crises. It was a macroeconomic crisis in the sense that it resulted from an external and internal disequilibrium. In particular, it was a balance of payments crisis or a foreign debt crisis since widening current account deficit and the subsequent shortage of foreign exchange supply was one of the main causes for the crisis. From the microeconomic point of view, it can be seen as a structural crisis, in the sense that it revealed the shortcomings of the economic system that had prevailed in Korea during the 1970s. It also had the characteristics of a corporate crisis and a banking crisis, because of the delinquencies of the heavy and chemical industry firms and the financial distress imposed thereby on banks.

B. Background of the Crisis

(1) Over-heating and Speculation

The direct causes for the deterioration in the domestic firms' competitiveness in the export markets were an over-heated economy, during the 1976~1978 period, and an accompanying speculative rally in asset markets. Thanks in part to the measures contained in the 1972 August 3rd Decree to stimulate business activities, and also in part to the stabilized oil prices since 1975, the Korean economy recorded high growth rates of around 10 percent on average during the 1976~1978 period. Exports expanded rapidly along with recovery of the world economy, and income from overseas construction increased due to the construction boom in the Middle East. However, the rapid growth of monetary aggregates – of around 40 percent a year – resulting especially from the inflow of liquidity from abroad, generated pressure for inflation. Speculative booms, meanwhile, occurred in the markets for real estate, stocks, and commodities in short supply[13]. These factors, i.e., over-heated economy,

[12] The government withdrew about 500 million SDR from the IMF based on the stand-by agreement, in which Korea's credits were increased from 20 million SDR to 649 million SDR.

[13] In those days, the prices of real assets rose so sharply that the period was called an "age of premium"; the price of human capital, i.e., wages, also increased rapidly due to a labor shortage (Korea Development Institute 1981, p. 5).

speculative boom in asset markets, inflation, wage increases, were what weakened the competitiveness of domestic firms in the international export markets.

(2) Duplicated and Excessive Investment in Heavy and Chemical Industries

The adverse effects of the policy of promoting heavy and chemical industries, and of the hasty and aggressive implementation thereof in the late 1970s, included the increases in the number of delinquent firms and distortions in industrial structure. These problems, among others, caused the 1980 economic crisis. Firms which had initially been skeptical of investing in the heavy and chemical industries till the early 1970s, rushed to participate in the investment projects after confirming the government's determination to foster these industries. The amount of investment was too large, however, compared to the sizes of the markets. The capacity utilization of firms investing in new projects was so low that they could not reach the break-even point. Stagnation of the domestic economy and the world economy alike lowered the profitability of firms further and drove the heavy and chemical industries into a state of potential delinquency. Moreover, concentration of resources on the heavy and chemical industries resulted in short supplies of necessities and other products of light industries, and eroded long-term growth potentials of those industries.

(3) Repressive Economic Policy

The Korean economy in the 1970s was a repressed economy[14], if not a completely planning economy, in the sense that there existed a large amount of government control and intervention in the operation of the economic system. Since the August 3rd Decree in 1972, the government controlled commodity prices, interest rates, and exchange rates and continually intensified its intervention in resource allocation.

Seen from a structural point of view, the crisis beginning in 1979 was a result of the vulnerability stemming from the structural weaknesses or inefficiencies of a repressed economy. The policy makers those days also shared this view. The Economic Planning Board, for example, in its Comprehensive Economic Stabilization Policy promulgated on April 17th, 1979, stressed that structural policy measures were in need for fostering the growth potential of Korean economy in the long run (Korea Development Institute 1981, p. 371). In a similar context, the Bank of Korea attributed the then crisis to structural problems (The Bank of Korea, *1980 Annual Report*, p. 1), and asserted that the managerial efficiency and financial structures of firms should be improved to enhance their competitiveness (p. 8).

Repressive policy measures might have been unavoidable in order to foster the nation's infant industries. It is also true, however, that they distorted and weakened the economic structure. For example, interest rate ceilings brought about such problems as excess demand for bank loans, prevalence of the curb money market, and decreased incentives to save. Policy loans and required approval of foreign borrowings led not only to economic problems such as over-borrowings by firms, but also to non-economic problems such as cronyism, i.e., 'intimate' relationships between firms and the government. Direct control by the government stifled the individual will to innovate and thus discouraged the spontaneity essential for a harmonious working of the market system. Due to the intensive government intervention in

[14] The term "repressed economy" refers to an economy in which the government severely intervenes in private sector's resource allocation via price and quantity controls. For details as to repression, see MacKinnon (1973), Krueger (1993), Fry (1995), and others.

the financial sector, financial institutions had little incentive to screen loan applicants and monitor borrowers, and also lacked initiative in developing new financial techniques. Firms tended to seek profit maximization not so much through managerial innovation as through lobbying the government. Consequently, it seems highly likely that the government's control weakened the private sector's adaptability to changing economic environment.

The government's control of the economy is also likely to have stalled growth in the sophistication of the economic system and to have made it fragile to external shocks. In order to increase the flexibility of an economy, it is necessary to allow for a variety of heterogeneous elements in the system. Strict control by the government, however, led to an unsophisticated or monotone economic structure, which was more fragile than a sophisticated one.

(4) Imbalances Between Real and Financial Sectors (Underdevelopment of Financial Sector)

From the beginning of its economic development, Korea chose an unbalanced growth strategy for economic development, and pursued it faithfully. This produced various inter-sectoral imbalances, among them imbalances between real and financial sectors, begotten by the policy of promoting industrialization through financial repression. These imbalances became one of the major background factors behind the 1980 economic crisis. The degree of imbalance had intensified all the more because of the August 3rd Decree in 1972, which forced the financial sector to sacrifice for the sake of the real sector, especially the large firms, by means of a compulsive conversion of debt contracts and rescheduling, with a suppression of interest rates to below the market rates. Even though the decree contained some measures to encourage financial development, such as the establishment of non-banking financial institutions, it lacked respect for market principles in development of the financial sector. Behind this lay the developmentalist view that financial development was only supplementary to industrial development. Since the government controlled the commercial banks, investors did not find any incentive to buy bank stocks, and this of course hampered issuance of stocks by the banks[15]. In the late 1970s, there were cases where no single nation-wide commercial bank had even as much capital as the amount needed to finance a large investment project proposal by a big business firm. Among the most harmful effects of these imbalances between the real and financial sectors were retardation of the banks' capabilities to monitor and check firms' activities, and inability of the banks to restrain over-borrowings and inefficient use of them by firms.

C. Measures to Cope with the 1980 Crisis

The set of economic policies implemented from 1979 to the early 1980s to cope with the economic crisis consisted of a macroeconomic stabilization policy, an export promotion and foreign exchange policy, deregulation, measures to correct inefficient and duplicate investment projects, and others as microeconomic measures.

First, the government implemented a macroeconomic stabilization policy, beginning from 1979 when the domestic economy showed stagnation along with steeply increased international oil prices. The policy was promulgated as the Comprehensive Economic Stabilization Measures on April 17th, 1979. It consisted of measures to stabilize the prices of

[15] At that time, the government was the largest stockholder in four out of the five nation-wide commercial banks.

products and the supply of necessities, fiscal restriction, restructuring of heavy and chemical industries, and increases in the interest rates paid on bank deposits. The basis of the stabilization was maintained relatively consistently thereafter. The only exception was the expansionary monetary policy sought after June 1980 to boost the economy. To counter the destabilizing effects of this monetary expansion, stronger fiscal restriction was pursued. In order to control increases in expenditures, the government adopted a zero-base budget formula from 1981 on. In line with macroeconomic measures, stabilization was pursued through direct and microeconomic measures such as release of government-stock rice, strengthening direct controls on prices of major products, and anti-speculation policy in the real estate market.

Second, the government implemented a policy to promote exports and support firms' repayments of foreign debts, to alleviate the burden of foreign debt servicing by firms. The Won was devalued in January 1980. At the same time, the government increased its subsidies to exporting activities by increasing the loan for trade. In order to help public corporations and the heavy and chemical industries repay their foreign debts, the government introduced a special foreign-currency loan program on April 3rd, 1980. It also opened the stock market as part of an economic liberalization program, and tried to induce foreign capital by establishing an investment fund exclusively for foreigners, the first ever vehicle for foreigners' indirect investment in domestic securities.

Third, the government pushed forward a liberalization policy, admitting that the economic difficulties at that time stemmed from structural inefficiencies formed by its own excessive economic intervention. In the financial sector, the government privatized the nation-wide commercial banks, attempted to allow for more autonomy for bank management, and reduced the extent of policy loans. On September 6th, 1979, it introduced a new system for setting interest rates at individual banks, utilizing spreads over prime rate replacing the previous system of government-set interest rate ceilings. Subsequently, the government introduced new financial instruments, whose rates of returns could supposedly be determined by market forces, such as commercial papers (CPs), cash management accounts (CMAs), and negotiable certificates of deposits (CDs). The Bank of Korea tried to shy away from direct control of the domestic credits of financial institutions and introduced an indirect mode of managing the money supply, utilizing the price function of the interest rate from January 7th, 1982. As for industrial policy, the government changed from a selective to a functional or across-the-board intervention mode. In 1986, it abolished the seven acts pertaining to promotion of seven individual industries and enacted the 'Industry Development Act,' which integrated and unified these former acts. The thrust of this move was to provide a means to support industries across-the-board. With this measure, it became possible for preferential loans to be provided to an unspecified number of firms in the way of supporting exports or purchases of domestically produced machines. The government also promoted trade liberalization in a trial attempt to outgrow the protective industrial policy. On behalf of securing the orderly operation of the market system, the Fair Trade Commission was established. In addition, the legal system was improved in such a way as to change the character of regulations from a positive system to a negative system.[16]

---

[16] Positive list system refers to the legal system in which activities allowed are listed. Those not listed are deemed to be not allowed. Negative list system refers to the legal system in which only those activities not allowed are listed and those not listed are deemed to be allowed. Thus, in general, the positive list system is a more strict and regulatory legal system than the negative list system.

Fourth, in response to worsening cash flows and excess capacity in the heavy and chemical industries, the government established measures to restructure these industries. On the basis of the Heavy and Chemical Industry Coordination Plan, drafted in May 1979, the government tried to coordinate business restructuring, so-called industry rationalization, in such industries as electrical generators, diesel engines, automobiles, electronic switchboards, and transformers. It also attempted to resolve excess-capacity problems in the overseas construction and shipping industries. For various reasons including excessive burdens to financial institutions and recession, however, the so-called industry rationalization policies were not fully implemented prior to the mid-1980s. Measures were also taken to make up for the losses sustained by banks, as these losses had resulted, by and large, from government intervention in the financial sector. On several occasions, the Bank of Korea paid interest on banks' reserve deposits held in accounts in the BOK. The government also allowed banks to enter into new businesses, such as the credit card business, with a view to improving their profitability.

Finally, the government implemented several measures to discourage speculation in real estate and reckless management of firms. For example, a measure to improve corporate financial soundness was announced in September 1980, which urged sales of land held for non-business purposes, disposal of affiliate firms and strengthening of external audits for joint-stock corporations. To stabilize the prices of real estate, the government also announced a long-term plan for construction of houses. It also expanded home financing for the lower-income classes.

Table 7. Trends of Major Economic Indicators around 1989

	1985	1986	1987	1988	1989	1990	1991	1992
Economic growth[1](%)	6.9	12.4	12.0	11.5	6.2	9.2	8.5	5.1
(manufacturing)	7.1	18.3	18.8	13.4	3.7	9.1	8.9	5.1
Consumption	6.3	8.4	8.1	9.7	10.7	10.1	9.3	6.8
Capital formation	4.7	12.0	16.5	13.4	16.9	24.0	11.8	-0.8
Exports	4.5	26.1	21.6	12.5	-3.8	18.4	12.8	11.0
Imports	-0.6	17.8	19.4	12.8	16.3	29.1	11.0	5.1
Current account (100mil.USD)	-8.9	46.2	98.5	141.6	50.5	-21.8	-87.3	-45.3
WPI[2](rate of change, %)	0.5	-2.6	2.7	2.3	1.2	7.2	1.9	1.6
CPI[2](rate of change, %)	3.1	1.4	6.1	7.2	5.0	9.4	9.3	4.5
M2(end of period, rate of change, %)	11.8	16.8	18.8	18.8	18.4	21.2	18.6	18.4
Consolidated budget balance/GDP(%)	-0.9	-0.1	2.3	1.2	0.0	-0.9	-1.9	-0.7

[1] Growth rate of GDP at 1995 prices.

[2] Compared with that of previous year.

Source: The Bank of Korea, *Economic Statistics Yearbook,* various issues.

The Ministry of Finance, *Government Finance Statistics of Korea,* various issues.

4. The Post-1989 "Grave Situation"

A. Unfolding of the Situation

The economic situation during the period from 1989 to 1992 worsened relatively compared to that in the 1986~1988 period, although not so bad as to constitute an actual economic "crisis." Government officials termed it a "totally grave situation" before others subsequently called it a crisis. Immediately after the high-performance in late 1980s, in which all three major macroeconomic targets – rapid growth, current account surplus, and price stability – had been achieved, things turned the other way; growth, the current account, and prices all worsened simultaneously. At this time, government authorities seemed to be at a loss, as changes in domestic and external conditions brought about many new difficulties for them in designing and implementing proper policies. The term 'grave situation' seems to have been used more to indicate the difficulties in policy implementation than to point to the economic difficulties themselves.

The main economic difficulties then can be described as a slowdown of economic growth, widening current account deficits, and inflation. The economy that had shown double digit growth rates during the 1986 ~1988 period suddenly slowed down in 1989, growing only 6 percent in that year. Owing to the grand government-promoted project of building 2 million houses, along with a rise in consumption, however, the economy recovered to a growth rate of 9 percent during the following period from 1990 to 1991. Meanwhile, the current account reversed to deficit in 1990 and recorded an even bigger deficit in 1991. The reversal from surplus to deficit reflected the loss of international competitiveness of Korean firms and a large increase in imports. Inflation rose because of excess demand resulting from increased expenditures by residents.

An unfavorable world economic situation at this time amplified the worries over stagnation. The dollar was weak in the international financial markets, while competition in the domestic and overseas markets had intensified. Domestically, Korea had to open its markets as promised in its liberalization plans[17], and the Won was on an appreciating trend reflecting the current account surpluses. International oil prices also increased substantially due to the Gulf War in 1990.

Despite the need to respond to this deteriorating economic situation, the government confronted many difficulties in doing so, as proper means were not readily available. Along with the political transition from an authoritarian regime to a democratic regime, public demand for wage increases and improvements in the quality of life became uncontrollable, so that the government could not find ways to constrain wages or consumption increases. Direct controls were unthinkable because of the economic liberalization trend. For example, after the government adopted a market average exchange rate system on March 2nd, 1990, its influence on exchange rates diminished to a great extent. Seen from this point of view, the economic crisis at that time was indeed actually more of a policy dilemma in nature, in that the government was unable to offer proper means to deal with the economic difficulties.

[17] After succeeding in opening the Japanese economy through the *Yen-Dollar Committee* in 1984, the US government pressed Korea for market opening.

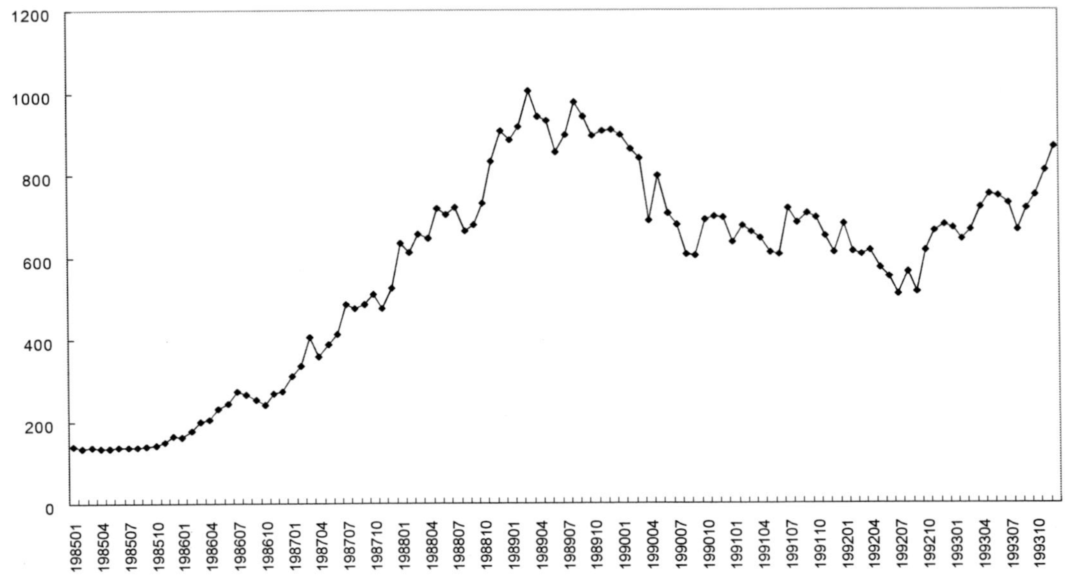

Source: Korea Stock Exchange, *Stock*, various issues.

Figure 2. Trends of Stock Price Index.

B. Background of the Situation

(1) Speculative Boom

Against the economic boom in the latter half of the 1980s, another round of speculative boom appeared in the stock and real estate markets. The stock price index, which had been 137 in October 1985, began to rise from around the end of 1985, and reached 1,003 in March 1989 (refer to Figure 2). This long-rising trend of stock prices was followed by jumps in the prices of land and houses from around 1988. The prices of land and houses increased 129 and 56 percent, respectively, during the period from the end of 1987 to the end of 1991 (refer to Figure 3).

These asset bubbles caused several disturbances to the economy as they spread, even though there were no cases of their sudden bursting. Speculative demand for credit increased rapidly as speculators financed their investments through bank loans. The resultant increases in interest rates eroded the international competitiveness of domestic firms. Due to the wealth effects of the asset appreciation, consumption and construction investment increased. The changes in the structure of aggregate demand from exports to domestic demand generated worries over erosion of the home base for export production. The proportion of GDP consumed by the private sector or invested in construction was 65.5 percent in 1988, but it increased to 76 percent by the early 1990s. Moreover, the firms sought capital gains from the real assets, while neglecting their needs to improve managerial efficiency, and this weakened their competitive edge even further.

Table 8. Demand Structure of GDP (Shares in GDP) (%)

	1980	1985	1988	1989	1990	1991	1992
Private Consumption(A)	63.4	57.5	50.0	52.0	52.3	52.3	52.9
Construction(B)	18.0	16.2	15.5	17.6	22.2	24.2	23.1
A+B	81.4	73.7	65.5	69.6	74.5	76.5	76.0

Source: The Bank of Korea, *National Account*, various issues.

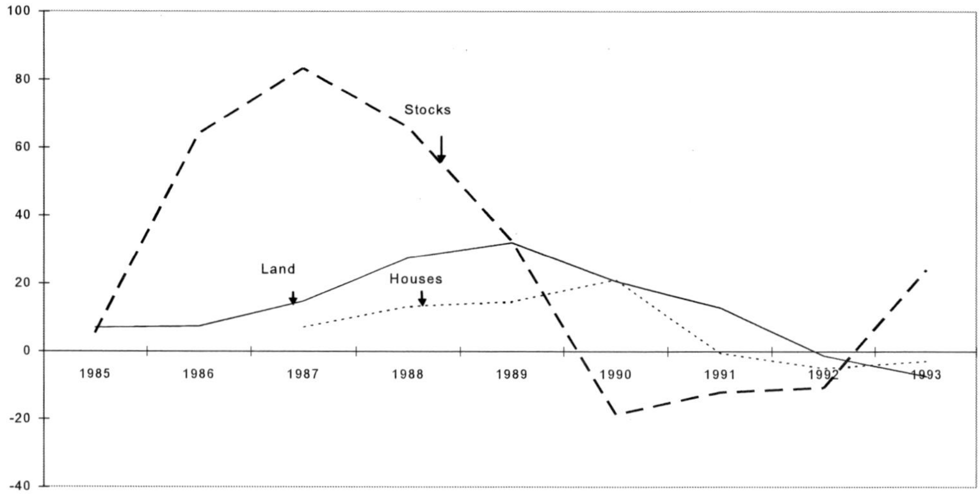

Source: Korea Stock Exchange, *Stock*, various issues. Ministry of Construction and Transportation, *Land Price Statistics*, various issues. Housing and Commercial Bank, *Survey of Urban Housing Price Trends*, various issues.

Figure 3. Changes in Prices of Stocks, Land, and Houses.

(2) Liberalization and Democratization Accompanied by Eruption of Demand for Basic Needs

While liberalization had been a basic theme since the early 1980s in the economic sphere, democratization had also progressed steadily in the political sphere. The June 29th Democratization Declaration in 1987 set the stage for a jump in the number of labor disputes. Rapid increases in wages[18], together with social unrest, caused a decline in the international competitiveness of Korean firms and lowered international confidence in the Korean economy. In this situation, an economic opening policy, including freed overseas travel and liberalization of luxury consumer goods imports[19], was also promoted in order to help manage the large current account surplus. Owing to income and wealth growth, and to the appreciation of the Won, these measures triggered increases in consumption, especially of

[18] It is highly probable that the wage rate would have increased, the democratization decree notwithstanding, since the unemployment rate in late 1980 stayed at the level of 2 percent, well below the projected natural unemployment rate of 3 percent.

[19] After travel abroad by elderly people was liberalized in January 1988, the policy was applied to all citizens. In addition, import of luxurious home electronic products, such as large refrigerators and large TVs, was liberalized in 1989.

luxuries. This in turn caused workers to ask for further wage increases and led to more labor disputes. The 1988 Olympics held in Seoul also brought about a laxity in social discipline.

(3) Changes in World Economic Environment

The worsening of the world economy and the Won appreciation together aggravated the difficulties of the government in conducting economic policies. By then, international pressure was growing for Korea to increase its role in the international community, commensurate with its improved economic status. Specifically, pressure from advanced countries mounted for the opening of Korean markets. This was a fundamental change in trade policy for these countries, which had previously preferred to stall rapid increases of imports from Korea. Moreover, as the WTO system was expected to come into effect before long, there arose worries about foreign firms' taking over domestic markets in agricultural products and financial services, as well as markets for manufactured goods.

(4) Lessened Effectiveness of Economic Policies

One of the background factors of the post-1989 grave situation was that the old-style economic policies could not respond effectively to the changes brought about by economic liberalization and movements in the domestic and world economic environments. The economic situation was nothing exceptionally severe, but the government nevertheless called the situation a grave one. The reason was that the policy makers felt ill-equipped to handle the situation. In fact, institutions, including an adequately working market mechanism, had not evolved sufficiently to incorporate the new economic order required under the liberalized system. The government had lost the use of its previous policy instruments and had not yet developed the capabilities needed to coordinate economic matters under drastically changed economic conditions.

In addition, it was hardly possible to come up with a solution to disentangle the combination of stagnant stock markets and over-heated real estate markets. An expansionary macroeconomic policy would help support stock prices, but it would hamper the efforts to stabilize real estate prices.

C. Measures to Cope with the Situation

The economic policies in this period comprised an industrial restructuring policy, a measure to stifle real estate speculation, and a policy to boost stock prices. A stabilization policy was also promoted, although not in the sense of managing macroeconomic demand, but rather in the sense of wage stabilizing, stock price stabilization, and asset prices stabilization, control of commodity prices, and stabilization of the living conditions of the common people. From the latter half of 1991, a traditional macroeconomic stabilization policy was pursued. Liberalization and opening were also among the main themes of the policy. During this period, the speed of promotion of liberalization went up.

The industrial restructuring policy aimed at addressing the issue of improving firms' profitability and competitiveness, which had deteriorated due to increasing wages, the Won appreciation, and inflation. As for the mode of policy implementation, the government advocated an indirect provision of support to firms; that is, it tried to remain basically a promoter of infrastructure, basic technology development, and an elastic supply of skilled labor, excepting that it might use direct measures to support the small and medium-sized firms. Despite the government's assertion, however, things were not done so differently from before, as the government provided support to targeted activities directly and frequently twisted the arms of banks to get them to supply the required funds for the preferred sectors. For example, to help firms invest in improving their equipment, the government created special equipment funds on November 14th, 1989 and April 4th, 1990, providing loans for this purpose on preferential terms. It also allowed a temporary investment tax deduction on July 4th, 1989, and requested that banks lend in foreign currency to firms which imported new equipment. The government also increased subsidies for exporting activities by increasing the Bank of Korea rediscount proportions applied to foreign trade bills. It also lowered interest rates. In addition, it promoted a policy inducing big business firms to specialize in their core business areas. In order to facilitate this policy, the credit control system was also modified.

One of the priority policy agenda items during this time was cooling the rampant real estate boom. This is well demonstrated by the fact that, during the three years from early 1989 to early 1992, almost twenty related policy measures were announced. This high level of concern was based on the government's judgment that an excessive boom in real estate markets would cause inefficient allocation of resources, trigger demands for wage increases, induce over-consumption, and bring about a sense of incongruity in society by destabilizing the lives of the common people. Thus, the government introduced four laws based on the concept of public ownership of land on December 30th, 1989, and this was meant above all to calm the real estate market[20]. In addition to this, regulations concerning the general land tax (June 16th, 1989), permission for land transactions (December 20th, 1989), and compulsory registration of real estate (April 13th, 1990) were introduced. A measure to encourage the sale of real estate held by big business firms and financial institutions, and one to prevent new acquisition were also introduced. Finally, there was the plan for construction of two million houses, promulgated on April 27th, 1989 with a view to increasing the supply of houses.

Varied measures to stop the steep decrease in stock prices were implemented as stock prices continued to fall after recording their peak in March 1989. On December 12th, 1989, the government announced a policy measure to boost the stock market, and this was followed by measures to control the volume of the stocks issued and to establish a stock market stabilization fund (September 18th, 1990) and a measure to open the stock market to foreign investors (November 30th, 1991). The government also arranged for commercial banks to provide 2.7 trillion Won to investment trust companies, so that these companies could buy stock in the market. On May 27th, 1992, the Bank of Korea supplied 2.9 trillion Won to the investment trust companies to help improve their profit earnings.

Meanwhile, a series of deregulatory measures was put in place with ever-increasing speed, in accordance with the long-term plan for financial liberalization and market opening. In December 1988, interest rates were fully liberalized. Although this policy soon underwent *de facto* repeal when the government's window guidance on determination of interest rates was resumed in response to the sudden economic recession in 1989, it reverted again to plan, when the first stage of the four-stage interest rate liberalization plan of August 1991 was implemented in November 1991. Capital market opening was only partly promoted until 1993, in the form of an increase in the amount of investment funds available exclusively for

[20] Included in the laws were the Ceiling on Housing Ownership Act, Restitution of Development Gains Act, Land Excess-Profits Tax, Special Account for Land Management and the Balanced Regional Development Act.

foreign investors. Then, however, the government announced a comprehensive blueprint for Korea's financial deregulation and capital market opening over the following five years.

Macroeconomic policy in those days was used so as to to boost economic activities, rather than as a tool to stabilize them. As for monetary policy, relatively tight money had been pursued through the introduction and operation of the so-called marginal reserve system until the first half of 1989, as a way of handling the large balance of payments surplus. From the second half of 1989, however, money began to be supplied to fuel an expansionary phase. The reason for this turn-around in monetary policy was a change in the basic goals of monetary policy to include that of providing sufficient funds to the private sector to activate corporate investment and stimulate the stock market. As the economy entered an over-heated phase under the influence of this expansionary policy from 1990 to 1991, the policy took a turn to contraction from the end of 1991. It turned around to expansion once again, however, when the New Economy 5-Year Plan was implemented in 1993.

5. The 1997 Economic Crisis

A. Details of the Crisis

The 1997 economic crisis took place through a complex process: beginning from recession and terms of trade deterioration, then moving to corporate bankruptcies, to banking crises, to contagion from foreign currency crises of South East Asian countries, and to a currency crisis. In addition, during the crisis resolution, a series of corporate bankruptcy and subsequent banking crises repeated itself. The 1997 crisis provided a window for looking at the problems innate in the Korean economic system. This is one of its distinct features.

Before going into the details of the 1997 crisis, this chapter first takes a look at the economic situation in 1996. Above all, it should be noted that the economy slowed down in 1996, after showing a high growth rate of over 8 percent a year on average in 1994 and 1995. At a first glance, the 1996 slowdown looked like a soft landing, since GDP grew almost 5 percent that year.

Looking at the details of economic growth in 1996, however, one can find problems in the Korean economy. The nearly 5% growth rate was mainly attributable to increases in inventories, which occurred as firms struggled to continue production under sluggish demand. The reason for this was that the cost of stopping factory operation was extremely high in processing industries such as the petrochemical, steel, and semiconductors, which are the major industries in the Korean economy. The volume of inventories began to weigh heavily on the corporate sector. The portion of inventory increases in GDP mounted up to 1 percent. Thus, if it had not been for the increase in inventories, the economic growth rate in 1996 would have ended up at the mere 3 percent level.

The current account deficit, which had been increasing from 1994 to 1995, amounted to 23 billion dollars, 5 percent of GDP in 1996. Decreases in the prices of major exports, such as semiconductors, and continuous increases in imports were main contributory factors to the widening deficit of the current account. Moreover, the decrease in the unit prices of exports, combined with increases in export volume, worsened the profitability of exporting activities.

Table 9. Trends of Inventories (in 1995 constant prices) (Billion Won, %)

	1990	1991	1992	1993	1994	1995	1996	1997	1998
Changes in Inventories	234.2	1,943.6	1,690.1	-1,767.5	2,170.9	1,825.7	3,914.4	-4,218.3	-27,983.1
(Ratios to GDP)	(0.1)	(0.7)	(0.6)	(-0.6)	(0.6)	(0.5)	(1.0)	(-1.0)	(-7.0)

Source: The Bank of Korea, "Recent Trends of Inventories," *Press Release* 2000-1-17.

Table 10. Decomposition of Exports

	Amount of Exports[1]	Amount Index[2]	Unit Value Index[2]	Volume Index[2]
1990	650.2	52.0	94.2	55.2
1991	718.7	57.5	94.7	60.7
1992	766.3	61.3	93.2	65.9
1993	822.4	65.7	93.6	70.2
1994	960.1	76.7	95.2	80.7
1995	1,250.6	100.0	100.0	100.0
1996	1,297.2	103.7	86.6	119.8
1997	1,361.6	108.9	72.8	149.6
1998	1,323.1	105.8	60.5	174.9

[1] In 100 million US dollars

[2] Indices express values relative to 100 in 1995.

Source: The Bank of Korea, *Economic Statistics Yearbook*, various issues.

Table 11. Trends of Major Economic Indicators around 1997

	1993	1994	1995	1996	1997	1998
Economic growth[1](%)	5.7	8.4	8.2	4.8	2.4	-7.1
(manufacturing)	5.4	10.8	11.3	6.8	6.6	-7.2
Consumption	5.4	7.1	8.2	7.2	3.2	-8.2
Capital formation	6.3	10.7	11.9	7.3	-2.2	-21.1
Exports	11.3	16.1	24.6	11.2	21.4	13.3
Imports	6.2	21.6	22.4	14.2	3.2	-22.0
Current account (100mil.USD)	9.9	-38.7	-85.1	-230.0	-81.7	403.6
WPI(rate of change, %)	1.5	2.7	4.7	3.2	3.9	12.2
CPI(rate of change, %)	4.8	6.2	4.5	4.9	7.5	0.8
M_2(end of period, rate of change, %)	18.6	15.6	15.5	16.2	19.2	19.0
Budget balance[2]/GDP(%)	0.08	0.53	0.45	0.03	-0.02	-2.97

[1] Growth rate of GDP at 1995 prices

[2] On the basis of the central government budget

Source: The Bank of Korea, *Economic Statistics Yearbook,* various issues.

The total foreign debt of residents was climbing rapidly at that time, increasing from 120 billion U.S. dollars at the end of 1995 to 160 billion U.S. dollars at the end of 1996. This was mainly attributable to the widening current account deficit, but it was also influenced by increases in foreign borrowings by domestic firms and financial institutions following capital account liberalization.

Table 12. Trends of Foreign Debt (end of period, 100 mil. dollars)

	1992	1993	1994	1995	1996	1997	
						11p	12p
<IMF criterion>							
Long-term	260	267	303	410	575	729	860
	(..)	(2.9)	(13.5)	(35.5)	(40.3)	(26.7)	(49.5)
	<41.2>	<39.9>	<34.2>	<34.2>	<36.5>	<45.0>	<55.7>
Short-term	370	403	584	787	1,000	889	685
	(..)	(8.9)	(44.9)	(34.9)	(27.1)	(-11.1)	(-31.6)
	<58.8>	<60.1>	<65.8>	<65.8>	<63.5>	<55.0>	<44.3>
Total Foreign Debt	629	670	887	1,197	1,575	1,618	1,544
	(..)	(6.4)	(32.4)	(35.0)	(31.6)	(2.7)	(-2.0)
<World Bank criterion>							
Total Foreign Debt	428	439	568	784	1,047	1,161	1,208
Long-term	243	247	265	331	437	545	696
Short-term	185	192	304	453	610	616	512

Numbers in ( ) denote rates of change and those in < > denote composition ratios.
Source: The Bank of Korea, *Statistical Yearbook of Foreign Exchange,* 1998.

Because of a recession with increased financial burdens of firms, entering 1997, cases of corporate insolvency began to propagate, and the banking sector's non-performing loans accumulated accordingly. Starting with the Hanbo Steel Company, which went bankrupt on January 23rd, 1997, the *chaebols* (Korean big business groups) began going under in a series consisting of Sammi, Jinro, Daenong, Hanshin-Gongyoung, and others. Accordingly, the portion of non-performing loans (classified as substandard, doubtful, and estimated loss credits) in total loans of banks rose from 4.1 percent at the end of 1996 to 6.0 percent at the end of 1997. These bankruptcies of big business groups revealed the evils of the Korean economy implied by cronyism or cozy relationships between political groups and businesses, and played a crucial role in the loss of Korea's economic credibility in the international community.

Under these circumstances, then, the Thailand Baht suddenly plummeted on July 2nd, 1997, signaling the beginning of currency crises in South East Asian countries. The Baht had been put under speculative attack as the Thai government attempted to maintain its value, while at the same time bailing out the troubled financial institutions in the wake of a bubble-like boom and bust, and collapse in the real estate market. Through contagion effects, the currencies of Malaysia, Indonesia and the Philippines, which were in similar situations or had close trade relationships with Thailand, also began steep depreciation. Afterwards, the speculative attacks on currencies spread to Taiwan and Hong Kong.

Immediately after the South East Asian currency crises, Kia Motors became insolvent, and foreign investors' confidence in the Korean economy was further undermined by the protracted resolution of the Kia Motors' problem. After the speculative attacks on the Taiwan and Hong Kong currencies took place, international credit rating agencies downgraded Korea's sovereign credit rating. From then on, international financial institutions would hardly agree to roll over their loans to Korean financial institutions. Korea's domestic financial institutions, no longer able to obtain finance abroad, were forced to purchase foreign currency on the domestic foreign exchange market for their daily settlements. The Bank of Korea accordingly provided them with foreign reserves, and the nation's stock of foreign reserves was rapidly depleted as the financial institutions failed to recover their credit-worthiness. In consequence, the Korean government asked the International Monetary Fund for emergency credits.

Immediately after the announcement of the IMF stand-by credit agreements and the associated IMF/IBRD economic reform program, the economic situation in Korea became genuinely critical due to break-down of financial intermediaries under the widening spread of business bankruptcies, to the point where normal operation of the economy was seriously threatened. Shortly thereafter, however, credits from international financial agencies flowed in, foreign debts began to be rolled over, and the balance of payments turned to surplus. In addition, the crisis began to be resolved, as Korean firms and financial institutions showed progress in restructuring. With these developments, the foreign exchange markets began to calm down, and Korea was able to emerge from the crisis situation.

The above discussions indicate that the 1997 economic crisis comprised a number of different characteristics – a corporate crisis, a banking (financial) crisis, a currency crisis, and a policy-driven crisis. It was nevertheless the typical type of economic crisis defined in Chapter 2, since the whole economic system was close to collapse.

B. Background of the 1997 Crisis

Since the nature of the 1997 crisis was so complicated, its causes may not be summarized by only one or two factors[21]. But for the sake of comparison with the other crises that happened in Korea, the following may be enumerated as important factors of the 1997 crisis:

(1) Over-investment

It is doubtful that the economy had been in an over-heated state in the period from 1994 to 1995, or that a speculative boom had occurred. The economic growth rates during the period were not as high as those in the past boom periods; investment showed no more than a mild increase. Thus, the economy at the time can hardly be viewed as having been in an over-heated state, let alone a speculative boom.

Table 13. Cases of Corporate Integration

	1991	1992	1993	1994	1995	1996	1997
Horizontal integration	43	39	36	40	58	73	78
Vertical integration	45	38	34	24	43	69	80
Conglomeration	66	72	53	131	224	252	260

[21] In light of this, discussions in the Korean media after late November, when the currency crisis began to emerge, attributed the crisis to political, social, and cultural factors as well as economic ones.

Note: Horizontal integration brings together similar or related business types. Vertical integration occurs between businesses that have a supplier-customer relationship. A conglomeration integrates firms whose products are largely unrelated to each other with each other.

Source: Korea Fair Trade Commission, *White Book of Fair Trade*, various issues.

From the viewpoint of industrial organization, however, the problem lay in the excessive-competition and over-investment in major industries, which resulted when many of the big business groups expanded their business areas by entering industries already full of competition. Heterogeneous business conglomeration, a type of business integration of companies whose products were largely unrelated to each other, increased rapidly from the mid-1990s. During this period, the firms seemed to have actively diversified their business areas in response to the trend toward globalization and domestic market opening. However, their strategy of entering new industries was ill-founded; the big business firms were seldom observed entering new and promising industries based on their own technological innovation. Rather, most of them entered industries in which other firms had already become established, and were known to be realizing high profit rates. The *chaebols* competed with each other in building petrochemical, electronic, and automobile factories, facilities for the distribution industry, and in the construction business. Such competition led to over- and duplicated capacity. Table 13 shows that heterogeneous business conglomeration, compared to other types of corporate integration, increased rapidly from the mid-1990s. Such over-investment resulted in over-production, and the profit prospects of the firms involved became dim. This over-investment underlined the inefficiency of the Korean economic system as a whole, and from time to time, triggered worries over the solvency of these firms.

(2) Over-borrowings and Maturity Mismatches

Deterioration in the financial structures of firms from the mid-1990s was one of the important factors behind the 1997 economic crisis. While firms expanded into new business areas, the economy began to stagnate, and corporate cash flows dried up. The firms thus attempted to meet their increased needs for funds through external financing. This practice was especially notable from 1996, when the economy entered a recession period. The debt-equity ratio in Korean manufacturing was 396 percent at the end of 1997[22], which was 110 percent points higher than that at the end of 1995.

In the midst of globalization and capital account liberalization, corporations placed securities in the international financial markets on the strength of their own credits and increased their short-term borrowings of trade credits. Table 15 shows a big increase in the non-bank private sector's foreign borrowings.

Excessive maturity mismatches of debts were among the main factors that caused the 1997 economic crisis. Firms suffered from liquidity problem because their investments had not yielded normal profits yet, while a lot of their funds were fixed due to investments. For

[22] The sharp rise in the debt-equity ratios of firms in 1997 was due partly to the steep depreciation of the Korean Won. But the *Financial Statement Analysis* of the Bank of Korea shows that the amount of debts denominated in foreign currencies owed by the manufacturing firms was about 10 trillion Won, which was not more than 3 percent of total debts. Even without the depreciation in 1997, the debt-equity ratio would have reached the level of 370~380 percent, considering that the loss from foreign exchange revaluation amounted to about 9 trillion Won and the capital stock was about 102 trillion Won.

Korean manufacturing industry, the current ratio, i.e., the ratio of liquidity assets to liquidity liability, was a mere 92 percent at the end of 1996, the lowest recorded during the 1990s[23].

Table 14 . Financial Indicators of Manufacturing in the 1990s (%)

	1990	91	92	93	94	95	96	97
Debt-equity ratio	282.5	306.7	318.7	294.9	302.5	286.8	317.1	396.3
Financial expenses-sales Ratio	5.12	5.69	6.31	5.93	5.64	5.57	5.84	6.39
Net income-total assets Ratio	1.48	1.41	0.89	1.04	1.90	2.83	0.50	-0.93
Current ratio	99.44	95.33	92.75	94.13	95.59	95.39	91.89	91.76

Source: The Bank of Korea, *Financial Statement Analysis*, various issues.

Table 15. Foreign Debt by Borrowers (end of period, 100 mil. US dollars)

	1992	93	94	95	96	97
Public Sector	56	38	36	30	24	180
	<8.9>	<5.7>	<4.0>	<2.5>	<1.5>	<11.7>
Non-Bank Private Sector	137	156	200	261	356	423
	<21.8>	<23.4>	<22.6>	<21.8>	<22.6>	<27.4>
Financial Sector	436	475	651	905	1,195	941
	<69.3>	<70.9>	<73.4>	<75.6>	<75.9>	<60.9>
Total Foreign Debts	629	670	887	1,197	1,575	1,544

Numbers in < > denote composition ratio (%).
Source: The Bank of Korea, *Statistical Yearbook of Foreign Exchange,* 1998.

The same problems of the maturity mismatches occurred in the external sector as well. Firms and banks came to rely more and more on short-term foreign debt during this period. The ratio of short-term to total foreign debt at the end of 1996 was 63.5 percent by the IMF criterion, and 58.3 percent by the World Bank criterion as shown in Table 12. The short-term debt increased because current account deficits were financed mainly through short-term borrowings by financial institutions and through trade credits by business firms. The financial institutions used too much of the foreign exchange funds that they financed on short-term bases to make long-term investments. Moreover, the domestic financial institutions' investments were concentrated in the markets of the South East Asian countries and Russia, which went sour when those countries experienced currency crises at almost the same time as Korea did. Meanwhile, official foreign reserves were allocated in such a way that sufficient reserves could not be secured. Fairly large amount of Korea's foreign reserves were deposited with domestic banks and their overseas branches, and deposits could not be withdrawn in an emergency.

[23] The current ratio decreased further to the level of below 90 percent in 1998 when corporate insolvencies increased steeply.

(3) Lack of Discipline

The lack of market discipline was another factor behind the 1997 crisis. Market discipline was at very disappointing level. Even though the country had already undergone such big changes as political democratization, economic liberalization, and market opening, Since government control or management had been able to deter economic agents from engaging in hazardous activities, the past government-led development system had at least been capable of sustaining itself, even if it could not attain the first best efficiency. With the results of economic liberalization and market opening, however, the government had been largely removed from such a role. Nevertheless, a new market discipline, the so-called market mechanism, had not been settled down.

Even after financial liberalization, for example, financial institutions remained too inactive to take on the role of checking and monitoring the behavior of customer firms. Nor were stockholders so active in monitoring managers as might have been expected, in light of the increased importance of the capital markets as the channel of financial resource allocation. Disclosure of information essential for checking management performance was also insufficient, while the role of credit evaluation agencies had not been established, either.

Regulation and supervision of financial institutions were still hardly developed. Prudential regulation was known to be essential in a liberalized environment, and some regulations had been established. In practice, however, they were neither sufficient nor effectively enforced. In fact, the playing field in the financial sector was tilted in favor of the non-bank financial institutions, leaving them with regulatory loopholes or loose supervision. Some of them, while lacking adequate capabilities to manage risk, nevertheless took extremely high risks in pursuit of high returns.

Failure to form a new disciplinary mechanism led to a situation in which individual actors' optimal choices conflicted with those of others or deviated from the social optimum. Making matters worse was the fact that there were no longer corrective actions which could be effectively taken. The government tendencies to gloss over the economic situation and practice excessive forbearance were never effectively corrected. Financial institutions took advantage of the implicit public guarantee of deposits, and engaged in gathering as much deposits as possible, while neglecting improvement of their profitability, or their capabilities to manage risk. Firms abused their increased ability to borrow, and engaged in high risk-high return strategies. The owner-managers of *chaebols* maximized their leverage and control, despite their small percentage shares of equity, by abusing mutual debt payment guarantees and cross-share holding. These owner-managers tended to manage a number of large firms dogmatically, or even despotically.

Such problems had been concealed by the brilliant growth performance of the Korean economy. Once revealed, however, they exposed Korean markets to sudden swings in investor confidence, i.e., to a crisis. The foreign – especially, short-term banking – capital that had previously flowed in, taking advantage of capital account liberalization and domestic market opening, abruptly withdrew from the Korean markets after confirming that the market's inefficiency stemmed from lack of discipline.

The lack of market discipline was certainly related to the continually accelerating promotion of liberalization before the crisis. One cannot say, however, that liberalization was the direct and fundamental cause for the absence of discipline. Even after liberalization, it takes time and effort – not only of the government but also of the market participants – to form market discipline. Thus, it is more to the point to say that a continuation of government control – different in form but similar in kind to that under the past authoritarian system – most impeded the formation of market discipline. To say it in another way, the liberalization was led by the government, and in the presence of government control or intervention in the financial sector, private sector initiative was not sufficiently exercised, especially in monitoring and checking the behavior of trade partners.

In this sense, it can be said that the predominance of government influence in the working of the financial sector was a cause for the sector's lack of discipline. The analysis here will not pursue this line any further, however, because termination of the so-called repression would not have automatically brought about market discipline. What is emphasized here is that lack of discipline and the resultant coordination failure exacerbated the adverse effects of the bounded rationality of economic actors, and thus provided a ground for the crisis.

(4) Loss of Confidence in Government's Policy

In some sense, inconsistency and ambiguity in the government's handling of the 1997 crisis exacerbated it. Proper action taken by the government in accordance with the circumstances would have prevented a critical situation from proceeding to a crisis or collapse. This had, in fact, always been the case in the past, when critical situations arose due to the government's pursuit of too rapid economic growth; through successful adaptations to the situations at such times, the government had always been able to preserve market confidence. In 1997, however, the government's policy response was unable to generate market participants' confidence. The government could not find its proper role in a market economy system. It failed to correctly diagnose the economic fundamentals, and to design the right prescription to cure what ailed them. It sometimes hid policy information that would have served the economy better if disclosed. It struggled to resist market forces even when it was obvious that accepting them was a better option. It failed to stop the propagation of the crisis; it did not heed the lessons of past experience, even after it had seen a few rounds of the crisis propagation process: corporate insolvencies leading to banking distress, and then to the near depletion of foreign reserves. In retrospect, there were several chances for the government to break the Korean economy's rolling in the vicious circle leading towards economic crisis in 1997. In this respect, the Korean government's policy mistakes during the years 1996 and 1997 can be listed as one of the factors behind the 1997 economic crisis

C. Policy Response

The government took varied measures to cope with the 1997 economic crisis, based on the recognition that the crisis resulted from accumulated structural imbalances in many areas. The main framework for crisis resolution, which was molded after the method of general IMF crisis resolution, was stated in the stand-by agreement, or letter of intent. It was composed of a macroeconomic stabilization policy and a microeconomic structural adjustment policy. The former was centered on restriction of domestic demand and expenditure-switching, to correct the balance of payments deficits. Exchange rates were thus allowed to depreciate freely and reflect market forces fully. At the same time, money market rates were raised sharply to control the inflationary impact of the Won depreciation. This extremely tight macroeconomic policy aimed at both restraining domestic expenditures and preventing capital outflows. The microeconomic structural adjustment policy, meanwhile, included measures to resolve structural problems in each market. Its fundamental theme was to establish the institutional setting for a well-functioning market mechanism.

Under the above framework, implementation of policies was practiced on the basis of a moving target approach, in which specific policy targets were changed according to circumstances. Right after the currency crisis, the primary target was to calm the foreign exchange markets through a sharp hike of money market rates, and to restore investors' confidence in the Korean economy through announcement of a restructuring plan, including the exit of troubled banks and the restructuring of industrial investments. From May 1998, when the foreign exchange market began to calm down and the Won stabilized, monetary policy was relaxed and the money market rates were lowered, in consideration of the by-then increased uncertainty in the domestic financial markets. The instability of domestic financial markets in mid-1998 reflected the credit crunch and wide-spread bankruptcy of firms at that time. The credit crunch resulted because all banks undergoing screening by the supervising authority, for possible market exits, refrained from lending. The widespread number of bankruptcy was due partly to this and partly to the high level of interest rates.

Table 16. IMF Reform Program

	Sector	Contents
Macro-Economic Policy	monetary and exchange rate policy	• tight money to contain inflation and limit downward pressure on the Won – large liquidity injection to be reversed, and money market rates raised – day-to-day conduct of monetary policy to be guided by movements in the exchange rates and short-term interest rates – targeting growth of M_3, reserve money, and net domestic assets of the BOK
	fiscal policy	• tightened to achieve a surplus – raising transportation tax, special excise tax, broadening the tax base – reducing current expenditures
Micro-economic Structural Adjustment Policy	financial sector	• comprehensive restructuring and strengthening of the financial system to make it sound, transparent, and more efficient – a clear and firm exit policy, strong market and supervisory discipline, increased competition
	trade and capital account liberalization	• streamlined import certification procedure and other trade-related regulations • acceleration of ongoing capital account liberalization program
	corporate governance and corporate financial structure	• improvement of corporate governance through financial reform and capital liberalization – easing restrictions on M&As, introduction of internationally accepted practices in accounting and consolidated balance sheets, revision of bankruptcy provisions, break from past policies of bail-outs
	labor market	• easing dismissal restrictions to improve labor market flexibility – facilitation of reemployment to ease the burden of layoffs

Source: IMF (1997).

Structural adjustment was largely divided into two stages. The first stage involved establishing basic institutions needed for smooth operation of a market economic system, and forcing insolvent firms and banks out of the market. For this purpose, varied policy measures were undertaken. The institutional capabilities for restructuring were enhanced by integrating the three extant financial supervisory agencies into one agency, the Financial Supervision Commission, and by expanding the function of Korea Deposit Insurance Corporation (KDIC), and establishing Korea Asset Management Corporation (KAMCO) to dispose of non-performing loans. Bankruptcy law provisions were amended and M&A restrictions eased. Disclosure requirements for accounting information were also strengthened, and measures to improve corporate governance introduced, to provide for better monitoring and supervision of corporate or bank managers by interested parties. The authorities also devised measures to restrain over-borrowing by firms, such as prohibition of mutual debt guarantees among firms in the same large business groups. The government forced extremely troubled banks to exit the market, and at the same time used public funds to buy non-performing loans from and recapitalize the viable ones. It let the main creditor banks lead the debt workout programs to liquidate delinquent firms.

The second stage structural adjustment plan aimed at improving the management and governance of firms and banks through their own initiatives. So far, however, firms and banks were not ready to enter this stage. This is mainly because the amounts of non-performing loans increased to an unexpectedly large extent, and because the first stage restructuring was delayed due to unexpected events such as the Daewoo Group's going into a workout program.

III. APPRAISAL OF POLICIES FOR RESOLVING THE CRISES IN THE PAST

1. The 1972 Crisis

The policies incorporated in the August 3rd Decree were evaluated by the authority as a success (The Bank of Korea 1973). The appraisal was based on economic performance, such as visible improvement in corporate financial structures and expansion of exports one year or so after the policies were implemented.

Seen from the present point of view, however, it can be said that the Decree was problematic in some ways; also, its effects were not so great in the long run. The nature of the economic crisis had been rightly identified as a corporate crisis, and the focus of policy appropriately put on improving the financial structure of firms and modernizing the financial system by introducing non-bank financial institutions. The problem lay in the methods used in pursuit of this policy. Especially, the write-offs of debts were obviously biased in favor of enterprises and against finance. The curb loan freeze and rescheduling did not leave room for autonomous financial transactions. It also violated the principle of private ownership and freedom of contracts. The root problem of worsening financial structure of corporations had been their strategies for unsustainably rapid expansion, despite their lack of internal funds. What was actually necessary to improve corporations' financial situations, therefore, was to slow down economic growth and restrain corporations from over-borrowing. Direct subsidies to firms, however, impeded the formation of a reasonable incentive mechanism, and deepened firms' prevalent tendencies to rely on external funds and government support.

The policy of fostering the establishment of non-bank financial institutions served to broaden the scope of the Korean financial system. However, the policy was ineffective in eradicating the curb market, which flourished again in the latter half of the 1970s and first half of the 1980s. Regulatory discrimination between banks and the newly established non-bank financial institutions brought about adverse side effects. The authority gave preferential treatment to the non-bank financial institutions, compared to the banks, in order to help these institutions grow out of their infancy. In this circumstance, the banks lost their market shares, which impeded their sound development. The fragility or weakness of the Korean financial system, a background factor of the 1997 economic crisis, seems to have originated from these policies in the 1970s.

At the time of the 1972 Crisis, the stabilization policy tended to rely on direct controls, rather than on orthodox macroeconomic tools. The government attempted to calm inflation by directly controlling the prices of products such as rice, construction materials, and living necessities. It managed the money supply through direct control of domestic credits from 1970. Unfortunately, this mode of policy implementation brought about adverse side effects afterwards, such as the spread of underground markets and dual prices, and supply shortages of important necessities. In particular, the direct control of domestic credits failed to prevent an excess supply of money in the late 1970s. It eroded the basis of the autonomous operations of banks as well. With regard to the basic stance of macroeconomic policy, in fact, it was expansionary. This was in some sense unavoidable, of course, as stimulating investment in the heavy and chemical industries was given a higher priority than resolving the problems associated with the over-heated economy in the late 1960s. However, the expansionary macroeconomic policy eventually caused over-heating and real estate speculation to spread widely in the late 1970s, and this was among the factors underlying the 1980 economic crisis.

Most of the 1972 crisis resolution measures shared characteristics of direct intervention and subsidies by government. For example, in relieving firms from financial distress, the government intervened directly by freezing their liabilities at the expense of breakdown of the curb market. Thus, the firms enjoyed a free lunch. In short, the crisis resolution measures in the early 1970s were effective to some extent in the short run, but in the long run deepened the structural anomalies of the Korean economy. These structural anomalies paved the way for both the 1980 crisis and the 1997 crisis.

2. The 1980 Crisis

The crisis resolution measures for the 1980 economic crisis contained a systematic blueprint based on a synthetic analysis of the various kinds of problems in the Korean economy. The government had at hand a stabilization plan prepared in 1979. The plan generally indicated the right direction for reforming the Korean economy, which was maintained even after the 1980s. Prices were visibly stabilized from 1982, and this contributed to the sustained surpluses in the current account in the latter half of the 1980s. Moreover, the liberalization policy after the crisis was quite consistently and gradually executed. Thus, it put in place a stepping stone for more aggressive liberalization policies in the 1990s.

The crisis resolution measures also laid the groundwork for financial development, both in quantity and in quality. Thanks to price stability, demand for financial assets increased, and correspondingly many new financial instruments were introduced. Especially, the stock and insurance markets, so underdeveloped previously, were able to grow substantially from the mid-1980s when inflation almost ceased. These developments in the financial sector in part reflected shift in emphasis in government's economic policy, from real to financial development, or its recognition of importance of both of them.

The public's perception of economic policy matters also changed as a result of the policy measures introduced in the early 1980s. In particular, the government campaign to deepen public understanding of stabilization policies succeeded, to some extent, in making the public to realize the importance of economic stability, among other objectives, and to accept the shift in policy focus from growth to stability. It seems that these consolidated efforts of the government and the public were rewarded by the country's excellent economic performance later.

Seen from the present point of view, however, the policy measures implemented following the 1980 economic crisis contained some problems as well. The trade-off between growth and stability was neglected, and both were pursued simultaneously. The policy tools for both were mixed together, causing considerable confusion. For example, in the latter half of 1980, about one year after implementation of the stabilization policy, expansionary monetary policy tools were used again. Once again, in the latter half of 1982, the government attempted, (through what were called the June 28th Measures) to activate the economy with a low interest rate policy similar to those in the 1970s. At the same time, the government sought economic stability through tight fiscal policy and direct control of prices. This combination of tight fiscal policy and expansionary monetary policy might be seen as an appropriate policy mix, in that the heavy and chemical industrialization plan required continuous investments by companies lacking internal funds. The fact that from the outset monetary contraction had been ruled out as a means of maintaining economic stability, however, implied that the policy means actually employed might not have been optimally suited to accomplish the policy goals. The fact that monetary policy tools remained only as a means for boosting the economy also indicates that the attitudes of the policy makers had not changed much; that is, they still put great importance to industrial development than to financial development.

The measures taken for liberalization also contained certain problematic aspects. It was then understood that liberalization was inevitable and necessary since the only way to cure the structural problems caused by repression or excessive government control was to liberalize. However, the actual liberalization measures included mostly deregulation of price controls, without serious consideration of need to provide the infrastructure for efficient markets. For example, interest rate liberalization, one of the major targets of liberalization policy, left much to be desired, in terms of stimulating innovation on the part of banks, because it was pursued in a narrow range with various forms of government intervention. It can also be pointed out that liberalization was a government-initiated process, rather than one initiated by private sectors. Thus, it was largely designed to meet the needs of the government, and not those of the private sector. Regarding the speed of the liberalization policy, it put too much importance to a gradual approach to bring about substantial effects. Moreover, it produced adverse side-effects, e.g., institutional disequilibrium such as the uneven playing field between banks and non-bank financial institutions.

In some senses, the nature of many of the economic policies remained largely similar to those in the past, in that such policy tools as controls and intervention were frequently used. Controls were applied to the management of prices, to restraining real estate speculation, and to improving corporate financial structures. In addition, selective industrial policies continued to be pursued through, for example, the Distribution Industry Modernization Plan, the Agricultural Machinery Import-substitution Plan, the Small- and Medium-sized Enterprises Promotion Plan, and the Electronic Industry Promotion Plan.

In short, even though the 1980 crisis resolution policy was rightly directed and performed well in the short run, it had only a limited effect in curing the fundamental problems of the Korean economy. This was verified in part by the similar crises recurred in the 1990s.

3. The Post-1989 "Grave Situation"

The government's attempt to overcome a policy-driven crisis by introducing the concept of industrial restructuring seems appropriate. It was also prudent for the government to have maintained consistency in its liberalization policy since the 1980s. There were problems, however. The policy goal was not clearly set, for one thing; and the same policy tools as in the past were applied.

The fact that the target of economic policy was not clear was, in part, due to the lack of a thorough analysis of the causes of the grave situation. The period was in the midst of revolutionary changes in political and social affairs; thus, a radical change in the goals, instruments, and mode of policy implementation was also required. Since the period had seen an eruption of desires that had previously been repressed, showing a stronger tendency for individual actors to pursue their own self-interests, a new policy paradigm, which would accord with these changes, was needed. Economic policy should have addressed such problems as the coordination of conflicting interests and the establishment of market infrastructure, rather than that of managing economic variables to optimal levels. It chose the latter, however; that is, policy makers addressed the short-term issues by making use of direct controls, as in the past. In order to sustain stock prices, for example, the government directly controlled the supply of and demand for stocks. In order to promote industrial restructuring, it provided preferential loans to borrowers importing equipment for factory automation and rationalization, through which many firms were induced to invest in equipment, the same kind pattern as observed in the past.

In another similarity to the past pattern, the government allotted macroeconomic policy to the objective of boosting the economy. Coming as it did after the long economic boom in the late 1980s, the period was characterized by big changes not only in political and social structures, but in consumption patterns as well. To facilitate the economy's adjustment, a dramatic change in policy tone was not desirable at the time, especially because uncertainty needed to be kept to a minimum. Macroeconomic policy, however, was operated in the manner of alternating, within a very short time period, between "stop(contraction)" and "go(expansion)." Furthermore, the economy was then confronted with contradicting trends, such as a slump in stock prices, a rally in real estate price, domestic recession, and a balance of payments deficit. Such a situation hardly yielded itself to a macroeconomic cure. Ideally, macroeconomic policy should have been kept neutral.

The nature of economic policy was not much different from the past, either. As mentioned above, the policy tools included direct controls, and were employed to temporarily address the problems revealed, rather than resolve them fundamentally. Preferential treatment of the real over the financial sector remained unchanged. Some policies were implemented in a manner that contradicted the trend of financial liberalization; for example, the policies for stabilization of stock prices, promotion of investment in manufacturing, and expansion of credits to small- and medium-sized enterprises were backed up mainly by using measures in the financial sector which might repress financial sector development.

In short, the substance of the policy responses to the grave situation in 1989 crisis was to employ direct control measures to resolve the problems which had surfaced. Policy makers neglected probing for a new policy paradigm appropriate for the new socio-economic structure and economic environment. Even worse, these problems innate in the economic system, rather than being fundamentally resolved, were covered over again after the New Economy 5-Year Plan was promoted in 1993.

4. Effectiveness of Crisis Resolutions in the Past

Crises of a similar type have repeatedly taken place under similar backgrounds, such as deterioration of the profitability of firms, over-investment and worsening financial structures, backwardness of the financial sector, and policy mistakes. The genetic processes of all the crises also resembled each other, since they all occurred after economic booms, or in over-heated economies. All in all, the economic crises in Korea may be regarded as having broken out as internal weaknesses – e.g., over-borrowings by firms – were exposed to external shocks – e.g., economic recession, worsening world economic environments, and so on. Similar policy measures were undertaken repeatedly to cope with the crises. In all cases, promotion of investment, through financial and fiscal incentives, was used immediately after the crisis outbreak, and macroeconomic policy was operated on an accommodating base. Moreover, direct controls on prices were frequently employed.

The mere observation that similar crises were being repeated implies that the past crisis resolution policies were not effective. In fact, the past crisis resolution measures consisted mostly of patching over the problems revealed, rather than addressing the root causes of the crises or trying to prevent crises beforehand. Instead, such measures tended more to deepen the structural problems. For example, most of the past crisis resolution measures focused on disposing of the losses incurred by firms and banks through such instruments as bail-outs. This might have lessened the difficulties facing firms and banks at those times; the effects were only temporary, however, and not of such kind as to help improve efficiency. Measures such as subsidies spoiled economic agents' independence and autonomy, eventually allowing them to stick to high leverage strategies or cronyism, distorting incentives and creating structural problems.

Delay of macroeconomic policy also tended to aggravate critical situations, rather than preventing further crisis. Before a crisis broke out, contractionary policy was introduced, but only after the adverse effect of the over-heated economy, or of the asset appreciation, had materialized. By the time the adverse effects are visible, the economy is already starting to slow down; thus, an expansionary, rather than a tight macroeconomic policy is needed. In Korea, however, a contractive policy has been adopted at this juncture, thus making the economy shrink rapidly. It has thus never been possible, however, for the contraction introduced to be promoted strongly enough or sustained long enough. This is because firms and banks have always asked for stimulus policies as production declined and profits decreased. Accordingly, immediately after the economic crises, governments had no choice but to relax macroeconomic policy. Pump-priming measures and favorable foreign economic conditions have then led to economic booms. This in turn sowed the seeds of a future crisis. Then, the story repeated itself.

IV. Characteristics of the 1997 Economic Crisis and Appraisal of Its Resolution

1. Main Characteristics of the 1997 Economic Crisis

The 1997 crisis differs from the previous ones in that the country could not resolve the critical situation with its own resources. There had been previous crises in which foreign debt had been the main problem, and in which the economy faced difficulty in inducing further capital inflow. At those times, however, the country had overcome the crises on the basis of its own creditworthiness. In 1997, in contrast, Korea could not borrow abroad any more. Thus, it had to depend on the liquidity facilities of international financial institutions and maturity rescheduling of foreign debts.

Another feature of the 1997 economic crisis is that even though the external shocks were weaker than those during the previous crises, e.g., the 1980 crisis, their effects were much stronger. As for the 1980 crisis, it was triggered by a number of large shocks. Externally, unstable international oil prices, turmoil in the international financial markets, and world-wide economic recession were all happening together. Internally, bad harvests were accompanied by political and social unrest. In 1997, however, the only shock was the instability in the international financial markets caused by the South East Asian currency crisis. The terms of trade had worsened in 1996, to a larger degree than expected, but they had then improved somewhat in 1997.

As for the impacts, that of the 1997 crisis seems to have been larger than that of the 1980 crisis, which was severe enough. The economic situations of 1980 and 1998 can be compared like this: in 1980, the growth rate was -2.1 percent and the unemployment rate 5.2 percent; in 1998, they were -6.7 percent and 6.8 percent, respectively. Moreover, the psychological impact seemed to be also larger in the 1997 crisis, because the crisis was a setback to Koreans who had taken such pride in the development of the Korean economy to join in the group of the advanced countries. The social impacts, such as damage to the middle and lower classes, were also huge.

The fact that the impact of the 1997 crisis was by far larger than those of other crises, even if the external shocks were relatively small, indicates that the main problem was weakness of the economic system as a whole. Of course, the extremely tight macroeconomic policy measures undertaken by the IMF program exacerbated the deep recession. However, the emergence of the crisis itself, even without any particularly large external shock, shows that the economic system was extremely fragile to shocks.

The extreme variety of types of crises involved in it may be another distinct feature of the 1997 crisis. Even though the 1980 crisis comprised many types of crisis factors, such as troubled firms, foreign debt-servicing problems, and inflation, it is analyzed as having been in essence a result of the simultaneous occurrence of external shocks. In the 1997 crisis, however, the sequence of events (firm insolvencies →non-performing loans of banks → loss of international confidence in the Korean economy) repeated itself twice or three times and generated corporate crisis, banking and/or financial crisis, and currency crisis in a series. To this list of crisis types might be added a balance of payments crisis, in that widening of current account deficits was one cause of those other types of crises. One trait of a policy-driven crisis may also be attached to the list, in that crisis resolution policy faltered over and again.

Considering the variety of features of the 1997 crisis, it seems to have resulted from all the problems remaining unresolved from past crises which all erupted at once by a relatively small shock from abroad. To put it another way, the innate problems of the Korean economic system finally came to greatly hinder the smooth operation of the economic system. The fact that a flaw in one sector could not be offset by the strength of another sector indicates that each part of the economic system was fragile. The variety of features of the 1997 economic crisis reflected these various weaknesses in almost all parts of the Korean economic system.

2. Comparison of the Structural Adjustment Policy since 1997 with the Past Economic Crisis Resolution

It appears too early to assess the policy responses to the 1997 crisis, since some of policy measures are in an ongoing process. In addition, its complexity would not allow an easy appraisal. One window to assess the recent crisis resolution measures may be provided, however, by comparison with the past crises. Compared with those adopted during past crises, the measures to cope with the 1997 crisis have some different aspects as well as some similar ones. Since most past crisis resolution measures were not effective, difference from them may be assessed as a positive feature, while similarity to past measures would be regarded as a negative feature of the recent structural adjustment policy. For example, the recent measures included an attempt to address the structural problems, something which was absent on past occasions. This can be evaluated as a positive feature.

A. Differences from the Previous Crisis Resolutions

The measures to resolve the 1997 crisis, unlike the previous ones, included attempts to provide indirect assistance to troubled firms and banks on the condition that they make their own efforts and take responsibility themselves to resolve their own problems. This differs from the unilateral provision of support in the previous crisis resolutions in that it has required the firms and banks being bailed-out to conduct restructuring. This is an improvement over the past crisis resolution measures, considering the fact that the past unilateral assistance tended to reduce the efficiency of the recipient firms and banks.

The recent crisis resolution policy also differs from the past ones in that the measures have spanned over a wide agenda and addressed fundamental issues. The measures included not only macroeconomic policy but also efforts to correct problems in the financial, corporate, labor, and public service sectors.

Another difference between the recent policy and earlier ones is that this time it addressed the issue of regulating the undesirable behavior of economic agent, for example, moral hazard, by adopting the global accounting standards and by strengthening the rule by law. This approach to curing the structural problems of the Korean economy should be highly evaluated.

The crisis resolution policy was so radical in a sense that it covered a wide-range agenda and touches the root causes of economic crisis. This was made possible by a social consensus, which was readily reached thanks to clear appearance of the structural problems as well as the wide-ranging impacts of the crisis.

The content of the policy was also different from those of previous ones in that it has included preemptive measures, to prevent recurrence of crisis, as well as *ex post* measures to cope with the troubled firms and banks. In the past, crisis resolution policy usually did not contain preventive measures. Nor was policy such as the clearance of non-performing loans of financial institutions promoted in a timely manner, right after the crisis breakout; rather, it tended to be implemented after the critical situation had somewhat calmed down. In contrast to this, the recent policy implemented the exits of insolvent banks and firms first, of all items on the agenda. Furthermore, policies taken at this time included changes in the laws and regulations, which was also *ex ante* in nature since it too aimed at preventing another crisis. Accordingly, the contents of the recent policy have also become different. In the past, the same policy tools as before were used again and again; in response to the 1997 crisis, however, new policy tools were adopted or old tools employed in different manners.

The mode of policy implementation this time changed to a radical reform or big-bang approach. This was because the government wanted to resolve the problems in many sectors within a short time span. Radical reform has the advantage of speeding up learning by all economic actors. It has the disadvantage, however, of requiring high adaptation costs. This contrasts to the gradual reform in the past, adopted mainly to reduce adaptation costs.

Another new feature in the recent crisis resolution is the improved variety and quality of policy instruments. In the past, financial instruments were almost the only measures used to cure any economic problem. In the 1997 crisis resolution, however, fiscal instruments and institutional rearrangements were added to the financial instruments, as new tools. Diversification of policy tools is meaningful; it has reminded policy makers that there are other policy tools than financial ones to achieve economic policy objectives.

In short, the 1997 crisis resolution policy can be highly evaluated in that it addressed the fundamental issues with various and wide-ranging policy tools.

Unlike the past ones, the recent structural adjustment policy has also attached more importance to the financial sector than to the real sector. Thus, the reform tends not to take the real sector's activities into account seriously. This is a cause for concern, because the source of long-run economic development in Korea has always been and still is in the real sector, and in the near future this situation does not seem likely to change dramatically; the Korean economy is still in the phase of economic development in which value is added mostly through industrial rather than financial competitiveness. In the increasingly competitive global environment, an economy is required to be very active in research and development in the real sector. Recently in Korea, however, investment has been extremely sluggish except in a few industries. This is partly because of the negligence of the structural adjustment programs in the real sectors.

B. Similarities to the Previous Crisis Resolutions

The *1997* crisis resolution policy also has some similarities with previous ones. Above all, it resembled past experience in that the government is playing a leading role in its design and implementation. The government first derived a consensus among workers and employers through the Tripartite Commission, and then promoted structural adjustment through the initiative of private actors. As time has gone by, however, the private sector agent's will to restructure has weakened, and in some cases the government has coercively pushed reforms to overrule disputes. Government initiation was certainly inevitable, because the reform was in its first stage (hardware reform) – a stage in which resolution of the troubled firms and banks was the focal issue[24]. However, the government has not been able to proceed to the second stage reform (software reform).

Since the reform was mainly led by the government, the effects were expected to be limited. For example, although firms have sharply reduced their debt-equity ratios, as the government forced them to do so, this did not necessarily mean that they had quit their old ways of doing business; in fact, they lowered their ratios largely through the revaluation of assets and issue of new stocks, rather than by redeeming debts or selling assets.

The operation of macroeconomic policy during the recent crisis resolution process resembled the past, too. Just as in the previous cases, the stabilization policy implemented in the early stage of the crisis exacerbated the situation further. It does seem, however, that while the switch of macroeconomic policy from a restrictive to an expansionary base from mid-1998 was similar to the past in its timing, it was different in its purpose. It was done not so much to boost the economy, as it had been in the past, as to stop the troubles in firms and banks from spilling over to others. The policy seemed to have amplified the intensity of the business cycle because it was so strong in magnitude and was introduced in an environment characterized by greater uncertainty. It also misdirected or lessened the effects of the restructuring efforts.

3. Implications for Structural Adjustment Policy

The main lesson from the above analysis of four crises in the Korean economy is that the problems intrinsic to the economic system should be cured fundamentally so that a crisis does not recur. The 1997 economic crisis was caused by over-borrowings by firms, financial sector weakness, inefficiency in the economic system, and policy mistakes. All of these factors are fundamental problems of the Korean economy; they had all been causes for past crises. Mishandling of the problems in the past might have contributed to the 1997 crisis. Measures to prevent future crises should focus on resolving these fundamental problems[25].

In order to prevent the same problems causing further crises, the methods used in crisis resolution should be different in nature from those employed in the past. In the past, similar

[24] The government's intention to distinguish between the first stage structural adjustment (hardware reform), which attempts at introduction and establishment of formal institutions such as laws and regulations, and the second stage structural adjustment (software reform), which aims at changing the behaviors of individual actors, may be interpreted as having resulted from neglect of the fact that institutions comprise not only rules, but also behavioral patterns.

[25] That an economic crisis may happen because of factors other than those so far discussed remains a possibility, of course.

policies were repeatedly used, such as subsidizing distressed firms and financial institutions. These policies were not effective, as is shown by the recurrence of similar crises afterwards. In other words, to protect, to support, and to foster firms and banks just because they are core components of the economic system, is not an appropriate way to go. On the contrary, such a policy aggravates the fragility of the economic system. Therefore, a crisis resolution policy should avoid using such bail-out measures, in order to prevent a crisis from coming back. The fact that structural adjustment policy following the 1997 crisis did not use unilateral subsidies to troubled firms and financial institutions should be highly evaluated.

It should also be noted that the measures initiated by the government, including the introduction of new laws and guidelines to improve the financial structures of firms and financial institutions, are not sufficient to prevent reoccurrence of a crisis. The measures so far were undertaken to establish the proper environment to enable firms and financial institutions to do business in a changed manner. The undertaking of such measures is one thing, and whether the firms and financial institutions will actually change their behavior is another. Firms and financial institutions should reinforce their business competence by themselves, lest they confront crisis again.

All economic agents, including firms and financial institutions, stakeholders, and the government, should make efforts together in order to complete the structural adjustment policy successfully. Above all, firms and banks must put their efforts into reducing their structural weaknesses. Moreover, the roles of stockholders, employees, creditors and customers, in checking and monitoring the behavior of firms or financial institutions, should also be strengthened. In addition, the government should enact regulations and laws ensuring that firms and financial institutions operate on their own initiative and exert their creativeness freely, and that they also assume responsibilities consonant with their new freedom to choose.

In this respect, introduction and implementation of the concept of the so-called second-generation reform is necessary for the success of the second stage structural adjustment policy. While the first-generation reform typically involves liberalization, stabilization, and selected structural reforms, the second-generation reform focuses on deeper and broader institutional reform, to enhance institutional capabilities (World Bank 1997). The first-generation reform can mostly be enacted through executive order, and thus the main actors are limited to the few elite technocrats. The second-generation reform, however, relates to all those affected by the institutional change. This implies that the government should refrain from initiating reforms, and ways should be opened for all interested parties to participate in the reform process, i.e., in identifying the problems, improving institutions, and creating a new economic order, all with the willingness for mutual understanding and compromise.

Macroeconomic policy, moreover, as a part of the crisis prevention measures, should be implemented in a manner different from the past. It is the timing of a stabilization policy that matters. In the past, poor timing of stabilization policy typically lessened the effects of stabilization policy. Stabilization measures were introduced just when the economy had begun to stagnate after a long period of boom, and seldom contributed to preventing recurrence of crisis. If a stabilization policy is to be used, it should be implemented in a preemptive manner so that it can prevent an exceptional boom or wide-spread speculation, which is one of the main macroeconomic causes of an economic crisis. Even in that case, of course, the authorities must remember that microeconomic means to reduce corporate over-borrowings and restrain banks' exposures are no less important in achieving the purpose than aggregate demand management

V. TENTATIVE CONCLUSION

This chapter employed an approach different from those lying behind the various common views of the recent structural adjustment policy in Korea. This chapter has first defined structural adjustment policy as a set of measures to prevent economic crisis from recurring, and then evaluated the effectiveness of the crisis resolution measures from this perspective. Utilization of this approach could probably do away with the confusions, which have arisen, among various reasons, from lack of a consistent analytic framework.

Another feature of this chapter is that it has attempted at finding some ways to enhance the effectiveness of the structural adjustment policy, based on analysis and comparison of past experiences. The successes or failures in past attempts at crisis resolution should be of great help in evaluating the recent one, considering the fact that there is no complete theory or experimentation on what constitutes an ideal restructuring program.

Finally, it should also be noted that historic facts are subject to different interpretations, depending upon what point of view they are seen from. The same is true of the interpretation of the ongoing Korean economic structural adjustment policy. A researcher may arrive at different conclusions or draw different policy implications from those contained in this chapter if he starts from a different point of view. Therefore, more effective assessment of the structural adjustment policy would entail analyses from many points of view, and then a synthesis of them.

Bearing all of these points in minds, this chapter can reach a tentative conclusion as follows: Korea has experienced four episodes of economic crisis since the 1960s. This chapter examined each crisis and found out that the same factors that caused one previous crisis later brought about another crisis repeatedly. This implies that the measures taken to resolve the previous crises were ultimately ineffective. Most of the past crisis resolution measures focused on disposing of the losses incurred by firms and banks through such instruments as bail-out loans. As far as macroeconomic policy is concerned, stabilization measures were introduced just when the economy had begun to stagnate after a long period of boom, and seldom contributed to preventing recurrence of crisis; rather, they amplified the crisis intensity.

These results suggest several lessons for the restructuring policy. First, it should be designed in such a way as to encourage private agents to take initiative, with the government abstaining from direct intervention such as bail-out loans. This would eventually strengthen private sector capacity to overcome adverse shocks. Second, if a stabilization policy is to be used, it should be implemented in a preemptive manner, so that it can prevent an excessive boom or wide-spread speculation.

ACKNOWLEDGEMENTS

The authors would like to thank their colleagues for their constructive comments and suggestions. This chapter is a substantially revised version of the working paper entitled "Korean Experiences of Economic Crisis Resolution" by the first author. The views contained in this paper are the authors' own, and do not necessarily represent the official views of the Bank of Korea.

REFERENCES

In Korean

The Bank of Korea, (1973). *A Comprehensive Report on The August 3rd Economic Emergency Decree,* Seoul: The Bank of Korea.

———, *Economic Statistics Yearbook*, various issues.

———, *National Account,* various issues.

———, *Financial Statement Analysis,* various issues.

———, (1998). *Statistical Yearbook of Foreign Exchange*, Seoul: The Bank of Korea.

———, (2000). *The Bank of Korea: A History of Fifty Years, Seoul:* The Bank of Korea.

Economic Planning Board, (1980). *Economic Policy in the Periods of Liberalized and Open Economy: 30 Years of the Economic Planning Board Π*, Seoul: Economic Planning Board.

Fair Trade Commission, *Fair Trade White Book,* various issues.

Kim, Jung-Ryum, (1990). *30 Years of Economic Development Policy in Korea: Memoirs of Kim Jung-Ryum*, Seoul: Jungang Ilbo

Korea Development Institute, (1981). *Collections of Economic Stabilization Policy Measures* (Book I and Book II), Seoul: Korea Development Institute.

Lee, Jong Kyu, (2000). *Economic Crisis: Causes and Genetic Process, Economic Studies Series, No. 2*, Seoul: Economic Studies Office, The Bank of Korea.

In English

Fry, Maxwell J., (1995). *Money Interest, and Banking in Economic Development* (2nd Ed.), Baltimore and London: Johns Hopkins University Press.

Goldstein, Morris and Philip Turner, (1996). *Banking Crises in Emerging Economies: Origins and Policy Options," BIS Economic Papers,* No. 46, Basle, Switzerland: Bank for International Settlements.

IMF, (1997). *Republic of Korea – Request for Stand-by Arrangement,* mimeograph.

Kang, David, (2002). Bad Loans to Good Friends: Money Politics and the Development State in South Korea, *International Organization* 56, 177-207.

Kindleberger, Charles P., (1996). *Manias, Panics and Crises: A History of Financial Crises,* 3rd edition, New York: John Wiley and Sons.

Krueger, Anne O., (1993). *Political Economy of Policy Reform in Developing Countries,* Cambridge: MIT Press.

Lee, S. and K. Cheong, (2007). The Political Economy of Financial Structure of Korean Firms, *Journal of Developing Areas,* forthcoming.

MacKinnon, Ronald I., (1973). *Money and Capital in Economic Development,* Washington D. C.: Brookings Institution.

Schandler, Susan et al., (1995). IMF Conditionality: Experience under Stand-by and Extended Arrangements, Part I: Key Issues and Findings, *IMF Occasional Paper,* No. 128, Washington D. C.: IMF.

World Bank, (1997). The State in a Changing World, *World Development Report* 1997, New York: Oxford University Press.

In: Korea: Economic, Political and Social Issues
Editors: P. H. Elwood, J. B. Albertus

ISBN: 978-1-60456-513-3

Chapter 2

The Role of the Exchange Rate in Inflation Targeting: A Case Study of Korea

Barry Eichengreen
University of California, Berkeley, CA, USA

Introduction

This paper is concerned with the conduct of monetary and exchange rate policy in Korea. It inquires into the best way of characterizing central bank policy since the financial crisis of 1997-1998, asking specifically whether the Bank of Korea should be portrayed as an open-economy inflation targeter. National officials will insist that the answer is yes – that the Bank of Korea has pursued inflation targeting since at least 2000 and that it no longer targets the exchange rate, either explicitly or implicitly. The central bank has adopted much of the apparatus of inflation targeting, complete with a band for target inflation and a Monetary Policy Report to the National Assembly. The 2004 version, the most recent edition available at the time of writing, stipulates an annual target of 3 per cent plus or minus 1 per cent, along with a medium-term (longer than one year) inflation target of 2.5-3.5 per cent; it makes little mention of the exchange rate. Trends in the dollar/won exchange rate are mentioned in passing, but no implications are drawn for the conduct of monetary policy.[1] From this it would appear that the exchange rate plays little role in monetary policy in Korea.[2]

---

[1] There is then a brief Chapter 5, entitled "Foreign Exchange Markets," again with a one-page review of trends in the dollar/won exchange rate in 2003, but no analysis of the implications for monetary policy. Equally revealingly, the first time the words "exchange rate" appear in Bank of Korea (2003) is some one hundred pages into this document, and then only in the context of a retrospective discussion of monetary and financial experience. The most revealing passage in this document is hidden on p.123, where it is written that "the Bank of Korea is obliged to change its monetary policy stance when the exchange rate is not in balance with the inflation target."

[2] The Bank of Korea's *Quarterly Bulletin* for the first quarter of 2004 (the latest available at the time of writing) does mention in the depreciation of the exchange rate in the context of import price inflation as early as p.16, although it then does not refer further to the exchange rate in describing the formulation of monetary policy. See Bank of Korea (2004b).

In a sense it would be surprising were this the case, for in an economy as open and sensitive to foreign trade and investment as Korea, movements in the exchange rate will contain information useful for forecasting movements in inflation and the output gap, the two arguments of the standard objective function of a central bank that engages in flexible inflation targeting. Movements in the exchange rate determine movements in import prices, which are passed through into the prices of domestic substitutes and thereby affect the prospects for inflation. Movements in the exchange rate also affect the short-to-medium-term evolution of the output gap, whether through changes in competitiveness (owing to incomplete passthrough) or balance-sheet effects (if a country's external assets and liabilities are dollarized). They may have implications for other valid concerns of the central bank such as the stability of the financial system. Hence, even if the central bank does not attach utility to the exchange rate itself (even if the value of the currency is not itself an argument of the authorities' objective function), the exchange rate can still be an important intermediate target for monetary policy. This in fact is the conclusion of virtually all recent analytical work on the conduct of inflation targeting in open economies.[3]

In addition, there is the conclusion of authors like McKinnon and Schnabl (2003) that when exchange rate changes are measured at high frequencies the day-to-day volatility of the dollar exchange rates of the principal East Asian countries, including Korea, is not significantly greater than before the crisis. To be sure, other authors have reached different conclusions: Oh (2004a) computes various measures of exchange rate volatility before and after the crisis (the percentage change in the absolute value of the end of day price between successive days, the difference between the highest and lowest price during the day as a percentage of the intra-daily average exchange rate) and finds more than a doubling of both measures between 1 March 1995-31 October 1997 and 1 April 1998-30 September 2003.[4] The same conclusion comes through even more strongly in Eichengreen (2003) when the standard deviation of the exchange rate is normalized by the standard deviation of reserves. Be this as it may, a number of authors have expressed surprise that the won exchange rate has not displayed more variability at high frequencies in the last six years and asked whether the Bank of Korea is not in fact a covert exchange rate targeter.[5]

In this paper I therefore revisit the question of how to characterize the conduct of monetary and exchange rate policy in Korea. Should the Bank of Korea be portrayed as a

---

[3] See Ball (1999), Eichengreen (2002) and Truman (2003).

[4] Excluding the crisis period 1 November 1997-31 March 1998.

[5] In addition, McKinnon and Schnabl regress the exchange rate of the won against the exchange rates of the dollar, the yen and the deutschmark (where all exchange rate rates are measured vis-à-vis the Swiss franc and expressed as log differences). They find that the U.S. dollar has been the dominant currency in the authorities' implicit target basket both before and after the crisis and infer from this that the Bank of Korea continues to severely limit short-run fluctuations in the dollar rate. (There is some evidence of an increasing weight on the yen in the Korean basket, but the dollar still remains far-and-away dominant, according to their results. Oh (2004b) similarly finds that the won maintains its correlation with the dollar while displaying an increasing correlation with the yen.) Some Korean commentators will observe that the country was officially floating before the crisis as well, but the reality then was that the Korean authorities attached considerable importance to the dollar exchange rate. They actively managed the dollar rate to the point where some observers referred to an implicit dollar peg or band. Thus, pre-crisis experience is not obviously a challenge to McKinnon and Schnabl's conclusion that the Korean authorities continue to heavily manage the dollar rates – that even if fluctuations in the won-dollar exchange rate seem to be permitted in the medium run, the Bank of Korea adjusts policy to rather strictly limit the currency's fluctuation in the short run.

flexible inflation targeter?[6] Does it use its monetary policy instrument – the overnight call rate – to target inflation and other variables potentially of concern (the output gap, the stability of the financial system) to while allowing the exchange rate to passively adjust to that interest rate setting, which is what would seem to be suggested by the Monetary Policy Report? Or does it attach independent importance to the exchange rate and modify its monetary policy stance when a putative setting for the overnight call right implies an uncomfortably large change in the exchange rate?

My answer to the first question is yes: a standard Taylor-type inflation targeting rule is a useful way of characterizing the Bank of Korea's policy. At the same time, movements in the exchange rate are too important for the objectives of central bank policy to effectively be disregarded, as they are in large, less open de facto inflation targeters like the United States. It is not surprising in this light that my analysis suggests that when setting the overnight call rate the Bank of Korea in fact responds to not just expected inflation and the output gap but also to movements in the won/dollar exchange rate. I thus prefer to think of its monetary regime not as a free float backed by inflation targeting but as a managed float accompanied by modified inflation targeting.

Having provided a characterization of Korean monetary policy, I next consider some special issues that arise in context of inflation targeting in a relatively advanced emerging market such as Korea. I ask whether the controversy over the role that the exchange rate has actually played in the conduct of monetary policy suggests that Korean policy has been insufficiently transparent. In addition, previously authors (like McKinnon and Schnabl) having asked whether Korea has to follow the United States, Japan and Euroland when formulating its monetary and exchange rate policies, I inquire into the implications of the emergence of China. Finally, I ask how the development of the Korean economy and its financial markets should influence the conduct of monetary and exchange rate policies going forward.

INFLATION TARGETING IN EMERGING MARKETS[7]

Inflation targeting entails an institutionalized commitment to price stability as the primary goal of monetary policy, mechanisms rendering the central bank accountable for attaining its monetary policy goals, the public announcement of targets for inflation, and a policy of communicating to the public the rationale for the decisions taken by the central bank. Central bank independence is needed to give the monetary authorities the leeway necessary to commit to price stability. And sound and stable fiscal policy and banking system are needed to avoid problems of fiscal dominance that would otherwise prevent the central bank from subordinating other goals to the objective of price stability or cause its independence to be undermined.

The multi-dimensional nature of this definition explains why there is no consensus about which emerging markets practice inflation targeting. Brazil, Chile, the Czech Republic, Israel,

---

[6] The distinction between flexible inflation targeting and the alternative (strict inflation targeting) is that under the former the authorities attach weight not only to deviation in inflation from its target but also to short-run fluctuations in the output gap, over which they have limited control.

[7] This section and the one that follows are drawn from Eichengreen (2004).

South Africa, Poland, Colombia, Thailand, Mexico, the Philippines and South Korea are all cited in this connection. While the length of this list would appear to pose a challenge to those who argue that floating, backed by inflation targeting, is not viable in emerging markets, there is the question of whether these countries are actually practicing inflation targeting or they are really just covertly pegging their currencies. That some, like Israel, also maintain bands for their exchange rates, while others, including South Korea, intervene to limit or offset exchange rate fluctuations, has been pointed to as evidence that they are really covert peggers, as noted above. But the fact that their central banks alter monetary policy when the exchange rate moves may not in fact mean that they are not really inflation targeting. Insofar as depreciation is a leading indicator of inflation, the standard inflation targeting framework suggests tightening monetary policy when the exchange rate weakens. This is the prescribed response when there is a change in the direction or availability of capital flows due to, say, a rise in foreign interest rates, or a deterioration in foreign investor sentiment toward the country. A higher foreign interest rate implies less capital inflow for a given domestic interest rate and therefore a weaker currency. As the exchange rate weakens, higher import prices are passed through into inflation. The appropriate response is thus to raise interest rates. This is not because the central bank cares about the exchange rate in and of itself, but because it cares about inflation.

If the disturbance is to the foreign component of aggregate demand (to the terms of trade or export demand), again the exchange rate will weaken, since export revenues will have declined while nothing else affecting the foreign exchange market will have changed in the first instance. In addition, demand will decline, since foreigners are demanding fewer of the country's exports. Now there are two offsetting effects on inflation: while higher import prices will be passed through into inflation, weaker aggregate demand will be deflationary. If the second effect dominates, then inflation will decline with the growth in the gap between potential and current output, and the appropriate response for an inflation-targeting central bank will be to cut interest rates regardless of the weight it attaches to output variability. The more policy-relevant case is probably the one in which this shock, by depreciating the exchange rate, is inflationary on balance. If the central bank attaches a high weight to output variability, it still may want to cut interest rates. If on the other hand it attaches a high weight to deviations of inflation from target, it may instead raise interest rates to limit currency depreciation and inflation in the short run while still allowing the exchange rate to adjust eventually to its new long-run equilibrium level. In other words, it will acknowledge that the weakness of demand requires a weaker exchange rate, but it will still smooth the downward adjustment of the currency by leaning against the wind in order to prevent a sharp spike in inflation.

This framework suggests a test of whether countries like Korea have really begun to practice inflation targeting. Find instances where the shock is to commodity rather than capital markets, since these are the cases where the weakness of output creates a case for interest rate cuts and for allowing the exchange rate to adjust. Consider not just the tendency for the central bank to lean against the wind in the short run but also its willingness to allow the exchange rate to adjust subsequently. 2001 is a useful data point insofar as the shock to the Korean economy came mainly from commodity markets (reflecting the U.S. recession, continuing Japanese difficulties, and the high-tech slump). While the won weakened considerably, fanning inflation, there were also worries of rising unemployment. An inflation targeting central bank will tighten as inflation heats up, but it should also allow the exchange rate to adjust if the slump persists. My reading of Korean experience is that the central bank did just that: while it was concerned with inflation, which was running just below the official 3 per cent target in mid-2001, it nonetheless allowed the won to fall – by fully ten per cent against the dollar in the six months from late November 2000 – as the economy has weakened. This behavior does not obviously resemble "fear of floating."

TECHNICAL ISSUES

A number of technical obstacles to inflation targeting have also been raised in the emerging market context. Here I consider three: the speed of passthrough, the difficulty of forecasting inflation, and credibility problems.[8]

High Passthrough

Calvo and Reinhart (2000) provide evidence that changes in import prices due to movements in the exchange rate are passed through into domestic prices faster in emerging markets than industrial countries. With high passthrough, a change in the exchange rate has a large short-run impact on inflation and a small short-run impact on output. For example, if there is a shock to the foreign exchange market that causes the exchange rate to depreciate and output to fall, the authorities will have less reluctance to tighten than in the case of slower passthrough, since they gain more in terms of disinflation as the currency stabilizes and strengthens, while losing less as output falls due to declining competitiveness.[9]

Under full (instantaneous, 100 per cent) indexation, monetary policy has no capacity to stabilize – or, for that matter, destabilize – output. It can simply be used to target inflation. With full indexation, that target can be hit immediately. Full indexation thus simplifies the inflation targeting problem since it reduces the central bank's objective function to the one variable that it can now influence and allows the authorities to hit that target immediately.

The implications for exchange rate management depend on the source of shocks. If domestic monetary policy is the source of the instability, then stabilizing the exchange rate will force the central bank to undo such shocks immediately. If shocks are external, then the exchange rate should adjusted to offset them. Foreign deflation will induce an inflation-targeting central bank to expand the money supply and allow the currency to depreciate, while an inflationary shock will induce the opposite reaction.

Thus, while rapid passthrough will modify the implementation of monetary policy by an inflation targeting central bank, it is not a fundamental challenge to the viability of that approach to its formulation.

---

[8] A fourth issue, liability dollarization, is not so relevant to the Korean case, at least since the crisis. For discussion of it see Eichengreen (2002) and other chapters in this book.

[9] This paragraph also makes clear that passthrough is not an exogenous parameter that can be regarded as independent of the monetary regime. If the credibility of the commitment to low inflation is enhanced by an institutionalized commitment to price stability, central bank independence and accountability, and policies of communicating the rationale for monetary-policy decisions, then agents will revise downward the likelihood they attach to the prospect that transitory shocks will be validated by policy and hence become permanent, and therefore how quickly they adjust prices in response to a weaker exchange rate. There is some anecdotal evidence of this for Brazil and Mexico (Mishkin and Savastano 2000) and Israel (Leiderman and Bufman 2001).

Difficulty of Forecasting Inflation

Disturbances make it difficult for observers to evaluate the central bank's commitment to inflation targeting, since it is often hard to determine the extent to which divergences between actual inflation and the target are due to the monetary policy implemented several quarters ago as opposed to shocks occurring during the control lag. This uncertainty may reduce credibility – it will not be clear whether the central bank is in fact following the announced policy. This is where the conditional inflation forecast comes in. The central bank announces a point or range forecast for inflation and explains how its instrument settings are consistent with its forecast. If it misses the target, it must then be able to point to unanticipated disturbances occurring during the control lag that can account for the discrepancy or risk losing credibility.

If reliable forecasting is not possible, then the markets may be unable to determine the intent of the authorities. A brutally-honest central bank might surround its point forecast with a wide confidence interval. But a wide range of outcomes will be consistent with a wide range of policies, complicating efforts to determine the authorities' intent. Nor will specifying a narrow forecast range and missing it repeatedly build confidence in the central bank's commitment to its target.

Are there structural features of emerging markets that complicate the forecasting exercise? Emerging economies are more commodity-price sensitive than their advanced-industrial counterparts, and commodity-price fluctuations can wreak havoc with the forecastability of consumer price inflation. There is the fact that foodstuffs, whose prices are affected by the weather, have a heavy weight in the CPI in low-income countries. The obvious solution to both problems is to target "core" (or underlying) inflation net of commodity prices, as is the practice of some industrial countries.

Then there is such countries' disproportionate dependence on capital flows. Sensitivity of domestic financial conditions to international capital flows is, in a sense, the defining feature of an emerging market. The literature on asymmetric information suggests that unpredictable volatility is especially pronounced in the financial sphere, and nowhere more than in international financial markets. Because information is costly to acquire and process, investors are imperfectly informed. They therefore herd in and out of markets in response to the movements of other investors, amplifying volatility. Because asymmetric information reduces the liquidity of financial assets in periods of distress (reflecting fears that assets liquidated in fire sales are damaged goods), illiquidity and balance-sheet problems may transmit financial difficulties across borders, with destabilizing repercussions for innocent bystanders. These phenomena will be most pronounced in international markets, where information must travel geographical and cultural distance, and in emerging markets, where the information environment is least developed.

The forecastability of inflation, ultimately, is an empirical issue. Hoffmaister (2001) has analyzed it in Korea, finding that inflation is roughly as forecastable there as in Sweden. Univariate models of inflation perform similarly in Korea and in the high-income inflation targeters in the period immediately preceding their adoption of the strategy, although there is some evidence of positive kurtosis, as if inflation is subject more frequently to larger shocks than would be expected given its standard deviation. Christoffersen and Wescott (1999) and Rivas (2001) similarly find evidence of kurtosis and skewness for Poland in 1992-98 and Nicaragua in 1988-98, respectively. But upon eliminating some of the largest and smallest price changes each month among the 33 main categories in Poland's CPI to derive a measure of core inflation, Christoffersen and Wescott find that a limited set of economic variables forecasts one-period-ahead core inflation reasonably well by international standards. Rivas similarly has considerable success in forecasting core inflation in Nicaragua so long as he focuses on the period of moderate inflation starting around 1993.

Thus, the difficulty of forecasting inflation may be an obstacle to effective inflation targeting in an economy in economic and financial disequilibrium. It is not realistic to hope to forecast inflation with the requisite reliability if the country is still bringing inflation down from high levels, comprehensively reforming the tax and public-spending systems, and radically restructuring the private sector. But where such reforms have been underway for some time and are proceeding at a measured pace – as in Poland, South Korea and Brazil – forecasting difficulties would not appear to be an insurmountable obstacle to inflation targeting.

Credibility Problems

We have already seen how the difficulty of forecasting inflation can lessen the credibility of inflation targeting in emerging markets. In addition, a history of arbitrary enforcement that lessens respect for constitutional and statutory law may limit the effective independence of the central bank, whose insulation from pressure to pump up activity before an election or to help meet the government's financial needs is a prerequisite for effective inflation targeting. Central bankers threatened with dismissal, notwithstanding laws ostensibly guaranteeing them long terms in office, will be more inclined to bow to pressure to purchase government securities on the primary market. And chronic budget deficits can convince even an independent central bank that it has no choice but to meet the government's fiscal needs if it wishes to preserve financial stability, sowing the seeds of time inconsistency.

To the extent that inflation targeting is less credible in emerging markets, its benefits will be less. Absent confidence that the central bank is committed to low inflation, interest rates will not fall to the levels of other low-inflation countries. Shocks will raise questions about whether the authorities are prepared to stay the course. Sharp changes in interest rates, exchange rates and international capital flows may feed upon themselves: financial variables will be volatile, with negative implications for the economy. If policy is not credible, then firms will not reduce price increases to meet the inflation target. Hitting it will require an increase in interest rates sufficient to deliver a substantial reduction in import prices (through a sharp appreciation of the exchange rate), with destabilizing output effects.

A wide variety of models of monetary policy point to the fact that there is a tradeoff between flexibility and credibility. Central banks most lacking in credibility will have an incentive to move along the frontier of feasible credibility-flexibility combinations in order to obtain it. In particular, imperfect credibility may require the central bank to target inflation rigidly. Absent credibility problems, a central bank faced with inflation in excess of its target may want to raise interest rates and damp down inflation only gradually in order to avoid causing or compounding a recession. Faced with a weak banking system ill prepared to absorb interest rate increases, which raise the cost of servicing its short-term liabilities and increase default rates by borrowers, it may want to limit interest-rate volatility and administer its anti-inflationary medicine in small doses. But if the monetary authorities fail to respond quickly when inflation heats up, observers may begin to wonder whether they are optimally trading off objectives or they are in fact not really committed to price stability. Asset prices and the variables they affect will not respond as hoped. Similarly, if the central bank targets core rather than headline inflation, observers may wonder whether this is because monetary policy should not attempt to offset temporary commodity price fluctuations, or whether the authorities are really just seeking an excuse to disregard inflationary pressures. Monetary policy will thus have to respond more sharply to exchange rate and commodity-price fluctuations than would be the case if it was being implemented by a highly credible central bank. The monetary authorities may not be able to afford even modest deviations from strict inflation targeting for fear of sending the wrong signal.

In addition, central banks in emerging markets will have an incentive to use transparency to further enhance their credibility. This will tend to push them in the direction of a fully-articulated inflation-targeting framework rather than the seat-of-the-pants approach preferred by, inter alia, the Federal Reserve. Its hard-won credibility allows the Federal Reserve Board to hint at its inflation forecast rather than announcing it. It allows the Fed to sketch the model used to link its policy instruments to that forecast rather than describing it in any great detail. Most emerging markets do not enjoy this luxury. To convince investors that they mean what they say, their central banks will have to publish the forecast and the model.

Another implication is that effective inflation targeting will require steps to eliminate fiscal dominance as a way of building credibility. In particular, inflation targeting must be supported by the reform and reinforcement of fiscal institutions as a way of delivering better fiscal outcomes. Fiscal-policy making processes and procedures should be centralized to reduce free riding. Vertical fiscal imbalances should be reduced. The budget constraints facing sub-central governments should be hardened. Where inflation targets are announced not by the central bank but by the government (Chile, Poland) or by the central bank and government jointly (Brazil, Israel), this can be understood precisely as a way for the government to commit to the fiscal discipline needed to achieve the target.

These implications are evident in the behavior of those emerging markets that have embraced inflation targeting. Such countries have generally moved toward the adoption of a formal framework. Their central banks have been reluctant to miss the inflation target even temporarily, or to slow the pace at which deviations between target inflation and actual inflation are eliminated, for fear of undermining their anti-inflationary credibility. The credibility problem has tended to dictate that the change in the CPI must be the operational measure of inflation, because it is widely understood and therefore more credible, even when core inflation purged of import-price fluctuations would be more appropriate in principle.

Credibility problems make inflation targeting less attractive. They imply more volatility and less flexible policy implementation. The question is then how quickly credibility can be gained and whether or not inflation targeting can be part of that process.

Inflation Targeting in Korea

The revision of the Bank of Korea Act that came into effect in April 1998 stipulates that price stability is the primary objective of monetary policy. It specifies that the central bank should set an annual inflation target and strive to achieve it. These arrangements superseded a system in which monetary indicators were the intermediate targets of policy (first M1, then the central bank's net domestic assets, then reserve money, then domestic credit of financial institutions, net domestic credit, again M1, M2, M2 plus certificates of deposit and balances held by investment trust companies, and finally M3 – it is hard to imagine a clearer illustration of the operation of Goodhart's law). The 1998 act then stipulated that the central bank should set an inflation target in consultation with the government and make that target public.

Initially, the target was framed in terms of the consumer price index; in 2000, after further study, this was changed to core inflation. For a time the Bank of Korea continued to set targets for M3 as well as inflation, on the grounds that "financial markets could have been thrown into confusion if the monetary targeting that had been utilized during the past 30 years were to be scrapped all at once."[10] From 2001, M3 was dropped as an intermediate target.[11] Policy decisions are delegated to an independent Monetary Policy Committee.[12] Consistent with modern theories of inflation targeting, the Bank of Korea began announcing its monetary policy decisions immediately, communicating its general intentions to the public, and submitting an annual report on monetary policy to the National Assembly.

The central bank's operating variable is the overnight call rate, the target for which can be raised or lowered on a monthly basis in response to fluctuations in expected inflation and other variables. The actual overnight rate fluctuates around the target call rate as a function of open market transactions in repos or monetary stabilization bonds (Figure 1). Other market rates move broadly in line with the overnight rate (Figure 2). The Bank of Korea's most recent report to the National Assembly suggests that it engages in flexible inflation targeting, in that it moderates the speed at which it adjusts the call rate in response to deviations between actual and target inflation with the condition of the real economy in mind. "Although the central bank's fundamental task is clearly that of ensuring price stability, that does not mean that it can ignore other policy goals. Even if future price increases are expected to be high, provided they remain within the target range, the central bank may not need to raise interest rates, basing its decision rather on the state of the financial markets or the real economy."[13]

One way of inferring how important inflation, the real economy and the exchange rate have been in the policy decisions of the Bank of Korea is to estimate an extended Taylor Rule.[14] Assume that the call rate partially adjusts to the target according to the function:

$$r_t=(1-\rho)r_t^* + - \rho r_{t-1} + \upsilon_t \qquad (1)$$

[10] Bank of Korea (2003), pp.17-18. In this respect its approach resembled the "two pillar" strategy of the early ECB. Thus, initially the Monetary Policy Committee decided on the basic direction of open market operations with reference to the movement of the monetary aggregates.

[11] M3 was subsequently used as an information variable only.

[12] Independence was buttressed by the revised Bank of Korea Act that came into effect in 1998, which made the Governor of the Bank rather than the Minister of Finance and Economics the chairman of the Monetary Policy Committee, limited to one the number of members that was appointed by the government, and removed provisions that might have been invoked by the government in order to force board members to resign.

[13] Bank of Korea (2003), p.33.

[14] Here I follow the approach of Clarida, Gali and Gertler (1998).

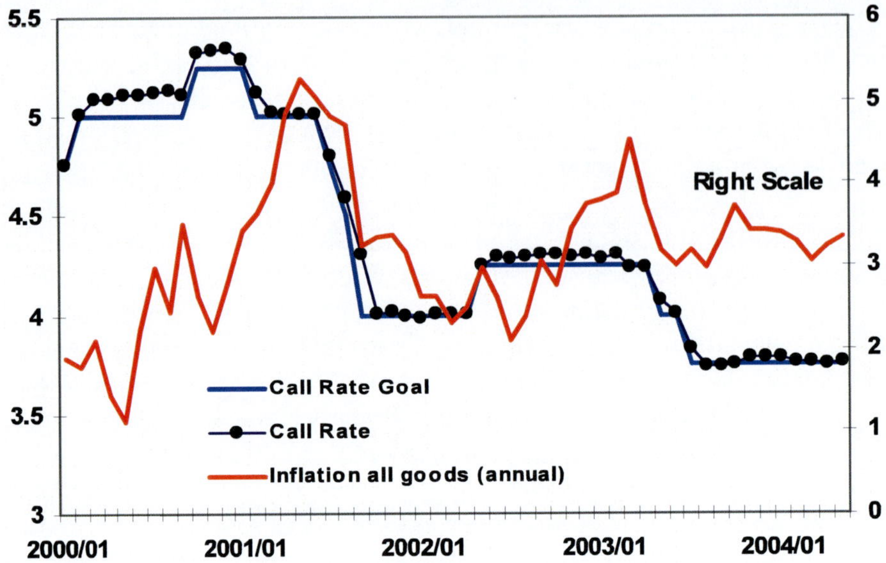

Figure 1. Observed and Target Call Rate and Annual CPI Inflation

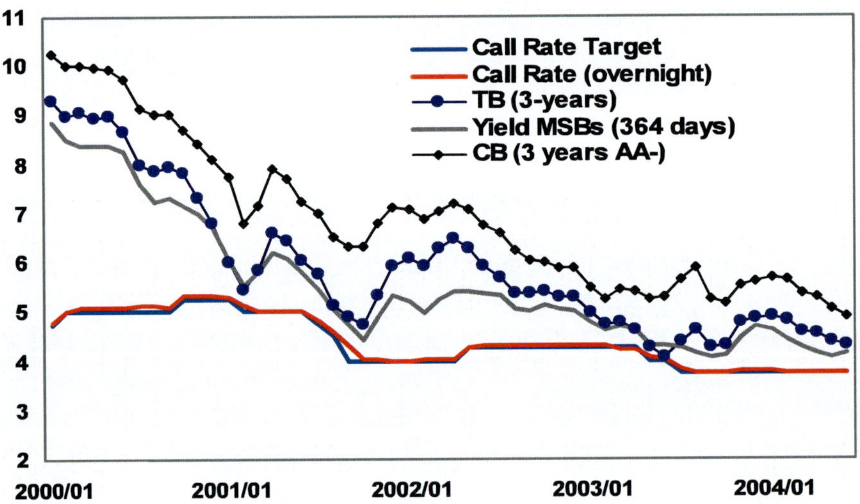

Figure 2. Call Rate, Treasury Bond 3 years, Corporate Bond (3 years) and Monetary Stabilization Bond Yields

where r is the call rate, r* is the target for the call rate, and υ is a random shock that is assumed to be i.i.d.[15] The coefficient $\rho\varepsilon^*[0,1]$ captures the degree of interest rate smoothing practiced by the central bank.

Assume now that:

$$r_t^* = r_t^{lr} + \beta(E[\pi_{t+n} \mid \Omega_t] - \pi^*) + \gamma\, E[\text{output gap}_t \mid \Omega_t] + \zeta E[z_t \mid \Omega_t] \quad (2)$$

where r_t^{lr} is the long-run equilibrium nominal interest rates, π_{t+n} is inflation between period t+n and period t, and z is another variable (or vector of variables) that may influence the reaction of the central bank (i.e. the depreciation of the exchange rate, as in Clarida et al. 1998).[16] Combining (1) and (2) and rearranging:

$$r_t = (1-\rho)[\alpha + \beta\,\pi_{t+n} + \gamma\,\text{output gap}_t + \zeta\, z_t] + \rho r_{t-1} + \varepsilon_t \quad (3)$$

where $\alpha = [r_t^{lr} - \beta\,\pi^*]$, and

$$\varepsilon_t = (1-\rho)[\,\beta\,(\pi_{t+n} - E[\pi_{t+n} \mid \Omega_t]) + \gamma(\text{output gap}_t - E[\text{output gap}_t \mid \Omega_t]) + (z_t - E[[z_t \mid \Omega_t]) + \upsilon_t$$

Let u_t be a vector of variables included in the central bank's information set at the time it sets the interest rate that are orthogonal to ε. In other words:

$$E[\varepsilon_t \mid u_t] = 0 \quad (4)$$

Equation (4) provides the orthogonality conditions (the moments) that we exploit in order to estimate the unknown parameters via GMM. In particular, the inflation forecast for period t+12 is constructed using the values of instrumental variables available through time t. In practice, we use lags 1, 2 3, 4, 5, 6, 9, and 12 of the overnight call rate, the index of industrial production, the inflation rate and the lagged rate of real exchange rate depreciation as the elements of the central bank's information set.[17]

The sample period for this exercise is January 1998-May 2003. Although we have additional observations through May 2004, these are needed in order to calculate forward inflation.[18] Since a lagged dependent variable is included on the right hand side of equation (3), the estimates are adjusted for heteroskedasticity and autocorrelation.[19]

A key step in this exercise (for the Bank of Korea as for the econometrician) is to estimate the output gap. Here the time series for industrial production is transformed into an

---

[15] I discuss and defend this assumption of interest-rate smoothing below.

[16] In this application we assume that the central bank cares about the current output gap but learns its value with a one-month lag, which seems realistic. It would, however, be possible to relax this assumption, as noted by Clarida et al. (1998).

[17] Lags longer than 12 months added little in terms of forecast accuracy. Similarly, eliminating lags 7, 8, 10, and 11 sacrificed little and reduced the extent of multicolinearity in estimation. Note that the rate of real exchange rate depreciation in the current month is not included in the posited information set because it is not uncorrelated with the current interest rate shock $\varepsilon_{t,}$, the exchange rate being a "jump variable" that can presumably move instantaneously in response to the shock.

[18] Given the 12 lags in the information set.

[19] The first step in the algorithm is to estimate the coefficients by OLS in order to compute an initial estimate of the parameters for use in computing the optimal weighting matrix. The second step uses the Davidson-Fletcher-Powell algorithm to find the line search in subsequent iterations.

output gap series in two ways: a) using the two-sided linear Hodrick-Prescott filter; and b) assuming a linear trend.

The results in Table 1 fit actual movements in the call rate well.[20] The first two equations show that the call rate rises with inflation, although as aggressively as suggested by Taylor's rule (with a coefficient greater than one) only when the gap is constructed assuming a linear trend as in the original Taylor (1993) article. The call rate also rises as actual output rises relative to capacity (which is how the output gap is operationalized here). The lagged dependent variable is significant and large, consistent with the considerable degree of smoothing evident in the Bank of Korea's setting of the call rate. Note that the same large coefficient on the lagged dependent variable has been obtained previously in studies of other countries. Thus, for example, Clarida et al. (1998) obtain estimates in the interval 0.90-0.97 for the United States, 0.91-0.93 for the Bank of Japan, and 0.91 for the Bundesbank.[21] This suggests that the interest-rate smoothing behavior evident in the Korean data is not peculiar to that country, although a number of the explanations that have been offered previously in the literature for why central banks smooth interest rates – fear of disruption of financial markets (Goodfriend 1991), for example – seem especially relevant to the Korean case. It is worth noting that differences between the predicted and actual values of the call rate are particularly large following the beginning of the Daewoo problem, which is consistent with the notion that the Bank of Korea smoothes interest rates with a view toward financial stability.

Table 1. GMM Estimates: Forward-Looking Inflation (adjusted standard errors in parentheses)

Equation	Alpha (constant)	Beta (Inflation)	Gamma (Gap)	Rho (LDV)	Zeta (Real depr.)	Gap computed by
1	1.086	0.772	1.103	0.956	–	Hodrick-Prescott
	0.881	0.288	0.139	0.004		
2	-0.716	1.384	0.412	0.944	–	Linear trend
	0.696	0.223	0.038	0.004		
3	2.493	0.370	0.129	0.937	0.123	Hodrick-Prescott
	0.672	0.228	0.099	0.005	0.010	
4	-0.073	1.169	0.409	0.933	0.054	Linear trend
	0.713	0.237	0.029	0.005	0.009	

Note: The rate of real exchange rate depreciation is lagged one month. The instruments are a constant and lags 1, 2, 3, 4, 5, 6, 9 and 12 of the overnight call rate, industrial production index, real exchange rate depreciation and inflation.

Source: see text.

Also note that despite the considerable explanatory power of the lagged dependent variable the coefficients on the inflation and output-gap variables are well determined (they have respectable t statistics). Although the presence of the lagged dependent variable explains

[20] The goodness of fit is of course heavily driven by the lagged dependent variable. I return to this below. Note that the dependent variable in these estimates is the actual call rate as opposed to the call rate target (see Figure 1 for information on their relative movement).

the success of these equations in tracking trends in the call rate, the other variables still appear have a role in explaining fluctuations around that trend.

The key result for present purposes is that the rate of change in the real exchange rate in the immediate past month also appears to influence the setting of the policy instrument in practice.[22] Note that the real exchange rate is measured as the bilateral rate vis-à-vis the dollar, since it is the dollar rate to which the Bank of Korea refers in its publications.[23] When the real rate depreciates, there is a tendency for the Bank of Korea to raise the call rate, other things equal (Figures 3 and 4). Adding the rate of currency depreciation reduces the magnitude of the other coefficients slightly but does not otherwise change the results.[24] Because the first lag of (the percentage change in) the real exchange rate is also included in the information set used to forecast inflation, the interpretation of this coefficient is that the Bank of Korea cares about the movement of the real exchange rate above and beyond its use in forecasting future inflation.

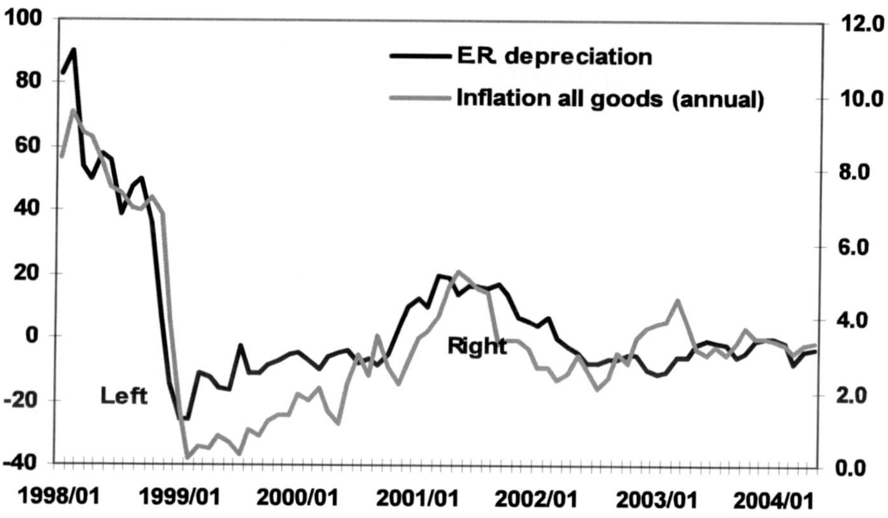

Figure 3. Observed Inflation and Annual Exchange Rate Depreciation

Some of these results are sensitive to alternative ways of estimating the output gap. When no extra (z) variable is included, the coefficient on inflation is larger than the coefficient on the gap when the latter is constructed using a linear trend, but the inflation coefficient is smaller than the gap coefficient when the latter is calculated used the HP filter. It is not clear which approach to estimating the output gap is more reliable in this context. The linear-trend approach will be particularly sensitive to structural breaks in the data, which are likely to be evident in an economy like Korea that has been passing through rapid structural change since

[21] In principle, the standard errors on these other independent variables should not be understated as a result of a combination of a lagged dependent variable and positive autocorrelation, since the results here adjust for autocorrelation.

[22] Note that similar results have been obtained for other open economies, e.g. for a number of Latin American countries by Corbo (2000).

[23] See below.

[24] The one change is that the coefficient on forward inflation just misses being statistically significant at the 90 per cent confidence level.

the crisis, while the sharp fall in output at the beginning of the sample period may tend to bias downward estimates of potential output obtained from the HP filter due to the end-point problem. Note, however, that the key result for present purposes – how the rate of change in the exchange rate affects the call rate – is not sensitive to how output is detrended.

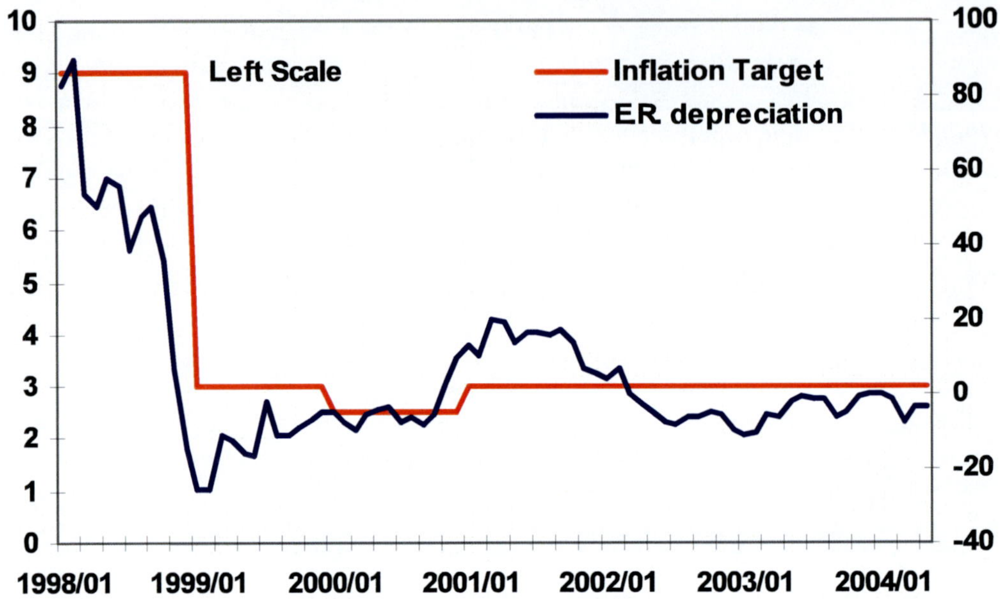

Figure 4. Inflation Target (%) and Annual Exchange Rate Depreciation

A number of other sensitivity analyses lent support to the robustness of these results. The two that did not where when actual inflation was substituted for expected inflation, and when the sample was limited to the second half of the post-crisis period. Substituting backward-looking behavior for forward-looking behavior produces a negative coefficient on the excess of actual output over capacity output, contrary to what one would expect (see Table 2). The difference in the two sets of estimates is thus consistent with the assumption that the Bank of Korea looks forward when contemplating the evolution of inflation and makes reasonably efficient use of the available information. Table 2 also provides support to the observation that estimates of monetary policy reaction functions framed in terms of backward-looking price movements can be seriously misleading.

Second, limiting the sample to the second half of the post-crisis period produces less precise estimates. This is not surprising, in that this leaves relatively few monthly observations and even fewer changes in the call rate, and given the fact that many of the changes in the call rate are concentrated toward the beginning of the period.

The bottom line is that in practice the Bank of Korea does not disregard fluctuations in the won exchange rate when operationalizing monetary policy. The rhetoric of inflation targeting and lack of reference to the exchange rate in its reports on monetary policy notwithstanding, it seems to take exchange rate fluctuations seriously when setting its operating target. This appears to be true even when the behavior of the exchange rate is included in the information set used to forecast inflation. This seems to indicate that exchange rate fluctuations matter not just for expected inflation but also for other variables of concern to the central bank, such as the relative condition of the traded and nontraded goods sectors, the stability of the financial system, and the overall development of the Korean economy, which has traditionally been linked to the level of the exchange rate through the mechanism of export-led growth.[25]

Table 2. GMM Estimates: Backward-Looking Inflation (adjusted standard errors in parentheses)

Equation	Alpha (Constant)	Beta (Inflation)	Gamma (Gap)	Rho (LDP)	Zeta (Real depr.)	Gap computed by
1	-0.523	1.259	1.555	0.947	–	Hodrick-Prescott
	0.555	0.138	0.175	0.005		
2	1.820	0.505	0.574	0.925	–	Linear trend
	0.295	0.071	0.055	0.004		
3	4.347	-0.318	1.034	0.939	0.133	Hodrick-Prescott
	0.442	0.137	0.115	0.004	0.018	
4	4.613	-0.453	0.422	0.910	0.128	Linear trend
	0.242	0.079	0.042	0.004	0.012	

Note: The rate of real exchange rate depreciation is lagged one month. The instruments are a constant and lags 1, 2, 3, 4, 5, 6, 9 and 12 of the overnight call rate, industrial production index, real exchange rate depreciation and inflation.

Source: see text.

The conclusion I draw is that the exchange rate matters for the conduct of monetary policy in Korea, rhetoric of free floating or not. It matters not merely in that it is useful for forecasting inflation, but in its own right, insofar as it is directly linked to the evolution of other variables also of concern to the central bank.

What this Implies About the Transparency of Korean Monetary Policy

The fact that the Bank of Korea says little about the exchange rate and its influence on policy decisions in its annual report to the National Assembly and in its monthly statements on monetary policy, issued following policy decisions, raises questions about whether central bank policy in Korea is as transparent in theory as it is in practice. If the central bank says one thing but does another (or, in the case of the exchange rate, it says nothing but does something), current practices may neither be an efficient way of communicating with the markets nor be an effective mechanism for holding the independent monetary authorities accountable for their decisions.

This is less of a problem for the annual report on monetary policy than for the monthly statements of the Monetary Policy Committee. Insofar as the annual report to the National Assembly is intended as a mechanism of accountability, it makes sense that this should focus

[25] Or perhaps the Bank of Korea cares about the opinions of the Ministry of Finance and Economy, which in turn has strong views about the level of the exchange rate that is appropriate for the growth of exports and the stability of the financial sector, and which is officially responsible for determining Korean exchange rate policy.

on the ultimate goals of policy – an acceptable average level of inflation and an acceptable tradeoff between inflation variability and short-term movements in the output gap – and that it should devote limited attention to the exchange rate per se. The Bank of Korea should be held accountable for its success in achieving its ultimate goals and crafting a socially-acceptable balance between them. The National Assembly should have something to say, and it may want to do something as well, if it sees the central bank too single mindedly attempting to minimize the variance of inflation while placing too little weight on short-term movements in the output gap, or equally if it sees the central bank as doing the converse. Movements in the exchange rate are not obviously of first-order importance for the balance between these variables (as distinct from affecting each of them). It is hard to imagine members of the National Assembly, or other observers, saying "Because we think you should be placing more weight on the output gap as opposed to minimizing the variance of inflation, we think you should be placing more weight on the exchange rate in your decisions," for it is far from clear whether the exchange rate affects the prospects for inflation or the output gap more strongly. Indeed, the precise answer may depend on circumstances. From this point of view, that the Bank's annual report to the National Assembly focuses on inflation, financial stability and the real economy rather, while saying little about the exchange rate per se, does not seem inappropriate.[26]

The monthly statements of the Monetary Policy Committee are another matter. These are a mechanism for communicating the intentions of the monetary authorities to the public and the market on a month-to-month basis. They are part of the basis on which the public and the market take their consumption and investment decisions. Typically, these statements make no mention of the exchange rate. If in fact the central bank is responding to movements in the exchange rate but it is not acknowledging this fact, private consumption and investment decisions may be taken erroneously, or at least they will be unnecessarily affected by uncertainty.[27] Best-practice open-economy inflation targeting suggests that MPC's monthly statements should contain more discussion of the exchange rate if this in fact is part of the basis for the committee's rate-setting decisions. This is especially important for a country with a highly competitive media, like Korea, where there is an incentive for journalists to engage in hyperbole in order to sell papers. In this case it will then be particularly important

[26] Faust and Henderson (2004) suggest a different problem with documents like the Bank of Korea's report to the National Assembly. In practice these focus almost entirely on the central bank's success in achieving an acceptable average rate of inflation, and do not analyze the policy tradeoff between greater inflation variance on the one hand and smaller variance of the output gap on the other. Like the Bank of Korea, they describe the optimization process in terms of a target for one variable (inflation) and adjusting the time horizon (moving from the short-run target to a medium-term target) to take into account the other (movements in the output gap). As Faust and Hednerson (p.15) put it, "this description fundamentally obfuscates" a trade-off that essentially involves using one instrument (monetary policy) to get close to a weighted average of two targets (the mean of inflation and the balance between the variability of inflation and the variability of the gap).

[27] Poole (2001, p.4) puts it too strongly when he asserts that there is no finding in the macroeconomic literature providing "a theoretical case, or empirical support, for the view that confusion or uncertainty in the private sector about the direction of monetary policy serves to better achieve policy objectives." In fact, there is a fairly substantial theoretical literature (surveyed by Geraats 2002) analyzing circumstances in which less transparency and/or more uncertainty about central bank policy may be welfare improving. Most of these special cases are elaborations of the theory of the second best, where an additional distortion (adding noise to the public signal about the intentions of monetary policy makers) is welfare enhancing because there exist other distortions working in the opposite direction. Most of these examples are, in my view, rather special cases with little practical relevance for policy. The most compelling such example assumes strategic interaction among private, resulting in a deterioration rather than an improvement in resource allocation. In practice, studies like Memertzis and Hughes Hallett (2003) provide little empirical support for these perverse cases.

for the central bank to provide market participants with the relevant information directly, rather than leaving it to the press to characterize the role of the exchange rate in monetary policy formulation.

WHICH EXCHANGE RATE?

Traditionally, these questions of how events in other countries affect Korean growth and inflation have been formulated in terms of the U.S., European and Japanese markets. When those markets are buoyant, the output gap narrows in Korea and inflationary pressure intensifies. There is then an argument for tightening monetary policy and letting the exchange rate strengthen. The new development on this scene is, of course, China. Where China accounted for less than one per cent of South Korea's exports as recently as 1990, it now accounts for roughly a fifth. (See Table 3.) This implies that the Bank of Korea should monitor developments in China as intensively as it monitors developments in the United States and other advanced industrial countries. This is an argument for the Bank of Korea moving away from its "dollar focus" in its policy statements and its call-rate policy. In particular, as Chinese economic growth decelerates in response to the monetary tightening implemented there in response to fears of overheating, there may similarly be an incentive for the Bank of Korea to loosen and allow the won to depreciate as necessary.

Table 3. The Percentage of Exports to China in Total Exports

	1990	1997	2002
Japan	2.47	6.38	11.69
Bangladesh	1.26	1.04	0.51
Cambodia	0.39	7.48	1.28
Sri Lanka	0.08	0.21	0.24
India	0.47	2.19	4.25
Indonesia	3.14	4.74	6.96
Korea	0.39	11.73	16.42
Malaysia	2.49	2.65	8.01
Pakistan	1.54	4.54	5.51
Philippines	0.94	1.11	6.90
Singapore	1.96	4.60	7.28
Thailand	1.62	3.25	7.46
Vietnam	0.06	3.80	6.61

Source: Eichengreen, Rhee and Tong (2004).

But Chinese trade in general and Chinese trade with Korea in particular differ from the trade of other countries in the magnitude of the country's imports of parts and components used as inputs into its exports of manufactures to third markets. China is an export platform for countries like Korea, assembling consumer electronics and other goods for sale in the U.S., Europe and Japan, using Korean machinery, parts and expertise. Thus, a deceleration in Chinese growth (like that which we are apparently witnessing at the moment) has two offsetting effects on Korea. On the one hand, it slows the growth of China's demand for Korean exports of components and capital goods. On the other hand, it slows the growth of

China's exports of manufactures to third markets, creating additional space there for Korea's own exports. It is not clear in the abstract which effect dominates. If the second effect dominates, then a soft or hard landing in China might in fact *intensify* inflationary pressure and *narrow* the output gap in Korea, providing grounds for tightening monetary policy and allowing the won to appreciate, rather than the other way around.

In Eichengreen, Rhee and Tong (2004), my coauthors and I estimate the impact of Chinese growth on China's demand for imports from its Asian neighbors, together with the impact of China's growth on that country's exports to third markets, and the propensity for Chinese exports to crowd out the exports of other Asian countries to those same third markets.[28] We use trade data disaggregated into exports of capital goods, intermediates, and consumer goods. A summary of the results is in Table 4. These show that the Chinese and Korean economies tend to move together. Thus, when China slows down, Korea slows down as well, due mainly to the impact on Korean exports of capital goods to the Chinese mainland. This suggests that the Bank of Korea should react to movements in the Chinese yuan in much the same manner that it reacts to movements in the dollar, the yen and the euro.

Table 4. Net Impact on Neighbors' Exports of China's Income Growth

	Capital Goods	Consumer Goods	Inter-mediates	Total
Japan	0.18	-0.24	0.05	0.03
Bangladesh	0.00	-0.32	0.05	-0.28
Cambodia	0.01	-0.32	0.09	-0.24
Sri Lanka	0.03	-0.32	0.00	-0.25
India	0.02	-0.30	0.06	-0.12
Indonesia	0.14	-0.30	0.08	-0.04
Korea	0.23	-0.19	0.12	0.06
Malaysia	0.11	-0.30	0.04	-0.01
Pakistan	0.06	-0.25	0.07	-0.21
Philippine	0.11	-0.30	0.05	-0.01
Singapore	0.11	-0.28	0.00	0.03
Thailand	0.11	-0.29	0.08	-0.07
Vietnam	0.04	-0.30	0.14	-0.14

Source: Eichengreen, Rhee and Tong (2004).

Note, however, that while the same result obtains for Japan and Singapore, the two other advanced economies in the region that are also heavy exporters of capital goods to China, it does not obtain for middle-income Asian countries such as, inter alia, Malaysia and Thailand (and it certainly does not obtain for low-income Asian countries). This is a reminder that the same formula for monetary and exchange rate policy that is appropriate for Korea is not appropriate for all Asian economies.

[28] The key methodological insight in this exercise is the recognition that Chinese exports are endogenous, and the use of the standard arguments of the gravity model, such as the distance from China to each extra-Asian export market, as an instrument for this variable.

The Role of the Exchange Rate and Economic and Financial Development

At the most basic level, the choice of exchange rate regime – equivalently, the weight placed on changes in the exchange rate in the central bank's reaction function – should be a function of a country's economic development strategy. Korea has long been committed to a strategy of export-led growth, in which it keeps the exchange rate of the won stable at competitive levels. The traded-goods sector has traditionally been seen as a locus of learning by doing and productivity spillovers. Thus, keeping the exchange rate from appreciating in order to stimulate capacity expansion and investment in this sector, while at the same time keeping interest rates low and utilizing government influence over the financial system to channel resources for capital formation in its direction, was the Korean strategy for stimulating productivity and economic growth. The positive results of this strategy create understandable worries that greater exchange rate flexibility might jeopardize the success of Korea's growth model. This explains, in the conventional view, why the Ministry of Finance and Economy has opposed an overly strong exchange rate and the Bank of Korea has accumulated such massive dollar reserves.

The rebuttal to this view is that the model of export-led growth has outlived its usefulness. To be sure, exports of manufactures still matter for Korea, as they do for the United States and every other advanced economy. But they are no longer disproportionately the locus of learning effects and productivity spillovers. Recent studies of the U.S. (e.g. Gordon 2002) have documented that the sector with far and away the fastest growing productivity growth rates is retailing: companies like Walmart have succeeded in using information and communications technologies to rationalize inventory control and otherwise streamline their operations in ways that have resulted in massive increases in productivity. While U.S. companies have also sought to export this technology, this is basically productivity advance led by the nontraded goods sector. A set of economic policies that encourages companies to concentrate on the production of exportable manufactures at the expense of nontradables production may pass up the most attractive opportunities for boosting productivity.

To the extent that growth in the 21st century will depend on a country's ability to train – and retain – knowledge workers, the argument for policies that encourage a better balance between traded- and nontraded-goods production becomes stronger still. Education is the obvious activity to be fostered in order to train knowledge workers, and education is a classic nontraded good (although those of us who teach at the University of California, observing the composition of our student body, may question whether such services are really nontraded). Retaining knowledge workers – and, even better, attracting them from abroad – requires investing in housing and urban amenities, which are similarly nontraded goods. All this suggests that a growth model tailored to the imperatives of the 21st century requires a better balance of investment in sectors supplying traded and nontraded goods.

Finally, a strategy of keeping the exchange rate from appreciating and keeping interest rates low in order to channel additional resources into the production of exports – or more generally into the production of those goods in which the scope for productivity improvement is greatest – works less well in a deregulated financial environment. Recent experience shows that countries that have imported low U.S. interest rates as a result of keeping their currencies stable against the dollar have seen resources flow not into increases in industrial capacity but into speculative investments in commercial and residential real estate. In a substantially deregulated financial environment, the government has little ability to prevent this. Construction booms can lead to an inferior allocation of resources with very long-lived effects (Field 1992). A concentration of speculative construction loans on bank balance sheets can pose a threat to financial stability. Even China, where the banking system remains substantially under the control of the authorities, displayed these symptoms in 2003, when the combination of a pegged exchange rate and substantial capital inflows led to signs of property-market overheating. Because China's banks still take instructions from the authorities, the latter can address the problem simply by directing the banks to stop lending.[29] For countries with more completely deregulated financial systems and open capital accounts, the only solution to this problem is a more flexible exchange rate.

The other reason besides their long-standing commitment to export-led growth why Korean policy makers may be reluctant to move to greater exchange rate flexibility is the worry that exchange rate stability is important for financial development – and for the development of bond markets in particular. The currency risk associated with volatile exchange rates may deter both local and foreign investors from holding long-term, domestic-currency-denominated debt securities. Hence there may be a conflict between allowing greater exchange rate variability and encouraging local bond markets, something that Korean policy makers see as integral to building a more robust and better developed financial sector.

Eichengreen and Luengnaruemitchai (2004) report some evidence that countries with more volatile exchange rates do in fact have smaller bond markets, holding constant a number of other potential determinants of bond market development. However, this result is driven by a few cases where exchange rates are highly volatile and unpredictable. In the range of more modest exchange-rate volatility relevant to Korea, there is little evidence that greater exchange rate variability is a significant impediment to bond market development. Part of the explanation may lie in the development of derivatives markets and structured instruments with which it is possible to hedge exchange rate risk (see e.g. Fernandez and Klassen 2004).

CONCLUSION

Korea's experience with inflation targeting since the implementation of the revised central bank act in 1998 and the shift away from targeting monetary aggregates after 2000 has been broadly satisfactory. The authorities have succeeded in maintaining a stable and moderate rate of inflation. The technical problems warned of by skeptics of the application of inflation targeting to Korea and other Asian countries (viz. lack of timely data, difficulty of forecasting inflation) have not interfered with the operation of this regime. Nor have inadequate financial depth and development seriously disrupted its operation.[30]

---

[29] Although there is still some scope for capital to flow into the property market through nonbank channels, as described in Eichengreen (2004).

[30] There is some evidence, for example in the large deviation between the policy interest rates predicted by the Taylor rule and those actually maintained by the Bank of Korea around the time of the Daewoo crisis, that financial fragility has figured in the conduct of inflation targeting in Korea. Be this as it may, the authorities' concern for financial stability has not conflicted seriously with their pursuit of a low and relatively stable

What has been the role of the exchange rate in this regime? The balance of evidence suggests that the won is now fluctuating more freely than under the pre-crisis regime. By and large these fluctuations have stabilizing: the won has strengthened in periods when the expansion of the Korean economy was accelerating and weakened when the expansion appeared to be losing steam. While the exchange rate does not receive much attention in the Bank of Korea's Monetary Policy Report to the National Assembly or its monthly press releases following decisions of the Monetary Policy Committee, there is the sense that the authorities are vigilant about its fluctuation – that they continue to care about how movements in the exchange rate affect their ultimate policy goals, and that they adjust policy accordingly. Movements in the real exchange rate are understandably important in an open economy like Korea, where they have direct implications for the future course of inflation. But my findings suggest that the Bank of Korea cares about the real exchange rate not just because the latter contains information relevant for its inflation forecast; in addition it responds to movements in the real exchange rate for other reasons like the balance of investment in traded and nontraded goods sectors and the implications for financial stability.

This is a sensible monetary regime for Korea. The exchange rate is not a suitable anchor for monetary policy in a large, diversified and financially open economy with the capacity and need to tailor monetary policy to local needs. A managed float backed by inflation targeting provides a sounder basis for the formulation and conduct of monetary policy in such a country. A central bank like Korea's cannot regard fluctuations in the exchange rate with an attitude of benign neglect. Movements in the exchange rate matter too much for future inflation, for the evolution of the output gap, for the stability of the financial system, and for the development of the economy generally. Inflation targeting in an open economy like Korea does not imply disregard of the exchange rate. Indeed, the opposite is true. Moreover, the central bank of a country like Korea whose real and financial sectors are sensitive to movements in the real exchange rate is unlikely to limit its attention to the exchange rate to its implications for the future evolution of inflation.

Many of the trends reviewed in this paper suggest that the Bank of Korea should now place less weight on the exchange rate, the dollar exchange rate in particular, in the formulation of policy, on the grounds that movements in that rate are becoming less closely tied to the ultimate objectives of monetary policy. As Korea exits the stage of export-led growth for innovation- and knowledge-intensive economic growth, it needs a better balance of investment in traded- and non-traded goods sectors. Keeping the exchange rate from appreciating will no longer be the obvious tonic for growth. As the yuan begins to move against the dollar, as will happen sooner or later, no one exchange rate will any longer be an appropriate focus for export competitiveness. As domestic financial markets develop and prudential supervision and regulation continue to be strengthened, corporate finances will no longer be as sensitive to exchange rate movements, enabling the authorities to allow the currency to fluctuate more without threatening financial stability. By how much the exchange rate should then move will depend on circumstances; it will depend on the specific constellation of domestic and foreign shocks to which the Korean economy is subjected. We should not automatically expect to see wider exchange rate movements in 2004-2010 than in

inflation rate, any more than, say, in the case of the Federal Reserve and Long-Term Capital Management in 1998.

1998-2004. But the considerations raised here do suggest that the Bank of Korea should place less weight on those movements than it has in the last six years.

ACKNOWLEDGEMENTS

The original version of this paper was prepared for a symposium at the Bank of Korea, 25 August 2004. I thank Raul Garcia for exceptionally able research assistance and discussions, and Seung-Cheol Jeon, Jung Sik Kim, Junggun Oh, Ramkishen Rajan and Nicoletta Batini for helpful comments.

REFERENCES

Ball, Lawrence (1999), "Policy Rules for Open Economies," in John Taylor (ed.), *Monetary Policy Rules,* Chicago: University of Chicago Press, pp.127-156.

Bank of Korea (2003), *Monetary Policy in Korea,* Seoul: Bank of Korea.

Bank of Korea (2004a), *Monetary Policy Report*, Seoul: Bank of Korea.

Bank of Korea (2004b), *Quarterly Bulletin* (March), Seoul: Bank of Korea.

Calvo, Guillermo and Carmen Reinhart (2000), "Fear of Floating," NBER Working Paper no. 7993 (November).

Christoffersen, Peter and Robert Wescott (1999), "Is Poland Ready for Inflation Targeting?" IMF Working Paper no. 99/41 (March).

Clarida, Richard, Jordi Gali and Mark Gertler (1998), "Monetary Policy Rules in Practice: Some International Evidence," *European Economic Review*, pp.1033-1068.

Corbo, Vittorio (2000), "Monetary Policy in Latin America in the 1990s," Working Paper no. 78, Santiago: Banco Central de Chile (August).

Demertzis, Maria and Andrew Hughes Hallett (2003), "Central Bank Transparency in Theory and Practice," DNB Staff Report no. 105, Amsterdam: De Nederlandsche Bank.

Eichengreen, Barry (2002), "International Monetary Options for the 21st Century," *Annals of the American Academy of Political and Social Science* 579, pp.11-25.

Eichengreen, Barry (2003), "What to Do with the Chiang Mai Initiative," *Asian Economic Papers* 2, pp.1-52.

Eichengreen, Barry (2004), "Can Emerging Markets Float? Should They Inflation Target?" in Lavan Mahadeva and Peter Sinclair (eds), *How Monetary Policy Works,* London: Routledge.

Eichengreen, Barry and Pipat Luengnaruemitchai (2004), "Why Doesn't Asia Have Bigger Bond Markets?" unpublished manuscript, University of California, Berkeley.

Eichengreen, Barry, Yeongseop Rhee and Hui Tong (2004), "The Impact of China on the Exports of Other Asian Countries," unpublished manuscript, University of California at Berkeley and Sookmyung University.

Faust, Jon and Dale W. Henderson (2004), "Is Inflation Targeting Best-Practice Monetary Policy?" International Finance Discussion Paper no. 807, Washington, D.C.: Board of Governors of the Federal Reserve System (May).

Fernandez, David and Simon Klassen (2004), "Choice of Currency by East Asian Borrowers," unpublished manuscript, J.P. Morgan.

Field, Alexander J. (1992), "Uncontrolled Land Development and the Duration of the Depression in the United States," *Journal of Economic History* 52, pp.785-805.

Geraats, Petra M. (2002), "Central Bank Transparency," unpublished manuscript, University of Cambridge (March).

Goodfriend, Marvin (1991), "Interest Rates and the Conduct of Monetary Policy," *Carnegie Rochester Conference Series on Public Policy* 34, pp.7-30.

Gordon, Robert J. (2002), "Technology and Economic Performance in the American Economy," NBER Working Paper no.8771 (February).

Hoffmaister, Alexander (2001), "Inflation Targeting in Korea: An Empirical Exploration," *IMF Staff Papers* 48, pp.317-343.

Leiderman, Leo and Gil Bufman (2001), "Surprises on Israel's Road to Exchange Rate Flexibility," *Emerging Markets Research,* Deutsche Bank, 23 March.

McKinnon, Ronald and Gunther Schnabl (2003), "A Return to Exchange Rate Stability in East Asia: Mitigating Conflicted Virtue," unpublished manuscript, Stanford University (October).

Mishkin, Frederic and Miguel Savastano (2000), "Monetary Policy Strategies for Latin America," NBER Working Paper no. 7617 (March).

Oh, Junggun (2004a), "Effects of Free Floating on the Foreign Exchange Market: The Korean Experience," paper presented to the Claremont Exchange Rate Workshop, Claremont Graduate School, Claremont California, 1-2 April.

Oh, Junggun (2004b), "Exchange Rate Disparities and Needs of Policy Cooperation in East Asia," paper presented at the WEAI conference, Vancouver, Canada, 30 June-3 July.

Poole, William (2001), "Central Bank Transparency: Why and How?" www.stlousfed.org (30 November).

Rivas, Luis A. (2001), "Underlying Inflation Measures as Short-Run Inflation Targets in Developing Economies: The Case of Nicaragua," unpublished manuscript, Central Bank of Nicaragua.

Taylor, John (1993), "Discretion versus Rules in Practice," *Carnegie Rochester Conference Series in Public Policy* 39, pp.195-214.

Truman, Edwin M. (2003), *Inflation Targeting in the World Economy,* Washington, D.C.: Institute for International Economics.

In: Korea: Economic, Political and Social Issues
Editors: P. H. Elwood, J. B. Albertus

ISBN: 978-1-60456-513-3

Chapter 3

HETEROGENEITY IN UNIVERSITY INCOMES FROM THE TECHNOLOGY TRANSFER AND COMMERCIALIZATION IN KOREA

Jaehwan Park* and Inha Oh†

ABSTRACT

Since the Korean government enacted the 'Technology Transfer Promotion Act' in year 2000 to enhance technology transfer and technology commercialization, the trends of university R&D in Korea have been drastically changed. One of the most dramatic changes was focusing on the entrepreneurial aspects of R&D, such as technology transfer and technology commercialization. And as a result, universities in Korea have enjoyed increased number of transfers and handsome revenues from their technology transfer activities. This paper aimed to identify the major factors related to the amount of revenues from the sales of research outcomes. Utilizing the panel data from Korea Association of University technology managers, accumulated from 2000 to 2004, we identified the influential factors to the revenues of universities, as the number of patents, the type and amount of subsidies from the government, the reputation of the universities and the location of Technology Licensing Offices (TLOs). The results emphasized the importance of the effective management of the TLOs in the early stage of commercialization and productive implementation of government and university policies.

JEL Classification Numbers: C24, L26, O34, O38
Keywords: technology licensing, intellectual property, entrepreneurship, government policy

* Tel: +82-11-9753 3449, jhpark88@snu.ac.kr
† Tel: +82-11-9025 3501, whistle3@snu.ac.kr

1. INTRODUCTION

Since the enacting of the Bayh-Dole Act in the year 1980, the government of the United States has considered the universities as an important source for the creation of technologically advanced firms. Accordingly, universities have played both the traditional role as organizations for education and the role as the entrepreneurial contributor to the local economic developments (Van Dierdonck and Debackrere, 1988; Lerner, 2004). The conventional main tasks of universities might be to research and to disseminate knowledge across scholarship and education, whereas the new mission of universities is to contribute directly and indirectly to technology transfer activities by providing advanced technology and qualified individuals to the industry (Geiger, 1993; Bok, 2003). Recently, universities put more emphasis on technology transfers and commercialization and this trend is spreading out worldwide, including Korea.

In the late 1990s, the Korean government realized that merely increasing the amount oft the national R&D investment had some limitation to activate commercialization of technology further. And in this vein, the Korean government changed the policy which focused on increasing budget in R&D investment to the policy which focused on the technology transfer and commercialization. In this regards, 'Technology Transfer Promotion Act' was enacted and the Korea Technology Transfer Center (KTTC) was established. The goal of KTTC is to activate participation in the technology market, to promote effective and efficient technology transfers and to buildup the network among research centers, universities, firms, investment companies and skilled individuals.

The researches dealing with the topic of the role of universities in technology transfer can be found from a comprehensive series of papers of Shane (2001, 2002, 2003). Through the series of studies, Shane tried to explain cross-university variations in the abilities to produce start-ups, and pointed out several factors responsible for these heterogeneities. First, inventions originated from the universities were the critical sources of knowledge transfer, and understanding the mechanisms of knowledge transfer from the university to technology licensing office (TLO) start-ups, which are firms stemmed from the technology, was of great importance. Second, the TLO start-ups tended to locate geographically close to the institutions which made them valuable entities for local economic development and agglomerated economies. Third, successful TLO start-ups should generate significant wealth through the initial public offerings, and the inventors and provosts in the universities would be benefited in capturing the wealth.

Shane (2001, 2003) also analyzed the factors influencing TLO start-ups and venture companies at the micro-level and the macro-level. According to his study, at the micro-level, the new companies were influenced by inventors' career experience, by their psychological make-up, and by their research skills. And at the macro level, technology regimes, the strength of patent protection in the line of business, and the university intellectual property transfer seemed to influence the birth of venture companies.

After the establishment of KTTC, government helped national R&D centers and universities by enhancing TLOs' own competitiveness of commercializing in-house patents and technologies. At the end of 2005, most of universities in Korea established TLOs, and some TLOs showed significant annual income results came from the technology transfer and commercialization. However, due to shortage in number of staffs and amount of subsidies from the university and the government, most of TLOs could not attain a satisfactory result from the technology commercialization. Compared to the number of TLO staffs in Stanford University (30), Columbia University (21) and MIT (25) in United States, most TLOs in universities in Korea have below 4 employees who held a temporary position with low wage, as can be seen in Table 1.

Under these circumstances, in order to improve the environment surrounding TLOs, the Ministry of Commerce, Industry and Energy (MOCIE) of Korea has given the large amount of subsidies to TLOs of universities through the various agencies. However, although TLOs produced significant results based on the supporting policies, there exist few examples examining the effectives of the subsidies and the properness of the general direction of policy, such as fostering establishment of the TLOs and accessing contribution of TLOs to the competitiveness of the Korean economy.

The purpose of this study is to address the factors influencing the performance of TLOs of universities in Korea, and the factors are divided into four categories as: (1) institutional resources (2) financial resources from government (3) financial resources from university, and (4) patent resources from the university.

The direct income originated from technology transfer for each university is set as the variable measuring the performance of TLOs. Our study considers the technology transfer of universities and followed commercialization as new and important financial tools to make profits for universities. To measure the income from the commercialization, we examined the annual income of universities' TLOs.

The remainder of this paper is consisted of several parts. We will introduce Korean technology transfer and commercialization environment in section 2. Then we will describe our data and variables in section 3, research methodologies are presented in section 4, and results will be dealt in section 5. Lastly, in section 6, we present the summary and discussions of the results, and limitations and the direction of future studies also. The paper will present some implications to government policy makers and university heads how to set up and manage its TLO in early stages of commercialization.

2. Technology Transfer in Korea

2.1. Technology Transfer in Korea

As it is shown in Table 1, according to the report from MOCIE, 46.9% of National R&D institutes have about 1 ~ 3 number of staffs in TLO, 29.7% of them had 4 ~ 9 staff in TLO and 11% of them have mere one staff in TLO. Most of TLO staffs are involved in administrative works, patent management, patent registration work, technology exhibition, technology transfer work, and investment forum work. It shows systematic problems that just a couple of staffs involved in too many work descriptions.

Table 2 shows income from technology transfer and commercialization in universities and national R&D institutes in Korea. The trend shows steady increase since Korean government have began to statistical work of TLO; until the year 2002, Korean TLOs had gained 11,191 million Korean Won (KRW) and at the year 2005, Korean TLOs had eared 6,878 million KRW.

The performances of university TLOs have been relatively low compared to the national R&D institutes. 114 TLOs of national R&D institutes have recorded income of 61,853 million Korean Won, compared to 3,177 million KRW in 2004 and 6,878 million KRW in 2005 from 145 TLOs of universities. The big difference in technology transfer records between universities and national R&D institutes is partly due to the extraordinary performance of the Electronics and Telecommunication Research Institute (ETRI). ETRI has made successful technology transfer, especially in the fields of mobile phone related technologies. And it seems that the system of technology transfer in universities could not be a match for that of national R&D institutes.

Table 3 shows the performance of 145 TLOs of universities in 2005 in details. National universities have recorded about 1,300 million KRW of incomes from 10 transfers. While private universities have recorded 320 million KRW of incomes from 37 transfers. TLOs of national universities also have recorded 1,625 million KRW from 154 cases by technology licensing.

Table 1. Number of Patent, R&D, Technology Transfer staff (in person)

	Number of Patent, R&D, Technology Transfer staff				Average
Number of Personnel	~1	1~3	4~9	10~	-
	16(11%)	68(46.9%)	43(29.7%)	18(12.4%)	4.8

Table 2. Licensing Income (million KRW)

	Sum Until 2002	2003	2004	2005	Total Sum
University	11,191	2,250	3,177	6,878	23,495
Nat'l R&D Centers	379,443	46,846	53,313	61,853	541,455
Sum	390,634	49,096	56,490	68,730	564,950

Table 3. All Universities Technology Transfer Outcome in 2005, (number, million KRW)

		Selling		licensing		Tech guidance	
		number	income	number	income	number	income
University	Nat'l	20	1,300	154	1,625	3	3
	Private	37	320	384	3,510	31	119
	SUM	57	1,620	538	5,136	34	122

Universities in Korea have generated their income mainly from licensing rather than selling or technology guidance; whereas national universities have performed somewhat similar ration between income from licensing and selling, private universities have made more than 10 times of income from patent licensing compared to that from the technology sale.

2.2. TLOs in Korea

Figure 1 shows the annual changes in the amount of government subsidy. Small and Medium Business Administration (SMBA) has allocated 2,233,500 thousand KRW for five years in commercialization of technology; 155,000 thousand KRW in year 2000 for the Technology Transfer Promotion Act and establishment of Korea Technology Transfer Center, 941,000 thousand KRW in year 2001. It is planning to cut down the budget to universities as the university budget allocation has increased. Based on the idea that the patent registration is the prerequisite of technology transfer and commercialization, University Industrial Technology Force (UNITEF) has continuously increased its subsidy to stimulate patent registration; 302,600 thousand KRW in 2001, 465,097 thousand KRW in 2002, 742,100 thousand KRW in 2004, and 884,394 thousand KRW in 2005.

Figure 2 shows how university has increased its budget for the patent management and the protection of intellectual property starting from the point of time when the Technology Transfer Promotion Act was enacted. Also, universities began to prohibit each professor from registering patents under their individual names for the researches conducted using funds from the government. Universities in Korea have established the TLOs to reclaim the ownership of each patents registered under the name of each individual professors.

Despite the increase in the cost of patent management, cost used for of the administrational works and personnel expenses of TLOs has not increased at all, as can be seen in Figure 2. Universities were in lack of the understanding of the necessity of professional personnel who can handle technology transfer and commercialization. During the last 5 years, staffs in TLO were mainly temporal employees with single year contract base and most of these costs were covered by the government subsidy. It showed that universities failed in recognizing the importance of professionals in TLOs.

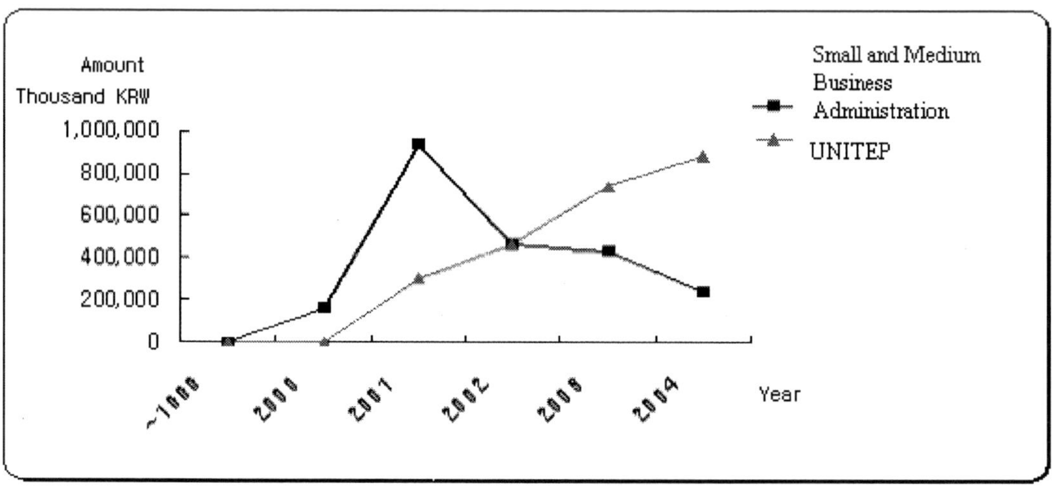

Figure 1. Subsidy from the Government.

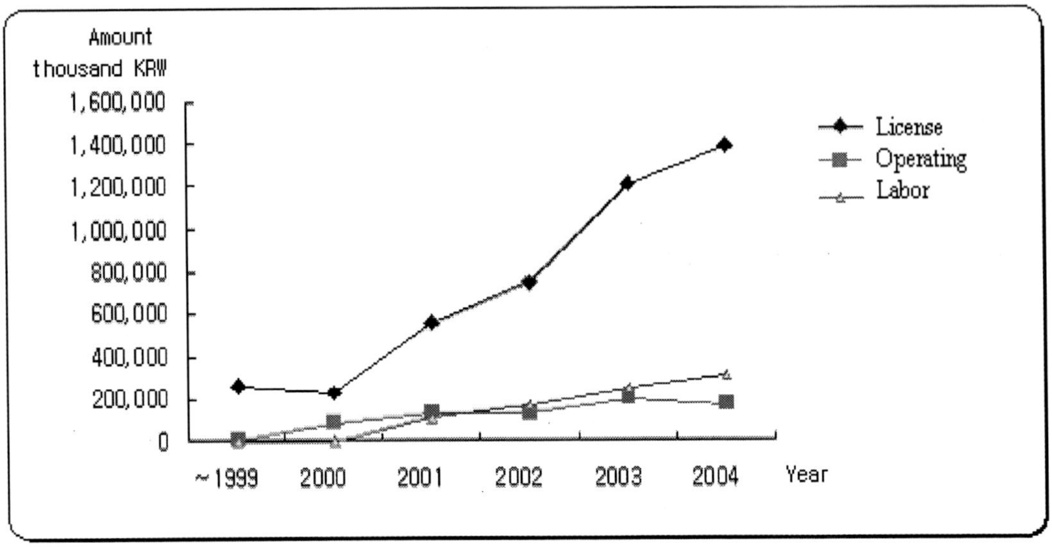

Figure2. Subsidy from the university.

3. Data and Variables

3.1. Data

This study is based on the balanced panel of 21 universities in Korea gathered by Korean Association of University Technology transfer Managers (KAUTM) during the period from years 2000 to year 2004. The 21 universities are mainly consisted of private universities which have their own TLOs. Due to the shortage of accumulated statistical data, we could not examine the effects of the Technology Transfer Promotion Act and KTTC. However, the data set included the age, the location of TLO, the different subsidies from government, the different subsidies from universities and patent from universities. For the direction of this study we exclude some factors which may be unrelated to the purpose of this paper.

3.2. Variables

As it was shown in Figure 3, under the purpose of observing the factors influencing the income from the commercialization process of each TLO, we set variables which would have potential relationship with these outcomes. Based on Shane (2003), the variables can be categorized into four parts; institutional resources, financial resources from government, financial resources and patents from university.

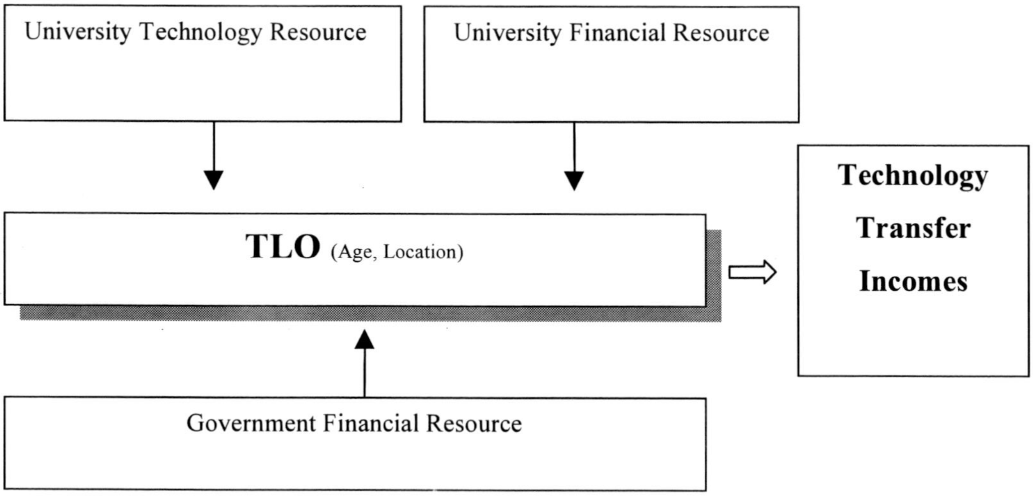

Figure 3. Model Design.

3.2.1. Institutional Resources

The institutional variables are set as the name value of TLO and the location of TLO. These variables were chosen to examine the effect of TLO in performances. TLOs can have independent organizational behaviors despite the fact that TLOs are regarded as one of the department in universities; TLO cannot be completely separated from the name value of the university. Therefore we assume that not the age of TLO but the age of universities affects the income of TLO.

About the factor of location of the TLOs factor, we hoped to examine the geographical influence of the venture capital accessibility and potential technology buyer accessibility. We measured the factor and most university TLOs were located in Seoul, where all the resources are congested. The measurement can tell us the tendency of TLO location in developing country. When the certain university is available in local area, it would reflect good indication of what the author is attempting to seek.

3.2.2. Financial Resources from the Government

The Korean government has invested various kind of funds in order to establish TLOs in universities through different departments and agencies; SMBA has invested the fund for running cost of TLO, including personnel expenses of TLO, and UNITEF has invested the subsidy for supporting the patent activities, except for the personnel expenses.

3.2.3. Financial Resources from University

Most budgets for TLOs from universities have been appropriated without proper evaluation processes. Budgets were allocated to support patents, running costs, and the labor costs of TLO. We evaluated these variables to find how to reorganize budget allocation to improve income.

Table 4. Variable Definition

Variable	Definition
Year	2000-2004
Sales	The sales amount of money through the technology transfer and the commercialization
Financial resources from the government	
SMBA Subsidy	The subsidy from the Small and Medium Business Administration(SMBA)
MOCIE Subsidy	The subsidy from the Ministry of commerce, industry and energy(MOCIE)
UNITEF Subsidy	The subsidy from the University Industrial Technology Force(UNITEF)
Financial resources from the university	
Patent Subsidy	The subsidy to manage its patents from the university
Running Subsidy	The subsidy to run its TLO from the university
Labor Subsidy	The subsidy to labor cost of its TLO from the university
TLO	
Established Year	The established year of TLO
Location	The TLO is located the Capital region or not
Patent	
Dom_pat	The registered number of patent in Korea each year
Inter_pat	The registered number of patent internationally each year

Source: KAUTM: Korean Association of University Technology transfer Managers

3.2.4. Patents from University

Both government and universities have believed that intellectual properties should be patented for technology transfer and commercialization. As a result, budgets were concentrated for these activities. To observe how patent holdings affected the income from technology transfer and commercialization, we selected registered patent numbers from each university for the analysis. Due to the lack of data, applying time lag had been skipped and the number of domestic and international registered patent was used as independent variables.

This study explored the data through looking at the descriptive evidence first. In Table 4 we can see the definition of various variables classified in four from 2000 year to 2004 year; 3 different financial resources from the government, three different financial goaled subsidies from university, name value of TLO, location of TLO, domestic and international patent numbers from each university.

4. Empirical Model

Because the dependent variable was truncated at zero value, we applied the Tobit model. The university specific effects were handled with dummy variables for each university and time specific effects were handled with trend variables. The model was aimed to examine the factors that influences to universities' incomes. The dependent variable was the direct income originated from technology transfer and commercialization of each university. And as for the explanatory variables, different combinations of variables listed on Table 5 were used to observe their effect on TLO performance.

Table 5. Descriptive Statistics

Variables	Mean	Std. Dev.	Minimum	Maximum
SMBA Subsidy	206.62	194.71	0	603.01
UNITEF Subsidy	223.83	507.35	0	1992.00
MOCIE Subsidy	9.34	26.79	0	138.06
Patent Subsidy	378.10	687.81	0	3593.59
Running Subsidy	67.97	99.19	0	480
Labor Subsidy	86.31	146.85	0	1085.42
Established Year	5.42	1.44	2	7
Location	0.57	0.49	0	1
Dom_pat	30.49	30.96	0	138
Inter_pat	5.68	16.48	0	99

5. Empirical Results

Table 6 presents summary of the regression results. We set up the 4 different models in order to get different understandings; model 1 for the effect of the only government's subsidies, model 2 for the effect of only the university's subsidies, model 3 for the effect of the university's subsidies with internal resources, and model 4 for the university's subsidies and the government's subsidies with internal resources.

First, among the government subsidies the fund for establishing TLO and for TLOs' labor cost are very positive in increasing the universities TLOs' incomes in Korea.

Second, it is found that the more the university register international patents, the less income recorded. This is because the early stage of technology commercialization, patent registration can affect future income but in the condition of running 3 ~ 5 TLO staffs, they would have no time to manage technology transfer in business. Reformation of TLO organization is necessary to generate additional incomes from technology commercialization.

Third, we found that the trend is very positive in increasing income of universities TLOs; as time passes the skill, know-how and infrastructure of technology transfer and commercialization have accumulated in TLO and the direction of government's policy was proper.

Lastly, the subsidies for patent registration funded from universities and government are somewhat positive in increasing the TLOs' incomes in universities in Korea.

Table 6. The result of FIXED EFFECTS Tobit regression

Variable	**1**	**2**	**3**	**4**
SMBA Subsidy	1.811293***			1.752489**
UNITEF Subsidy	-0.3611061			-0.6138385*
MOCIE Subsidy	-1.0885722			-1.158377
Patent Subsidy		0.3927074	0.8939727**	0.8818401*
Running Subsidy		1.795775	2.513355	2.848337
Labor Subsidy		1.021105	-1.335722	-1.902028
Established Year			16.38884	79.07524
Location			-936.8743	-709.8557
Dom_pat			7.048539	8.410811
Inter_pat			-35.44007**	-36.45375***
Trend	536.483***	105.8808***	330.7541***	487.4262***
Number of Observation	105	105	105	105
Log likelihood	-519.70906	-520.74861	-517.08963	-513.30389

Standard errors in parentheses are based on the Newey-West autocorrelation-consistent covariance estimator with a maximum of one lag.

* Significant at 10% confidence level, ** Significant at 5% confidence level; ***Significant at 1% confidence level

6. Discussions

6.1. Summary and Implications

First of all, among the different types of government subsidies, the fund served by SMBA was most effective and positively affect on the income of TLO. The goals of the SMBA funds are establishing TLOs and hiring more TLO staffs. The purpose of SMBA fund was very successfully accomplished and now it is the main factor influencing income of TLO. In the developing country, the universities don't want to pay for the labor cost of TLOs. Therefore, the government in developing country should focus on providing the subsidies for the labor cost of TLOs.

Second, due to the restricted numbers of staffs, TLOs in the developing countries could not focus on neither applying patents internationally nor activity of the technology transfer and commercialization. Therefore, TLOs in the developing countries should hire enough staffs for patenting and commercialization and

If the university hopes to increase the income through technology transfer, the school should either increasing the number of staffs and separating the work description by managing patents team and technology transfer team, or outsourcing technology transfer to professionals.

Third, we found that the trend is very positive to income of TLOs in universities; as time passes the skill, know-how and infrastructure of technology transfer and commercialization have accumulated in TLO and the direction of government policy was proper.

Finally, regardless of the source, the subsidies for patent registration is positive in increasing income of TLO; despite the limited staffs in TLO, the basic policy of protecting intellectual properties in universities were proper. However, for more income of TLO, universities should not only increase the fund for patent registration but also increase the TLO staffs.

6.2. Discussion

Promoting technology commercialization in Korea is worth watching despite the fact that Korea is the late runner on this field. Success rate of technology commercialization is deeply related to the quality of technology and it seems that Korea has been successful setting up the legislation support, research institution, and infrastructure for technology transfer and commercialization during last six years. Policy amendment cycle of the policy and regulation is very short; it takes only six years from the first legislation to second legislation. Likewise, the national strategy of Korean government on the technology transfer and commercialization is very flexible and is quick to react.

About the labor cost in TLO, in the early stage, the government could subsidize the cost in order to reduce the risk. However, after the early stage when the TLO tend to have some feasible outcome through technology transfer and commercialization, the universities should hire the TLO regular staff, not temporary staffs and endure whole expenses of TLO staffs to effectively manage intellectual properties.

TLO managers of TLO in Korea established Korea Association of University managers (KAUTM) following AUTM in the United States. Through on-line and off-line meeting of the organization, the TLO managers could share the know-how and information of technology transfer and they consider each other not competitors but partners in obtaining the national goal of technology transfer. TLO did not gain the big income during last five year, but this trend of TLO is very positive to the future income.

It is hard to find the similar model as KTTC except the British Technology Group in the early 1980. Korea Technology Transfer Center (KTTC) has showed the leadership as main organization of technology commercialization and technology transfer in Korea. Thanks to the role and the works of KTTC, Korean government has propagated the concept of the technology transfer and commercialization not only to the engineers and professors, but also to ordinary inventors. KTTC has built excellent results on the infrastructure of technology transfer, commercialization, and the education system of TLO. Without the effort of KTTC, Korea could not have revamped the technology transfer and commercialization. Nonetheless, KTTC has yet to show it can help increasing more income for universities TLO.

6.3. Limitation and the Direction of Future Study

This study has some limitations which should be reflected in the next study. First, there are missing results from two universities, Seoul National University (SNU), and Korea

Advanced Institute of Science and Technology (KAIST). Both of these universities are believed to have successful commercialization programs comparing to other universities.

Second, 'Technology Transfer Promotion Act' is very important and critical in discussing technology transfer and commercialization in Korea. However, there is no statistical data explaining what happened after the administration of the act. This paper didn't examine the effect of Technology Transfer Promotion Act.

Third, Korean government has organized twelve Techno-Parks on respective regions since 1997, to enhance the competitiveness of region through collecting human and intellectual resources, and bridge regional universities and industry sectors. This study did not examine the policy factors affecting technology transfer in regional universities. The next study should include the examination of the influence of Techno-Parks on technology transfer.

Therefore, in order to suggest better policy implication, future study should include the sales through technology transfer and commercialization of the two universities and examine the effect of 'Technology Transfer Promotion Act' and of Techno-Parks.

ACKNOWLEDGEMENT

We deeply appreciate all the advices and critical review provided by professor Almas Heshmati.

REFERENCES

Allen, T. J. and S. I. Cohen (1969). "Information Flow in Research and Development Laboratories." *Administrative Science Quarterly*, 14(1):12-19.

Allen, T. J. (1979). "Managing the Flow of Technology: Technology Transfer and the Dissemination of Information within the R&D Organization." *Cambridge, MA: MIT Press.*

Bok, D. (2003). "Universities in the marketplace." *Cambridge, MA: Harvard University Press.*

Dante Di Gregorio and S. Shane (2003). "Why do some universities generate more start-up than others."

Geiger, R. L. (1993). "Research and Relevant Knowledge: American research universities since World War II" *New York: Oxford University Press.*

Korea Government, MOCIE (2005). "The Survey on the Technology Transfer of Public Research Institutes".

Korea Association of University Technology Managers (KAUTM) (2005). "KAUTM White Paper on Technology Transfer in Korea."

Rosenberg, N. and R. Nelson (1994). "American universities and technical advance in industry." *Res. Policy* 23, 323-348.

Segal, N.S. (1986). "Universities and Technological Entrepreneurship in Britain: Some Implications of the Cambridge Phenomenon." *Technovation* 4, 189-205.

Shane, S. (2001). "Selling university technology: Pattern from MIT." *Management Science* 48(1) 205-20.

Shane, S. and T. Stuart (2002). "Organizational endowment and the performance of university start-ups." *Management Science* 48(1), 151-71.

Scott Shane (2004). "Encouraging university entrepreneurship? The effect of the Bayh-Dole Act on university patenting in the United States" *Journal of Business Venturing, Volume* 19, *Issue* 1, *January* 2004, *Pages* 127-151.

Shane, S. and D. Cablr (2006). "Social relationships and the financing of new ventures." *Management Science, forthcoming*.

Utterback, J. (1994). "Mastering the Dynamics of Innovation: How Companies Can Seize Opportunities in the Face of Technological Change." *Boston, MA: Harvard Business School Press.*

In: Korea: Economic, Political and Social Issues
Editors: P. H. Elwood, J. B. Albertus
ISBN: 978-1-60456-513-3

Chapter 4

COMPARING THE STRUCTURE AND COMPETITIVE PRIORITIES OF TAIWAN AND KOREA TFT-LCD INDUSTRY

Pao-Long Chang, Han-Chi Chiang and Ying-Chyi Chou

1. INTRODUCTION

The TFT-LCD industry started in Japan, where during 1992-1994 companies invested in eight 2~2.5 generation TFT-LCD production lines. At the time, the main application was in notebook panels. Once Korean firms entered the fray against their large Japanese competitors, the market became overly competitive and supply exceeded demand, leading to repaid price drops. During 1995-1996, the three largest Korean firms Samsung, LG. Philips and Hydis set up four 3~3.5- generation TFT-LCD production lines within the period of one year, following which switched their LCD focus from notebook computers to the monitor product market. Yet fluctuations in international economic trends led to the 1997 Asian economic meltdown, which seriously harmed Japanese and Korean firms. Taiwanese firms were less seriously affected, and although they lacked the large dimension panel production experience of their Japanese and Korean counterparts, Taiwan firms had their advantages. They had the capital, and the downstream industries to support the development of the notebook and monitor industries. Taiwan firms engaged in technology partnerships with Japanese firms and in 1998-1999 established seven 3~3.5-generation TFT-LCD production lines. This was their formal entry into the TFT-LCD arena.

Before 2000, Japan was the dominant producer in the large size TFT-LCD industry, holding 49.5% of the global market, with Korea second with 36.8%. Taiwan only had 13.7%. Yet Taiwanese and Korean firms invested more aggressively in new factories while Japanese firms remained more conservative, which allowed Korea to overtake Japan in the large size TFT-LCD industry in 2001, with a 40.5% share internationally. Japan fell to 33.5% while Taiwan enjoyed 26.1% [6]. As Japanese firms were withdrawing from production of large size TFT-LCD panels and switching to high resolution and low power consumption LTPS (low temperature poly-silicon) display development, Taiwanese firms wrestled 38% of the world market in the first quarter of 2004, while Korea still holding over 45% [7].

In light of the fact that the three main producers in the large size TFT-LCD product market are Taiwan, Japan, and Korea, the commercial behavior of firms in these countries will intimately influence the development of this industry. Moreover, Taiwan and Korea occupy a process technology niche position in the large size TFT-LCD industry; both nations focus on panel manufacturing. Japan, on the other hand, has a system specification niche position and has emphasized technology R&D, thus taking control of the development of components and manufacturing equipment. This allows Japanese firms to avoid the price slashing competition with Taiwan and Korea and to increase their production technology royalty earnings. Taiwan and Korea firms are Japan's largest technology transfer customers, and the strategic alliances between Japanese and Taiwanese firms are very close. Therefore, there is now more cooperation than competition between Japan and Taiwan.

This study focuses on the large size TFT-LCD industry in Taiwan and Korea, investigating the structures these two countries possess in the industry and the differences in their manufacturing strategies. Future development suggestions for Taiwanese firms will also be presented.

2. Research Methodology

This paper adopts the case study approach. The cases chosen are the most competitive large TFT-LCD panel and module manufacturers in Korea and Taiwan, including the main Taiwanese and Korean panel firms: 1) Taiwan: AU Optoelectronics, Chi Mei Optoelectronics, Chung Hwa Picture Tube, Hanstar Display, Quanta Display, Innolux; 2) South Korea: Samsung, LG. Philips.

This research mainly relies on primary and secondary data. Primary data is gathered through in-depth interviews with personnel working in Taiwanese or Korean companies or academic positions. Main interviewees from Taiwan include a senior manager in Cell Engineering Department, AU Optoelectronics Corp., and a senior manager in Marketing Development Department, Hannstar Display Corp. Korean interviewees include a sales manager, Supreme Electronics, Samsung's Taiwanese Agent, and a researcher in Taiwan Samsung Electronics. Academic interviewees include a professor at Institute of Electro-optical Engineering, National Chiao Tung University, and a research manager in Display Research Group, Industrial Technology Research Institute (ITRI).

Secondary data has been obtained through the ITRI's Industrial Technology Intelligence Services (ITIS) Project as well as from the following sources: company briefs and relevant materials, conferences, newspapers, research reports, journal articles and website materials, etc.

This study relies on its sources to compare the structure of the TFT-LCD industries in Taiwan and Korea and to investigate both the competitive priorities used in Taiwan and Korea TFT-LCD industry and also future development orientations.

3. TFT-LCD Industry Structure in Taiwan and Korea

The structure of the TFT-LCD industry can be divided into three levels, which are upstream material components manufacturing, midstream panel manufacturing and downstream product application channels. Downstream application channels are companies that apply midstream products in salable goods. For example midstream panels are applied downstream in notebook monitors or standalone monitors. (See Figure 1)

In terms of midstream panel manufacturing, three subdivisions can be distinguished: TFT circuit array engineering, top/bottom cell engineering, and module engineering. The array engineering stage is mainly semiconductor fabrication. The cell engineering stage is the main determinant of TFT-LCD panel yield rate. Due to the difficulty of the technology for integrating components made of different materials, this stage requires rich accumulated experience. The third stage is module engineering: this stage requires more manpower than any other in the TFT-LCD industry. Although fabrication is not particularly difficult, there is no way to automate the process. The work has to be finished by hand, so the manpower cost is higher.

In terms of upstream material components, array industrial process material components are mainly the glass substrate, ITO (indium tin oxide) conductive glass, photoresist, and other chemical materials. The main material components for the cell process are liquid crystal materials, color filters, polarizer film, alignment film, and spacers. The main components involved in the module process are driver/control ICs and backlight modules, etc.

In terms of downstream product application channels, large diagonal size TFT-LCDs are presently mainly applied in notebooks, computer LCDs, and LCD TVs, the last of which has the most repaid growth.

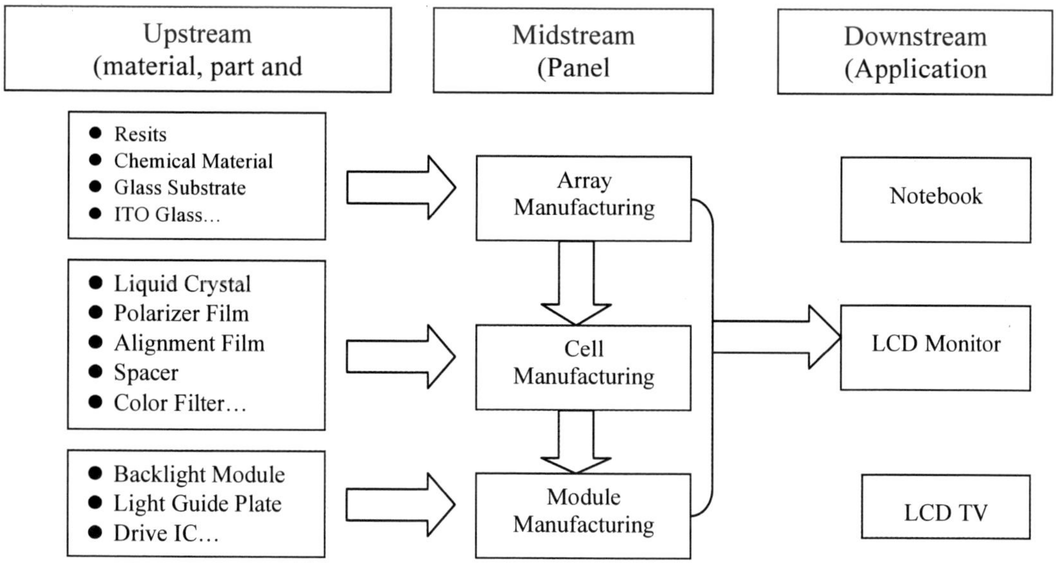

Figure 1. TFT-LCD industry structure.

3.1. Taiwan's TFT-LCD Industry Structure

In Taiwan's TFT-LCD industry structure, there is a significant number of large midstream panel manufacturers, including AU Optoelectronics, set up with BENQ and UMC investment, Chi-Mei Corporation's subsidiary Chi Mei Optoelectronics, Tatung's subsidiary Chung Hwa Picture Tube, Quanta Computer's subsidiary Quanta Display, Walsin Group's subsidiary Hannstar Display, and Innolux of Hon Hai Precision Industry. In the small diagonal size panel industry, there are Prime View, Toppoly, and Wintek Corp. As most of the professional involved in the TFT-LCD industry thin firm manufacturing process come from the semiconductor industry, whose companies have ample experience and mature technology, the yield rate during the array stage can reach 95% or higher. In terms of the cell stage, Taiwan invested in the TFT-LCD industry 4-5 years later than Korea. This is why Taiwan's yield rate for this stage still cannot reach 85%, which is the area where Taiwan cedes the most to Korean firms. As for the module stage, manpower cost is relatively high, so both Korea and Taiwan have transferred the LCM (liquid crystal module) factories for this stage to Mainland China to take advantage of lower labor cost. Generally speaking, the overall yield rate is pretty much 99%.

In addition, Taiwan panel manufacturers obtain their technology mainly through technology transfer arrangements with Japan, such as AU Optoelectronics obtaining technology from IBM Japan and Panasonic, Chi Mei Optoelectronics from Fujitsu and IBM Japan, China Picture Tube from the Japanese firm ADI and Hunet, Quanta Display from Sharp, and Hannstar from Toshiba [6]. Due to this type of relationship, Taiwan firms must pay high royalties to Japanese firms.

In terms of upstream material components, there are more than seventy suppliers, with the self-sufficiency rate of domestic manufacture around 70%. The technology involved in the manufacture of these material components is sourced in Japan and obtained through technology transfer. For example, the glass substrate needed during the array manufacturing process is produced by about five firms, only two are domestic firms: China Optoelectronics and Picvue Electronics. The other three firms are set by Japanese companies: Asahi Glass Fine Technology, Taiwan Nippon Sheet Glass, and by American company: Taiwan Corning [7].

In the middle stage cell manufacturing process, there are nine firms engaged in color filter production. The self-sufficiency rate of domestic manufacture has reached 80/% in 2004. In terms of light polarization technology, there are six firms. Among these, three have been established in cooperation with Japanese companies. For the module process, there are about twenty drive/control IC producers. Taiwan firms already have a lot of experience in the IC manufacturing industry and in packaging and testing technology. This gives them a competitive advantage in this field. However, for control ICs there is a lack of domestic expertise in analog technology, so Taiwan firms universally lack the capacity to develop analog-to-digital converters and must purchase it from foreign companies. There are 31 firms engaged in backlight module production, so that each Taiwanese panel firm is supplied by several backlight module firms. In sum, the rate of domestic manufacture for backlight modules is 95%, the highest proportion for any material component, but other material components require further localization.

For downstream product application channels, Taiwan's notebook computer and display production figure places it first in the world. There are thirteen notebook companies and sixteen display companies. With such excellent downstream product application channel relationships, Taiwan has a significant competitive advantage, but as some international PC firms have selected Korean panels and have signed long-term agreements with Korean firms, Taiwan's advantage in this area is not absolute.

The above description of Taiwan's TFT-LCD industry structure informs us that the industry is vertically disintegrated. This is so because in Taiwan SMEs are prosperous and downstream product application channels firms are numerous.

3.2. Korea's TFT-LCD Industry Structure

In terms of midstream panel manufacturing, there are two main Korean firms: Samsung, LG. Philips. Samsung Electronics produces TFT-LCD panels through its subsidiary Samsung Monitor. According to the words of a highly experienced manager formerly at Hydis for two years and presently at Samsung's Taiwan distributor/reseller, Samsung Monitor's most striking feature is that its capacity to mass-production is extremely strong. In recent years, Samsung has played a guiding role in bringing out new generation production lines. In 2002, LG. Philips Display LCD became the largest TFT-LCD manufacturer in the world. According to a highly experienced manager at Samsung's Taiwan distributor/reseller, LG. Philips Display LCD Co. most important characteristic is its strength in R&D capability and product quality. This company and Samsung Electronics have different mass production capacities.

In terms of the supply of upstream material components, this is mainly taken care of by the corporate organizations themselves. The self-sufficiency rate of domestic manufacture is 90% or higher. The technology involved is also internal to the corporate organization. Samsung Group provides an illustration of this: its subsidiary Samsung Corning (the second largest picture glass bulb case and LCD glass manufacturer in the world) produces glass substrate, Samsung SDI (the largest picture tube manufacturer in the world) produces color filters, Samsung Electro-Mechanics produces printed circuit boards, and Samsung Semiconductor (the world's largest memory chip and LC panel manufacturer) produces drive/control ICs. This provides Samsung Monitor with a powerful upstream supply system.

In terms of downstream product application channels, Korea's main customers are international brand name PC system giants, and firms have signed long-term agreements with these brand name companies. For instance, Samsung signed a long-term purchase agreement with Apple Computer and Dell worth upwards of 10 billion US dollars. This order not only assured Samsung a dominant position in the large TFT-LCD industry but also gave it the impetus to invest in fourth generation production lines even after weathering the serious financial crisis. LG. Philips LCD cooperates with international display giant Philips in order to keep a handle on downstream application market demand. It also has long-term high level product ordering agreements with American aviation parts suppliers and medical equipment firms.

The above elaboration of the structure of the industry in Korea shows that large corporations dominate the industry and the industry is highly vertical integrated.

4. Vertical Integration versus Vertical Disintegration

Since staring with a few downstream assembly plants in the 1960s, Taiwan IC industry has developed into a comprehensive industrial system with vertical disintegration pattern. It consists of sub-industries in designing, photomask manufacturing, wafer fabrication, IC packaging and testing, with each sub-industry specializing in their own area of expertise. Most of the sub-industry players are located in northern Taiwan (centered around the Hsinchu Science Park), with an intensive interaction between them that creates a highly efficient industrial value chain in terms of goods/material flow, information flow and the accumulation of human resources and capital.

The success of Taiwanese IC industry led Taiwanese firms to adopt a vertically disintegrated development pattern when they launched into the TFT-LCD industry [11]. In the IC industry system specifications are highly unified, so there are publicly recognized and respected standards for devices. This arrangement lowers the costs involved in searching for mutually acceptable specifications during the negotiation of contract terms. However, the TFT-LCD industry is different. The objective for establishing specifications for such TFT-LCD features as resolution, viewing angle, brightness, contrast radio, color, weight, diagonal size, and power consumption is to allow 1) the user to enjoy a comfortable and enjoyable visual experience and 2) the industry to benefit from high production quantities for a limited variety of products. The problem is that all companies need to do is meet specifications; inner mechanism specifications are left up in the air. Thus, there is a plurality of inner mechanisms and internal devices are left un-standardized. In addition, TFT-LCDs themselves are semi-manufactured products that are to be applied downstream by notebook and monitor manufacturers. For many specifications and designs, midstream firms must pair up with downstream firms and accommodate their requirements. In the vertically disintegrated development pattern used in the Taiwan TFT-LCD industry, upstream material components firms and midstream panel manufacturers are numerous. Without system specifications and publicly recognized standards for internal devises, specifications have to be determined during the negotiation of contract terms. This significantly increases the transaction cost incurred by companies competing in this field [8].

In addition, TFT-LCD industry materials cost is over 50% of overall cost, far more than the 30% materials cost which is the norm in the semiconductor industry. The rate of domestic manufacture self-sufficiency of upstream raw material components becomes very important. The level of precision in the process is lower than in the IC industry, but all links of the process must be well connected in a specific order. If at one stage of the process there is a lack of materials or components or a defect in the process itself, this will render the entire panel unusable. Therefore, the materials, components and process technology at every stage are crucial. In other words, continuity in production is stressed. Add to these factors the fact that TFT-LCD panels are large and fragile, not suitable for long-range transport like IC chips. Thus, during the production process, the locations of upstream and downstream firms must be very close together.

The TFT-LCD resembles the DRAM industry in that it is characterized by a quick product lifecycle. Although Taiwanese firms do OEM production for Japanese companies, with contracts where the Japanese companies will buy back a maximum of around 30%, Taiwanese companies cannot restrain Japanese ones. Japanese firms determine the market situation by deciding whether or not to buy back the products produced by the Taiwanese OEM firms. Thus, for a midstream panel firm to possess its own distribution channels and thus achieve downstream integration will help it to understand downstream product requirements, and adjust production capacity to lower its cost. If the panels a company produces are not salable, its future is grim.

Thus, differentiation is very hard to manage in the TFT-LCD industry. Success is only possible by continuously bringing out new generation production lines, engaging in mass production competition, raising yield rates and lowering costs. This is another reason why the TFT-LCD product life cycle is short and the rate of replacement of production line technology is rapid.

To sum up, the TFT-LCD industry is different from the IC industry. Taiwan firms started with vertical disintegration as the TFT-LCD industrial development model. Yet because upstream material components and midstream panel manufacturers were so numerous, there was redundant competition among firms, involving talent stealing and employee defection. Add to this the problem that individual firms were small with inadequate resources and financial strength: they had a very limited capacity to invest in technology R&D and brand name creation. This caused Taiwan to slip behind Korea in terms of cost efficiency and product quality.

Korean firms, on the other hand, have adopted vertical integration, a corporate group management mode of operation. This enhances their economies of scope and scale. Moreover, through corporate group affiliated research institutes, they emphasize long-term R&D and personnel training. Thus, in terms of process technology, patent numbers, and the learning curve effect, Korean firms are more competitive.

According to a highly qualified flat screen researcher at ITRI, "There is no benefit to the large size TFT-LCD industry in specialized OEM outsourcing; vertical integration would suit this industry." Taiwan began with vertical disintegration as its industrial development model, which falls short of the vertical integration industrial development model adopted by Korean firms.

5. Competitive Priorities

Looking at manufacturing strategy from the perspective of competition helps to define the competitive priorities. Sharma [10] believed that a company's competitive priorities could be the basis on which operations should outperform competitors. Identifying competitive priorities help to integrate corporate and business strategies with the goals pursued by company operations. Leong et al. [9] held that competitive priorities might be defined as a consistent set of goals for manufacturing. Buffa [2] has looked at manufacturing strategy in terms of four competitive priorities, which are: cost, quality, dependability of supply and flexibility/service. In addition to the four, Bolwijn and Kumpe [1] proposed that price and product innovation are also important priorities. Crowe and Nuno [5], for their part, content that there are four competitive priorities, which are flexibility, cost, quality, and service. Chang and Tsai [3] in investigating the manufacturing strategies of Taiwan's IC design industry argued that its competitive priorities were speed, cost, flexibility, and quality.

Table 1. Competitive priorities in TFT-LCD industry

Priority	Explanation
Speed	New generation production line development speed New large diagonal size panel release speed
Cost	Unit panel manufacturing cost
Quality	Able to maintain product stability or products with superior features
Price	Product market sales price
Flexibility	Flexibility in matching customer specifications and support requirements

This study considers the special features of the TFT-LCD industry and analyses the differences in Korean and Taiwanese manufacturing strategy in terms of five competitive priorities: speed, cost, quality, price, and flexibility. Table 1 explains the significance of these competitive priorities in the TFT-LCD industry.

5.1. Speed

Korean firms such as Samsung Group possess abundant financial resources, so it is easier for their subsidiaries to raise the funds necessary for new generation production lines than it is for independent Taiwanese firms. Moreover, Korean firms have signed long-term agreements with international PC giants, and they do not build new generation production lines until they have an order in hand. With this arrangement, they have taken a lead of 1-2 years over Taiwan in production line development. For example, in a one year period from 1995-1996, Korea brought four 3~3.5-generation plants into service. From 2001-2003, they brought four 5th generation plants into service, and then one 6th, three 7-7.5 generation plants from 2004-2005. By contrast, Taiwanese firms brought seven 3~3.5- plants into service in two years from 1998-1999, while from 2002-2005 they brought eight 5th generation plants, and another four 6th, and one 7th generation plants in 2005 and 2006 [7].

The application product market is very responsive to new generation production lines and production technology. With improvements in new generation production lines, the individual glass substrate size can be increased. When considering the economic cutting rate of panel, the newer generation production lines are most beneficial to large diagonal size panel development, as they lower the single unit panel manufacturing cost. For example, if you use a 3.5-generation plant to produce 15-inch panels, you can get 6 panels out of a single substrate, while a fifth generation plant provides more economic cutting, giving 15 panels per substrate. Because Taiwan develops new generation production lines slower than Korea, Taiwanese companies fall far behind Korea in terms of economy of scale and efficiency.

This also allowed Korean firms to take a half to one year lead over Taiwan in bringing out large diagonal size panels. For example, Korea firm had in 1999 already developed 15.4, 15.7, and 16.5-inch SXGA notebook computer panels, while at the time the notebook mainstream was still 13.3-inch. With the release of larger panels, competition is not fierce at the beginning so the prices can be higher and a wider profit margin enjoyed. Since Korea took the lead in bringing out large diagonal size panels and so enjoyed better profit margins than Taiwanese firms. This is another reason why Korean firms make more money.

5.2. Cost

Korea firms have taken vertical integration as their mode of operation. This is corporate group management operation, which creates favorable economies of scale and scope. Moreover, through corporate group affiliated research institutes Korean firms stress long-term R&D and personnel training. Thus, in terms of process technology, patent numbers and the learning curve effect, they are more competitive than Taiwanese firms. For instance, for the manufacturing process, Korean firms now make use of only four masks, while Taiwanese firms still use 5-8. As for production line manpower placement, a senior manager of the Cell Engineering Dept. at AU Optoelectronics, commented, "A Korean production line needs only about 250 personnel, while a Taiwanese line often needs 400." This is why Korean firms bear a much lighter manpower cost.

In addition, an ITRI's project [4] contended that if the production lines were operating under the same conditions, since the upstream component system in Korea is more integrated, companies there have a materials cost advantage over Taiwan. As for manpower cost, Korean companies bear 0.76 of the burden of Taiwanese companies. This allows Korean firms to achieve a lower single unit manufacturing cost. However, because Taiwan firms are smaller and have inadequate resources and finances, they have less R&D expenditure than Korea firms. In addition, Taiwan is less aggressive than Korea in brand name creation. Thus, in sales expenses Korea spends 1.6 more than Taiwan.

Because Taiwan's science parks are directly under the jurisdiction of the central government, there is no need to pay property or income tax. Thus, the tax load for companies within the boundaries of the science parks is lighter than for Korean firms. Since Taiwanese firms have a tax advantage and have limited investment in R&D and brand name creation, so that in the end they earn a higher percentage of net profit to revenues than in Korea. This is also why Taiwanese firm are always stuck in an OEM mindset.

5.3. Quality

In Korea, the corporate groups themselves handle the supply of upstream material components. Thus, they can control both the source and quality of components, and more easily keep a handle on process development and product stability.

In addition, in terms of panel exports, Taiwan's TFT-LCD panel firms mainly sell monitor panels, while Korea dominates notebook panels. Generally speaking, monitor quality requirements are lower and the brand name effect is not as strong. Profits are also lower. Notebook panels, on the other hand, have stringent requirements for both quality and specifications, and the brand name effect is very strong. Notebook panel producers enjoy higher profits.

Although Taiwan's downstream notebook firm production volume is number one, international brand name PC system giants have not shown any desire to deal with Taiwan midstream panel firms but have instead determined Samsung and LG-Philips as their notebook panel suppliers. Korean firms were selected because they have been professionally certified and their product quality and stability is high. In addition, when consumers purchase notebooks, they pay more attention to brand name reputation than when buying monitors.

Thus, when deciding upon panel firms, international brand name PC system giants will stress brand name reputation.

5.4. Price

Price has a key impact on overall market share in the TFT-LCD industry. Korea firms use their market strength to control price and to maintain a strategy of price slashing. This puts enormous pressure on Taiwanese firms. Taiwan and Korea's price competition from 2001 to 2003 will be explained below:

In 2001, TFT-LCDs were oversupplied and the economy was still in a slump. Korea firms noted that the yield rates at Taiwanese 3.5-generation plants were too low and panel single-unit manufacturing cost too high, and so proceeded to slash prices. Taiwan firms were well aware that they could not match Korean firms in terms of speed, cost, and quality, so they slashed prices even lower than Korea just to survive. Market prices dropped even lower, and with equipment depreciation in their 3.5-generation plants, Taiwanese firms were losing money. At the same time, Samsung was still profitable.

In 2002, the TFT-LCD market was more prosperous and prices rose. Taiwanese 3.5-generation plant yield rates improved and equipment depreciation was reduced. Facing a sturdier competitor, Korean firms would not lightly start a price war. Thus, in 2002, Taiwanese firms were pretty much all profitable, with AU Optoelectronics making 5.785 billion NT dollars and EPS 1.46 NT dollars. Yet Korean firms made even more. Taiwan firm were profitable in 2002, but combined with its losses in 2001 AU was 1.115 billion in the red for 2001-2002.

During 2003-2004, the yield rate at Korean fifth generation factories fell short of expectations, and Taiwan firms have been making money in both halves. Yet once the market is oversupplied and Korean yield rates improve, there will be probably another price war.

5.5. Flexibility

Korea TFT-LCD firms' main customers are all international brand name PC companies, with which they sign long-term agreements. Thus, the unit quantity for single orders is 200-300 thousand. Product specifications are fixed, so Korean firms are less willing to accept orders with different specifications or quantities.

Taiwan firms have adopted a "division of labor" as their development model, so they all have middleman distributors. When lower downstream firms can only place orders of 1-2 thousand, they band together to place orders of 10-20 thousand with TFT-LCD panel firms. For example, AU got 6.5% of its revenues through Promate Electronics, a middleman distributor.

Since many of the customers of Taiwan TFT-LCD firms are downstream firms affiliated to the corporate group itself, they are all pretty much scattered around the Hsinchu Science-based Industrial Park and the Southern Taiwan Science-based Industrial Park in Tainan. This placement gives Taiwan's TFT-LCD industry an obvious advantage. With numerous upstream and downstream firms, Taiwan is extremely flexible in providing customization and service/support to customers.

The preceding explanation shows that with a division of labor as development model, Taiwan firms have cultivated flexibility and excellent service and support capability. These advantages have been the narrow niche where they have competed.

6. Measures for Taiwan TFT-LCD Firms

At present, Taiwanese TFT-LCD firms are struggling to overcome problems brought by the industrial system with vertical disintegration pattern by moving towards a vertical integration industrial development model. Major changes for firms are observed as follows:

1) Panel Manufacturers Invest in Upstream Key Components to Facilitate Firm-Internal Integration

AU Optoelectronics is already self-sufficient in color filters, and has invested in the production of backlight modules (AU's Suzhou factory), drive ICs (Novatek), polarizer film (Daxon), and cold cathode fluorescent lamps CCFL (Wellypower). AU Optoelectronics is presently 70% self-sufficient in the manufacture of upstream material componets. Chi Mei Optoelectronics has also invested in the production of upstream key componets, such as color filters (CMO), drive ICs (Himax), etc. It has reached a self-sufficiency level of about 70%.

2) Develop a "Virtual in-House" Mode of Operation

Speaking of panel dimensions, panels produced by fifth generation plants and after will became thinner and larger, which will increase the risk of damage during shipping. If production is moved close to market demand, such risk and the associated cost can be significantly reduced. Focusing on this trend, Taiwanese firms have adopted a "zone within zone" or "factory within factory" approach, developing an original mode of operations. For example, backlight module firm Coretronics is stationed in an Chi Mei factory, color filter firm Sintek Optoelectronics is stationed in Longtan Park and is engaging in "virtual in-house" cooperation with Chung Hwa Picture Tube, and Toppan CFI (Taiwan) Co. Ltd. is stationed in the Sourthern Taiwan Science-based Industrial Park where it produces color filters. These methods will allow an application channel and service cost savings of 3-5% per panel.

3) Develop Own Channels

Taiwan firms do help Japanese firms with OEM production, but they have started to abandon their earlier OEM mindset. The stress is now on firm integration and on firms gaining their own application channels. For instance, Chi Mei Electronics spends 1/3 of its production capacity helping Japanese firms with OEM production, while 2/3 of production is sold through its own channels. Chi Mei Optoelectronics has in fact invested in the Arch Computer as its domestic downstream product application channel.

Promoting vertical integration among firms, developing a corporate group-style model of operation are tasks that demand the immediate attention of Taiwan's TFT-LCD industry. Of the major TFT-LCD producing nations, only Taiwan adopts the vertical disintegration as its industrial model. Even Mainland China, which got moving later than other countries, is now developing its gradually maturing LCD industry with "corporate group management." A star among mainland companies is North Caijing Group, formed of over ten businesses and having overall assets totaling 1.6 billion RMB. This group oversees over ten production and research organizations, including Jilin Beifang Caijing Digital Electronics Limited, Jilin Zijing Electronics Co. Ltd., Jilin Caijing Digital Hi-Tech. Panels Ltd., and Jilin North Academy of Optoelectronics.

7. Conclusion

The mode of operation in Korea TFT-LCD industry is corporate group management, which is vertically integrated, and enjoys favorable economies of scale and scope. Furthermore, it invests in long-term R&D and personnel training through the corporate group affiliated research institutes. These measures help Korean firms outstrip Taiwanese firms in process capability and patent quantity. In developing new generation production lines and releasing large diagonal size panels, Korean firms are speedier than Taiwanese firms. They also rely on their process technology and learning curve advantage, possessing a competitive advantage in product quality, manufacturing cost (pre-tax), and profit earnings. Thus although Korea falls behind Taiwan in terms of downstream product application channels, Korean firms have signed long-term agreements with international PC giants and have adopted a mode of operations where they wait until they get an order before developing new generation production lines. This is how Korean firms have taken first place in the TFT-LCD market.

For the Taiwanese TFT-LCD industry, it has commodious downstream firms which produce more notebook and LCD monitors than anyone else in the world. On top of this, Taiwan's market is mainly SMEs, so Taiwan has an advantage over Korea for customized design and product variety. Over the past couple of years, the state of the industry has trained a special flexibility in Taiwan's entrepreneurs, an ability to respond to change and to provide excellent service and support.

However, since there are too many firms in Taiwan's TFT-LCD industry and competition among these firms in combination with redundancy in production line investment have led to inadequate economy of scale for individual firms and relative competitive weakness. Thus, Taiwanese firms should engage in cooperation as a replacement for pernicious competition. By reducing firm numbers through mergers, the economy of scale of individual firms would be enhanced and they would not only be able to invest more energy in R&D but would also strengthen the upstream material components supply chain. The TFT-LCD industry would benefit by pursuing vertical integration. It is a large industry that could maintain or improve its position through this strategy. Therefore, if Taiwanese firms want to overtake Korea and become the key global TFT-LCD industry panel manufacturers, a strategy of corporate mergers is the first step.

REFERENCES

[1] Bolwijn, P.T. and T. Kumpe. "Manufacturing in the 1990s: Productivity, Flexibility and Innovation." *Long Range Planning*. 1990: 23 (4), pp. 44-57.

[2] Buffa, E.S. *Meeting the Competitive Challenge: Manufacturing Strategy for U.S. Companies.* Homewood, Illinois: Richard D. Irwin, 1984.

[3] Chang, P.L. and Tsai, C.T. "Finding a Niche Position-Competitive strategy for Taiwan's IC Design Industry." *Technovation.* 2002: 22, pp. 101-111.

[4] Chen, M.C., He, H.C. and Yeh, H.C., ITRI IEK ITIS Project: *Development Opportunities for Taiwan in Second Generation TFT-LCDs* (in Chinese), July, 1999.

[5] Crowe, T.J. and Nuno, T.P. "Deciding Manufacturing Priorities: Flexibility, Cost, Quality and Service." *Long Range Planning*. 1994: 24 (6), pp. 86-95.

[6] ITRI IEK ITIS Project: *2002 Flat Screen Display Annual Report* (In Chinese)

[7] ITRI IEK ITIS Project: *2005 Flat Screen Display Annual Report* (In Chinese)

[8] ITRI IEK ITIS Project: *TFT-LCD Industry Co-opetition and Management Format* (In Chinese). August, 2002.

[9] Leong, G.K., Snyder, D.L. and Ward, P.T. "Research in the Process and Content of Manufacturing Strategy." *Omega: International Journal of Management Science.* 1990: 18 (2), pp. 109-122.

[10] Sharma, D. *Manufacturing Strategy: An Empirical Investigation.* 1987.

[11] Yeh, H.C., "Analysis of LCD Industry Business Model Trends with the History of the IC Industry (In Chinese)." *Chemnet*, April 2001: pp. 42-47.

In: Korea: Economic, Political and Social Issues
Editors: P. H. Elwood, J. B. Albertus ISBN: 978-1-60456-513-3

Chapter 5

A "HOT" DEBATE: FINANCIAL CRISES IN TURKEY, MEXICO AND SOUTH KOREA

Nilgün Erdem[*]

Dr. Frankenstein (the policy maker), after creating the monster (external financial liberalization), observes its destructive activities (uncontrolled debt growth); but instead of putting the monster back to sleep (bringing back traditional controls), uses all the means under its control (interest and exchange rate policies) to tame the untameable creature. This is, in short, the dismal story of external financial liberalization in developing countries during the past decade (Boratav, 1993:17).

1. INTRODUCTION

Following the trend started in the 1980s and became quite distinctive during the 1990s, the financial systems of the center and the periphery converged towards the Anglo-Saxon market-based model. Let it be so: *prima facie* reason for all evils in the age of the so-called globalization is the unstable character of capital accumulation in the central economies, especially in a world with no limitations to finance capital. For the sake of its own profitability, global finance capital has always been seeking to overcome the devaluation of capital by penetrating into developing and underdeveloped countries. Along with the hegemony of neo-liberal policies and *laissez-faire* ideology, these countries, which are now called "emerging markets" in neoliberal parlance, liberalized capital movements across borders and reduced or totally eliminated foreign exchange controls. This paved the way for deregulation of the domestic financial markets. Thus, offered high arbitrage incomes brought about the large scale short-term capital inflows to such countries, especially in form of "*hot money*". Consequently, the hot money inflows themselves became the cause of instability with high and growing volatility which finally resulted in serious financial crises. Meanwhile, the advocates of neo-liberal policies anticipated that liberalization policies would inevitably

[*] The author would like to thank Korkut Boratav, A. Haşim Köse, Fikret Şenses, Aydın Ördek and Ceyhun Gürkan for their valuable comments on the paper.

remove inequalities between countries and result in convergence. As a matter of fact, convergence has taken place, but not in the way as anticipated by the neo-classical approaches. The "trinity" of financial liberalization, deregulation and integration with international markets has made many countries converged in financial crises; in line with that, instead of reducing intra-national and international income disparities, it has sharpened them.[1]

Triggered by such instability, repeatedly were observed the financial crises, some major of which outburst in Turkey in 1994 and 2000-2001, in Mexico during the years 1994-95, again in 1995 and later in 2001 in Argentina, in 1997 in Southeast Asia, in Russia in 1998, in Brazil in 1999 and 2002. Financial instability as a global fact, on the one hand, is experienced as a very geographical peculiarity; it is, on the other, with abraded border of the "nation", experienced with common features. Thus, from a point of view centered on above mentioned phenomena, not only the detection of similarities but also of differences enables us to elaborate on the present condition of the world and her future, at least it gives us the clues to understand. Turkey, of course, from the geographical standpoint should have been focused on; since the introspection is possible with the case. So, this study aims to make a comparative analysis of the financial crises of Turkey in 1994 and 2001, Mexico in 1994-1995, and South Korea in 1997.

Mexican and South Korean financial crises were selected for a comparison due to two reasons: Firstly, before the 1997 Asian crisis, two regions were distinguished on how they were affected by financial circumstances in developed countries, and on the impact of their own financial policies. These were Latin Americas where financial liberalization policies were implemented rapidly (*big bang* with the sole objective of international market integration) and East Asia where financial policies were designed in order to serve the objectives of economic development. In this context, Mexico can be considered as a typical country in the first category, while South Korea emerges as an important country in the second one. Therefore, the South Korean and the Mexican experiences have been selected for a comparison with Turkey with which they have some similarities. Secondly, fundamental macroeconomic indicators of these two countries can allow the exposition of the hot money flows resulted in instability and financial crushes. When the pre-crisis macroeconomic indicators are taken into consideration, as will be made explicit later, although Mexico and South Korea, unlike Turkey, had quite fiscal balances, they could not avoid the financial crises. Over and above, even the South Korea's incompatible industrial strategy and her proper economic indicators could not preclude the crisis. That is, why the selection of Mexico and South Korea as somewhat reagents provides us with the chance of searching out the reasons Turkish crises. In spite of exhaustive analysis of both Mexican and Korean cases (and recent ones on Turkish case), there will be some methodological and empirical novelties in this study: (i) a detailed analysis of the balance of payments data utilizing a useful and functional conceptual framework will enable us to distinguish arbitrage-seeking ("hot") capital movements from other inflows/outflows[2]; (ii) a decomposition of inflows/outflows into the resident and non-resident components will generate a framework by means of which parallel (pro-cyclical) and diverging (counter-cyclical) behavior of residents/non-residents

[1] For theoretical debates (from the Orthodox line to the structuralist, post-Keynesian and Minskyian approaches), see Krugman (1998), Stiglitz (1989), Akyüz (1993), Boratav (1993, 1999, 2003), Boratav and Yeldan (2001), Burkett (1987), Diaz-Alejandro (1985), Ffrench-Davis (1993), Grabel (1995), Kregel (1996), Taylor (1998).

[2] Boratav (1999) developed a method of calculation of these magnitudes based on IMF's new (1993) BOP (Balance of Payments) statistics.

can be distinguished; (iii) although it is usually possible to find out the destination of resident outflows, non-resident "hot" inflows can, in some countries, be decomposed into the types of asset[3] in which they are invested. Such decompositions can provide the basis for further causal or policy-based analysis.

There is another vital conceptual point to be mentioned: It is the term *new cycle*. A number of economists critical of the neo-liberal policy recipes have emphasized the role and importance of capital movements (and particularly their "hot" components) and their reversal in generating a new type of cycle which, in some cases, incorporates a financial crisis. The large increase in capital inflows leading to a boom and the reversal of it, accompanied, in some cases, by banking and/or currency crises is the typical pattern that explains our *cycle*. Residents may aggravate or dampen the cycle. Although the composition of inflows to developing countries and their maturity has varied over time and by countries, and such variation has affected the overall volatility of the flows, the common feature during the 1990s has been a rapid expansion of private short-term capital flows into and out of developing countries. Accordingly *the new cycle* guides us to the very simple understanding (by empirical means) of our three cases.

The following section compares the financial systems and the process of financial liberalization and deregulation in each country prior to the crises and overviews the path financial crises have followed in each economy. Section three undertakes to set forth the method of calculation of the magnitudes of capital flows and examines the empirical data. A general assessment in the light of the findings of previous sections, in section four, urges us to conclude.

2. An Overview of Structural Shifts in the Financial Policies Framework

A glance at the three countries examined in this study reveals that, as already described above, in each, their financial systems were liberalized *(Dr. Frankenstein -the policy maker- created the monster -external financial liberalization-)* during the pre-crisis periods. In this context, it should be pointed out that with respect to structural transformations experienced during the last twenty years, the economies of Turkey and Mexico resemble each other in large, while South Korea displays quite a different path.[4] In this framework, the section serves to fulfill our expectation of having a very simple historiography of the policy shifts in the countries in question for the last quarter, which make financial environment homogenous, and consequently ground for the financial crises.

Like of many others of the post-war period Turkey's import substitution industrialization strategy continued from the 1960s through the 1970s, and came to an end with the crisis of

[3] "The individual constituents of short-term inflows undertaken by non-residents (generating liabilities to the recipient country) are: portfolio investment in equity (essentially in stock markets) and short-term debt (money market) instruments (e.g. Treasury bills); short-term loans to banks and 'other sectors'; change in currency and deposits in the national currency held by external agents and other short-term external liabilities of banks. The same cross-border transactions undertaken by residents are considered outflows" (Gabriele, Boratav and Parikh 2000: 1044).

[4] For details on the fundamental transformations in the financial policies of Mexico, South Korea and Turkey see: Lustig and Ros (1999); Chang, Park and Yoo (1998); Türel (1993) and Williamson and Mahar (1998).

1977-79. Following the major balance of payments crisis, facilitated by the military coup of September, the 1980 program were to be implemented. One of the central elements of the 1980 stabilization/liberalization program adopted in Turkey was the internal liberalization.[5] In July 1980, deposit and credit interest rates were deregulated. This led to "Ponzi" type financing that caused an intense pressure over interest rates, which resulted in "bankers crisis". In 1986, the Istanbul Stock Exchange was established along with an interbank money market and foreign exchange market, and the Central Bank diversified its monetary instruments by starting open market operations. Financial instruments were diversified and the use of credit cards became widespread followed by the increasing availability of consumer credits. In 1985, the Treasury began to auction bills and bonds, thus giving rise to substantial increases of interest burden on public finance. These all led to difficulties in financial supervision.

The 1989 regulation on "convertibility" was a critical step towards external liberalization. Foreign exchange controls on capital outflows were removed, and both the current[6] and capital accounts were completely liberalized. Thereafter the combination of the overvaluation of the Turkish Lira and high interest rates became instrumental in attracting short term capital. The expansion that accompanied this state of world led, in 1993, to an unprecedented high level of trade, thus the current account deficit. In addition, the burden of high interest payments also worsened the fiscal balance[7]. Ultimately, the Turkish economy with such a fragile character made the way for the major financial crisis of 1994.

This situation continued with the exchange rate dis-inflation and stabilization program sponsored by the IMF till the year 2000. Thereafter, under no-sterilization policy rule capital inflows led to decline in interest rates and increase in domestic credits. The appreciation of the Turkish Lira was accompanied by an "explosion" of net capital inflows by non-residents during the first ten months of 2000. The appreciation of the TL caused the rapid deterioration in the current account deficit by the end of 2000. The economy became vulnerable to speculative attacks and, finally the program collapsed with two attacks on the domestic currency (TL) in 2000 and 2001. Analytically, "during the 1980s, the linkages between these variables appear to be in the direction of growth-current account deficits-capital inflows (...) The 1990s appears to have transformed the direction of foregoing linkage into capital inflows-growth-current deficits" (Boratav and Yeldan, 2001). And when capital inflows are not sustained, or turn into capital outflows, the process is reversed, as was witnessed during the financial crises of 1994 and 2000-2001.

From a more micro perspective, such steps towards financial liberalization changed the behavior of economic agents, contributing to the conditions that laid the groundwork for a financial crisis. For example, after the liberalization, credit interest rates rose to excessively high levels. The high credit interest rates in turn seriously increased the costs of firms relying

---

[5] Our discussion of financial liberalization in Turkey draws heavily on Akyüz (1990), Boratav (1995), Boratav and Yeldan (2001) and Türel (1993).

[6] By the mid 1980s, import quotas were mostly removed, customs tariffs reduced, and generous incentives were offered to exports. During the 1980s, "fictitious exports" scandals emerged, with the increase of export incentives.

[7] "The new issues of securities by the state increased from 6.9% of GNP in 1988 to 38.7% in 1999" (Boratav and Yeldan, 2001:6). This development contributed to a rise in interest rates. Paradoxically, it was the orthodox recipes on financial liberalization which, through rising interest payments, caused unsustainable fiscal imbalances blamed, later on, as the main cause of crisis by orthodox analysis.

heavily on credits.[8] Meanwhile, it became increasingly difficult for banks to find reliable customers with such high interest rates on loans. Non-performing loans rose substantially. Another development from the banks' point of view was a serious increase in speculative activities and banks inevitably started to act as institutional rentiers. Given the situation, the capital inflows gave rise to appropriate financial instruments such as "repos".[9]

Repos were legalized, but without any requirement obligations for banks; besides the tax-exemption to government bonds and treasury bills rendered these operations highly profitable. In the meanwhile, external financial liberalization made it possible for banks to start borrowing foreign currency abroad and to invest these funds domestically in kind of financial instruments mentioned above. Furthermore, repos were not confined with transactions between the Central Bank and other banks, the tax-exemptions encouraged any agent enjoying the funds to invest them in a similar fashion. As a result, some banks were unable to meet their liabilities on time, thus increased the "open positions" and eventually raised the liquidity risks. After the 1994 crisis, when banks began to go bankrupt, savings deposits started to be insured 100 % to cease the deposit flights. Throughout 2000, the number of banks that were transferred to the Saving Deposits Insurance Fund (SDIS) kept on increasing. It soon became apparent that in addition to open market operations, interbank money market operations also became a source of large profits and losses.[10]

To sum up, after 1980, when both internal and external financial liberalizations were implemented, and when financial deepening took place in large, private sector debts increased and the public sector could borrow only at very high interest rates. Thus, while only three banks and several intermediary institutions went bankrupt in 1994, the bankruptcies were much more widespread and the crisis was much more severe in 2000-February 2001.[11]

Having the same transformations with the Turkish economy, Mexico too abandoned import substitution industrialization in the early 1980s after fundamentally redefining the role of the state in economic sphere. After the debt crisis of 1983 that profoundly concussed the Mexican economy (as other Latin American economies), Mexico began to implement an orthodox stabilization program (Aspe, 1993). After a short while, in the mid-1985, at the time the country faced a balance of payments crisis, she was forced to devaluate the peso. On top of it, the drop in oil prices in 1986 aggravated Mexico`s foreign debt problem. Consequently, Mexico became the first country to sign a memorandum of understanding on borrowing with commercial banks in 1990, under the sponsorship of the Brady Plan (Lustig and Ros, 1999).

---

8 During the period of 1986-88, interests as a percentages of the gross value added of large private firms was substantially over the share of wages. Furthermore, it was observed that large companies still operated with high debt/net asset and debt/equity ratios, and a large portion of their debts were short term (Türel, 1993:148; 155).

9 In situations where the market has a temporary liquidity problem, banking system reserves are temporarily increased, and on the date of transaction, the State Domestic Debt Bonds are bought by the Central Bank, with a promise to sell at a certain price in the future. Thus, the Central Bank provides money for the market with a repurchasing agreement, and withdraws money from the market with an inverse repurchasing agreement.

10 In 1994, the share of overnight transactions in proportion to total transactions had reached 98,56% (Annual Report of CBRT, 1994). The importance of this figure emerges when we take into consideration the fact that in the month of March, the share of overnight operations reached 350%. On the other hand, in the months of May and June after the crisis, the Treasury was forced to make sales with an interest rate that reached 200%.

11 Respectively, *Marmarabank, TYT Bank, Impexbank; Türk Invest, Çarmen, Pasifik; Türk Ticaret Bankası, Interbank, Bank Ekspres, Yaşarbank, Esbank, Egebank, Yurtbank, Sümerbank; Etibank, Bank Kapital, Demirbank.*

Fortunately, the recipe was at hand: financial liberalization. Steps such as the removal of reserve requirements and interest ceilings in 1988 taken towards the deregulation of financial markets were followed by the opening of the stock market to foreign investors in 1989. In December 1989, state banks were opened up to foreign partners and codes restricting foreign ownership of financial institutions were abolished (Ros, 1994). In the early 1990s, the "Pacto" succeeded in bringing inflation down and public sector reforms swiftly proceeded. However, Mexico's recovery still depended on foreign savings to finance trade deficits, and there was a need for policies that would "shake up" the foreign capital owners' expectations (Lustig and Ros, 1999). The first step in adopting such policies was the decision taken to liberalize the financial sector even further.[12] The liberalization of trade, the reduction of obstacles to foreign ownership and the harmonization of Mexican laws with "international standards", along with the decision to participate in GATT in 1986, were the essential components of the new financial policies. The second step that would change the expectations was the beginning of the NAFTA with the USA, at mid-1990s.

The "measures" combined with the drop in interest rates in the USA led to an increase in the flow of portfolio investments towards Mexico. Between the years 1983 and 1993, the gross capital inflows rose from 3.5 billion dollars to 33 billion dollars. Although, to some extent those inflows were the repatriation of capital which had fled in the previous years, a large proportion was due to the new portfolio investments, of which worrisomely in large portion were made up of short-term inflows (Lustig ve Ros, 1999). Influenced by factors such as the political shock caused by the assassination of presidential candidate Colosio, a highly fragile banking system and reversed expectations, the course was to banks' ruins. In March 1994, just after the assassination of Colosio, the foreign exchange reserves dropped from US$ 26 billion to US$ 18 billion almost overnight. The monetary authorities decided to "sterilize" the fall in international reserves by increasing net domestic credits, keeping the monetary base approximately constant, and more importantly indexing domestic debt to the dollar. The peso-denominated *cetes* (short-term treasury bills) were replaced by the exchange rate-indexed tesobonos (short-term treasury bills denominated in dollars). The endeavors for sterilization and debt management triumphed in intended objectives of stopping capital flight and of relieving the pressure on domestic interest rates – at least for a while. The inevitable outburst of the crisis was the outcome of many other significant factors (Griffith-Jones, 1998: 100): the drop in domestic interest rates while interest rates in the USA were rising, the current accounts deficit growth to 8 % of the GDP in 1993 and 1994, the relatively high value of foreign exchange rate due to the fixed exchange rate commitment, the evaluation of the transfer of a significant portion of public debt into dollar-denominated papers as a reflection of inadequate reserves, and unanticipated political developments.

[12] Two of these measures were particularly important (Motamen-Samadian, 2000): i) The privatization of banks which started in May 1990 and ended in June 1992. ii) The relaxation of capital controls in November 1991, which was accompanied by a quasi fixed exchange rate regime. Although the privatization of the banking sector in Mexico with these reform programs helped the government reduce the public debt, it did not lead to greater competition and efficiency in this sector. Rather, it contributed to a greater concentration of capital in the financial system and the main outcome of the privatization was the change in the structure of banking industry from a state monopoly to a private oligopoly. Banks that were privatized in this process began to take advantage of falling international interest rates, and began to borrow from outside the country with low interest rates, and lend domestically with high interest rates. In addition to this, a significant increase in short-term capital inflows was permitted. Between 1992-94, external debts of commercial banks and of the non-banking private sector increased by 34.2% and 62.5%, respectively (Motamen-Samadian, 2000).

The short-term character of the capital inflows is determinant over the occurrence of financial crises, regardless of their autarchic exertions. In Mexico, large capital inflows were used for unproductive purposes such as supporting the peso, fuelling speculative investments in real estate and financial assets, encouraging private and public consumption, financing domestic capital flight, and consequently there remained no room for investments in tradable-goods sectors. Besides, it has been suggested that in the early 1990s, Mexico, with its semi-stagnant economy and large current account deficits, displayed symptoms of the so-called Dutch disease which is caused by resource-based export booms. But the Mexican case was different: instead of catching the disease through the trade account, it caught it through the capital account of the balance of payments. Although the same symptoms of fragility were present in other reforming Latin American economies, Mexico was a leader in attracting capital flows. Hence Lustig and Ros (1999) suggested that this phenomenon be called the "Mexican disease."

The Korean tale was somewhat different: a plan dominant one. Along the process that started with the first plan after the World War II, especially between 1962 and 1966, there was the objective of changing the price matrix faced by the private sector in a direction preferred by the planners.[13] The state was generally transferring investible funds at low prices from depositors to investors (mostly to *chaebols*).[14] Until the financial crisis that emerged in East Asian countries in 1997 and spreaded rapidly over the region, South Korea had significantly progressed in her productive structure with the determined industrialization efforts since the 1960s, and had "miraculously" improved her world trade share. Unanimously, South Korea accomplished this developmental leap by intervening in financial markets. In the early 1960s, the state borrowed abroad in order to finance the import of capital goods, and this took place with the intermediary role of publicly owned banks under government approval and guarantee, implementing a strict program of restrictive regulations of direct foreign investment and foreign exchange rate controls (Haggard and Maxfield, 1999). The balance of payments problems, encountered in 1971, called for some domestic financial reforms, before long the balance of payments was quickly recovered without any fundamental change in external financial policies. The oil crisis of 1973-74 led to more interventionist state in South Korea. Thus situated, during this time foreigners were being allowed only indirect investment through mutual funds like the "Korea Fund" and the "Korea Europe Fund". Although deregulation of interest rates started in 1981, during most of 1980s the state retained the right to set financial prices while successfully controlling inflation. Even so, the interest rate deregulations were speeded up towards the end of 1988.

In the early phases of the deregulation, the liberalization of capital inflows was emphasized more than that of capital outflows, and a full liberalization of capital accounts could not be even imagined until the early 1990s. Until the second half of 1980s, domestic firms were not allowed to transfer their funds abroad. In accordance with the State's

---

[13] It is clear that the success observed in the Korean economy was a consequence of state management using development-oriented planning as a tool. In Amsden`s (1989) characterization the developments referred to as "late industrialization" are quite interventionist experiences in which selective import controls are widely used to protect certain export-oriented activities, and serious obstacles were placed on the entrance of foreign investors.

[14] "This arrangement was terribly irrational from the perspective of allocative efficiency, but efficiency itself was never a virtue in Korea. The Koreans wanted industrialization, and they got it by giving cheap money to the *chaebol (-*is a group of firms owned and managed by a family that has oligopolistic or monopolistic control in an industry-*)*, forcing them to build industries and to export more" (Woo-Cumings, 1997: 79-80).

preferential regulations related to *chaebols*, 14 large corporations were allowed to issue bonds with the approval of the Ministry of Finance. In a closed and highly regulated financial system, there was an extremely protectionist attitude vis-a-vis foreign financial intermediaries. From 1985 to 1988, South Korea had amounts of large current account surpluses. The surpluses constituted 8 % of the GDP in 1987 led the government to loosen controls on capital imports, and in 1988, she encouraged firms to pre-pay their debts and invest abroad. In 1989, when the current account surplus turned to a deficit, controls both on capital exports and inflows were re-installed (Woo-Cumings, 1997). Throughout the 1980s, capital account operations were tightly regulated. The government placed many restrictions on capital inflows and outflows to minimize the destabilizing effects of short term capital flows and to ease the country's industrialization policies.

However, all this began to change in the early 1990s. Despite the absence of foreign exchange shortage, the liberalization of South Korean economy was quite gradual. It is clear that the financial liberalization process in South Korea was more influenced by global processes and the developments taking place in New York and Washington than a process that would go along with economic modernization and the correction of "errors" committed during the heavy industrialization period in the 1970s, as suggested by traditional analysts (Woo- Cumings, 1997). The pressure on South Korea was not originating from the balance of payments, but from developed countries, especially the USA.[15] In 1988, the US Treasury, given the authority to identify countries who were manipulating foreign exchange rates identified South Korea as such. In February 1990, financial policy discussions started between the USA and South Korea and progressed very slowly (Haggard and Maxfield, 1999). The deregulation and opening up of the financial markets started seriously in 1993, and this gained speed with Korea's entry into OECD, as the 29th member (Park, 1999).

Eventually, South Korea, like Turkey and Mexico, making ground for the maturity mismatch problem, arrived at the gates of the financial crisis. The combination of deregulation and opening up of the financial markets in South Korea and the Latin American tempest of 1994-1997 led to a rise in foreign capital inflows that were mostly short term and speculative (Park, 1999). Early in 1994, if the ceilings on banks' medium and long term borrowing from international markets had not been reduced, the ceilings on short term borrowing of foreign currency would have been removed. This forced commercial banks to finance long term domestic loans with short term foreign loans. While in 1993, 65 % of total liabilities of commercial banks were short-termed, this ratio rose to 79 % in 1994 (Park, 1999:151). Since commercial banks lent the funds (that they borrowed on short term money markets) to their clients as long term loans, a serious maturity mismatch arose, just as it had arisen in Turkey and in Mexico. As disclosed by the financial crises, the short term debts could not be rolled over indefinitely and the short term credit facilities should not be used as tools of finance of long term investments.

[15] A larger number of American and European banks demanded liberalization in order to enter the Korean market and expand their operations. The Reagan government put great pressure on the Korean government on behalf of American banks. By the end of 1993, the number of foreign banks in Korea had almost doubled: from 40 in 1981, to 73. (Woo-Cumings, 1997:81).

3. Analysis Based on Balance of Payments Data[16]

3.1. The Method of Calculation for Capital Flows and Related Definitions

Because of the role and importance of capital flows (especially their "hot" components) and their reversal in generating a new type of cycle which, in some cases, incorporates financial crises, the calculation of the magnitudes of capital flows gives us important and interesting findings, revealing some similarities and dissimilarities between these experiences. The initial impact of international short term capital movements on a national economy takes place through the gross volume of cyclical inflows and outflows (Boratav, 1999; Boratav and Yeldan, 2001; Balkan and Yeldan, 1996). Thus, in what follows, empirical analysis starts with the gross amounts of capital inflows and outflows. The new classification of the balance of payments data given in the 1993 systematic of the IMF Balance of Payments Statistics (BOPs) provides us with a fairly detailed framework for the decomposition of capital flows. On the basis of this classification, Boratav (1999) developed a method of identifying short term arbitrage-seeking capital which was also used in UNCTAD's *Trade and Development Report* dated 1999. The estimates of capital movements in this paper are based on this method.

In line with this, resident/non-resident decomposition of capital flows will ensure the 'net' and 'gross' distinction. The agents who carry on arbitrage-sensitive activities as a result of the liberalization of external finance are resident and non-resident rentiers, domestic firms, resident and foreign banks. A further classification may be made according to the tools and sectors towards which the funds are directed such as the funds directed towards public financing, stock markets and the banking sector by means of treasury bonds and bills, equities and deposits. This classification can be extended to other sub-groups as far as the data permit. Thanks to the new systematic of the IMF, "it has become possible i) to distinguish between resident vs. non-resident capital flows, ii) to separate components that originate from official and private sources, and to identify the kinds of assets and liabilities that constitute capital flows" (Boratav, 2003:18). Within this framework, *capital inflow* refers to the acquisition of assets by non-residents and a positive sign, while the sale of domestic assets by non-residents is considered as a negative capital inflow. Thus, net capital inflow is obtained by balancing the purchases and sales of assets by non-residents within a country.[17] Capital flows according to the IMF balance of payments statistics include items under the categories of *capital and financial accounts* of the balance of payments. *Capital outflow* refers to the acquisition of foreign assets by residents and a negative sign. The sale of foreign assets is depicted as negative capital outflow, and refers to a positive sign. The term "net capital flow" indicates the difference between these two:[18] the difference between the gross values of capital inflows

[16] This section is based mostly on Boratav (1999; 2003) and UNCTAD (1999).

[17] Inflows that do not create debits are made up of foreign direct investments and portfolio investments in equities. What remains behind from private inflows are bonds and bank credits.

[18] In IMF Balance of Payment statistics, capital outflows are made up of debt items under the headings of: "direct investments outside the country," "capital transfers," and asset items under headings such as "portfolio investments" and "other investments."

and outflows. When the total net capital inflows are larger than total the net capital outflows, this term appears to be positive (UNCTAD, 1999: 100).[19]

In the balance of payments identity of a typical under-developed country, we observe that net capital flows originating from non-residents should be equal to the "current account deficits" and "leakages" (Boratav, 1999; Boratav, Yeldan, 2001:13). "In other words, the difference between the net inflows and the financing of the current account deficit is made up of three items of leakage: the recorded and unrecorded (net errors and omissions) resident outflows and accumulated reserves. Negative values for both reserves and the net errors and omissions items, in this regard, should be considered as anomalies. In case of large-scale capital inflows exceeding current account deficits, some items of capital inflows that result in reserve accumulation may not be recorded. Such a contradiction may be "corrected" by means of a positive sign for the net errors and omissions item. Those inflows represent unrecorded capital and are not reflected in the reserves. The negative values of both items point to capital outflows (unrecorded outflows) that take place along with the massive inflows" (Boratav, 1999). The method developed by Boratav to estimate capital inflows/outflows and the "hot" components of them is summarized below with the items that correspond to the IMF new balance of payments statistics. As observed (see appendix), the items have been decomposed to the extent permitted by the IMF standard balance of payments classification.

3.2. Empirical Findings on Capital Flows[20]

There remains the analysis of capital flows on the basis of annual data for Turkey, Mexico and South Korea. First of all, we have a double distinction: i) the pro-cyclical/counter-cyclical capital movements by resident/non-resident agents' and ii) their "hot" components.[21] All these become 'clear and distinct' in the boom/bust analysis. To this end, the boom/bust cycles associated with capital movements are to be distinguished by the years capital flows were controlled or liberalized. As seen on Table 1, while in Turkey during

[19] Normally, the positive (+) sign of liabilities indicates the capital inflows of non-residents, and the negative sign (-) of "assets" indicates the capital outflows of residents. Typically, in a developing economy, (Boratav, 2003:19):

Accounts of Bops: Signs: Meanings:
Net capital flows by non-residents (NKI) (+) the capital inflows of non-residents
in exceptional circumstances and
under heavy crisis conditions (-) the capital outflows of non-residents
+ capital flows by residents (NKO) (-) the net recorded capital outflows of residents
+ the balance of current accounts (CA) (-) chronic deficits
+ reserve movements (DR) (-) the increase
+ *net errors omissions (EO)* (-) unrecorded capital flows of residents
= 0

"When the capital outflows of residents are valid over a long period from the point of view of accumulated values, it means that this economy is continually exporting capital to the outside world, and therefore as far as the systematic of the balance of payments is concerned, it has acquired characteristics of developed capitalist countries" (Boratav, 2003:21). As will be discerned later, the above situation appears applicable in an analysis of the situation in South Korea.

[20] For abbreviations see the appendix.

[21] The most descriptive of which are net errors and omissions and reserve movements that would "normally" be pro-cyclical, that is, capital flight with financial instability and capital inflows otherwise; however, the data show that there may be exceptions unique to each country.

the pre-liberalization period, i.e.1980-89, 67 % of the capital inflows financed the current account deficit, this ratio (CA/NKI) fell to 24 % during the 1990-1999 period as a whole, and to 22 % after the crisis of 1994 (1994-1996). In the post-crisis period of 2001-03, this ratio remained around 29 %. As for Mexico, it appears that during the 1990s, the total capital inflows by non-residents have financed a larger proportion of the current account deficit compared with the 1980s. This can be reasoned on the ground of the 1980s' debt crisis. Despite serious hot money outflows, compared to 1994, the non-resident inflows increased in 1995; nonetheless, it financed only 6 % of the current account deficits (CA/NKI). Since South Korea, unlike Turkey and Mexico, had a current account surplus, it would be meaningless to attempt to interpret this ratio for her.

A general comparison of developing countries between the 1980s and the 1990s reveals that in the latter period, a lower proportion of the net capital inflows were used for the current account deficits finance and the remaining constituted the leakages.[22] (UNCTAD, 1999:111). Unlike Mexico and South Korea, Turkey followed this common trend. As mentioned earlier, in Turkey, capital inflows, far from financing current account deficits, tend to set off a cycle that increases current account deficits. To have a more concrete view of the crises in this respect, following subsections, for sake of subtlety, quarry the hot money along with the leakages for our three cases.

i) Leakages from Inflows by Non-residents

In Turkey, the net capital inflows by non-residents had positive values before financial crises, at times of crises however, capital outflows became the norm. The difference in values between the years 1993 and 1994, and 2000 and 2001 has reached approximately the level of -19 billion dollars (Table 1).

In Mexico, whereas net capital inflows by non-residents increased in the crisis year, and as opposed to Turkey, this is a counter-cyclical movement; and in spite of hot money outflowing, the NKIs take a positive sign. This is largely due to the fact that the credits provided by the IMF are found under "other investments" liabilities item, (with code no.4766), on the IMF balance of payments statistics. On the other hand, foreign direct investments (FDIs) to Mexico were in large amounts; even though in 1995 the amount of FDI dropped a little, NKIs continued to have the positive values.

In South Korea as well, despite the massive drop of the post-crisis period, the amount of capital inflows by non-residents (NKI) maintained its positive sign. What's more, this was accomplished while non-residents' hot money components were outflowing (just as happened in Mexico). Even in cases of no increase (as seen in Mexico), it's possible to talk about two elements of continued capital inflows by non-residents. Those are the IMF credits and FDIs. An elaboration on FDIs to South Korea reveals an unexpected shift. While in 1997, there were FDI worth $ 2,844, in 1998, the figure went up to $ 5,405 millions. Since under normal conditions foreigners will not invest in a country experiencing crisis, the situation can be explained by the acquisition of domestic assets by foreigners through the "fire sale" of the assets in the post-crisis phase.[23] The capital inflows by non-residents handled in the lines above are to be detailed for its portion that is comprised of recorded/non-recorded capital flows by residents and reserves, leaking out of the current account financing.

---

[22] This observation is valid for developing countries that chronically have current deficits.

[23] See UNCTAD, 1999, 2001 and 2003.

a) Recorded Capital Flows by Residents

In Turkey, net capital outflows by residents proportional to net capital inflows by non-residents (NKO/NKI) has increased during the period of 1990-2003, compared to the period 1980-89 of capital controls. While the net capital outflows by residents (NKO) increased during the crisis (the pro-cyclical magnitude and sign) in Mexico and South Korea, the case was reversed in Turkey during the first financial crisis. Capital exporting residents during the pre-crisis period executed capital inflows during the 1994 crisis. As for the years 2001-2002, the outflows kept on in reduced amounts.

Compared to the 1980s, the cumulative quanta of the net capital inflows by non-residents in Mexico decreased in the 1990s. This higher NKO/NKI ratio of the 1980s may be explained by the debt crisis of early the 1980s and the large scale of capital flight that accompanied the crisis. However, a glimpse at different sub-periods reveals some striking figures. In Mexico, the net capital outflows by residents during 1989-93 amounted to 9% of the net capital inflows by non-residents, and during 1994-1996, 36% of non-resident inflows were assigned to finance outflows by residents. By contrast, the NKO/NKI ratio for South Korea attained high levels in the 1980s. This resulted from the high level of South Korean investments to other countries (notably to those of Southeast Asia).

Hereby it may be observed that the net capital outflows by residents —the leakage from net capital inflows by non-residents— have increased after the liberalization of capital movements in Turkey. Despite the Mexican and South Korean exceptions, a trend similar to the one in Turkey has been observed in many countries.[24]

b) Non-recorded Capital Flows by Residents (EO)

In Turkey, the non-recorded capital flows by resident/ net capital inflows by non-residents (EO/NKI) ratio was positive during the 1980-89 period; and in the period 1990-93, the non-recorded outflows reached 12% of capital inflows by non-residents. Non-recorded capital outflows were observed in both Mexico and Turkey in the pre-crisis years. The process accelerated in Mexico in 1995, whilst it was reversed throughout the 1994 crisis in Turkey, but an outflow of $1.6 billion was experienced during the 2001 crisis. As for South Korea, a positive value was observed during the pre-crisis period and a pro-cyclical change was observed in the crisis year.

The exceptions are still to be stated. It is possible to explain the Turkish situation by factors specific to the country. According to Boratav (1999), the reason for the incident of 1994 may be the non-recorded money movements from the dollar towards Treasury bills offering high interest rates. A high negative value of EO/NKI in Mexico between1980-89 may be reflecting a preference for foreign assets during and immediately after the debt crisis that affected Latin Americas entirely. As was expected with liberalization, non-recorded outflows decreased in the 1990s. In Korean case, however, the ratio of EO/NKI increased somewhat all along the 1990s compared to the period 1980-93. The ratio increased seriously during the crisis years and reached a level indicating 67 % of the capital inflows by non residents. Therefore, it appears that non-recorded capital flows by the residents are affected by reasons each country's differentia specifica.

[24] See Boratav (2003).

Table 1. Financial Boom/Bust Indicators

		Years	NKI	NKO	NKOE	CA	EO	DR*	DR/NKI	NKO/NKI	EO/NKI	CA/NKI
Turkey	Cumulative	1980-89	15529	-3471	-561	-10408	2910	-4561	-0.294	-0.224	0.187	-0.67
	Cumulative	1990-99	58292	-20184	-23468	-13981	-3284	-20843	-0.358	-0.346	-0.056	-0.24
	Cumulative	1990-03	91444	-31673	-34068	-28646	-2395	-28732	-0.314	-0.346	-0.026	-0.313
	Cumulative	1989-93	24788	-10021	-11984	-8844	-1963	-3960	-0.16	-0.404	-0.079	-0.357
Boom	Cumulative	1990-93	24536	-10333	-13265	-9782	-2932	-1489	-0.061	-0.421	-0.12	-0.399
Bust & after	Cumulative	1994-96	9615	288	2627	-2144	2339	-10098	-1.05	0.03	0.243	-0.223
		1993	12831	-3868	-6090	-6433	-2222	-308	-0.024	-0.301	-0.173	-0.501
		1994	-6259	2409	4175	2631	1766	-547	0.087	-0.385	-0.282	-0.42
	Minus	1994-1993	-19090	6277	10265	9064	3988	-239	0.013	-0.329	-0.209	-0.475
Boom	Cumulative	1995-97	27173	-4832	-6853	-7454	-2021	-12866	-0.473	-0.178	-0.074	-0.274
		1997	11300	-2711	-5305	-2679	-2594	-3316	-0.293	-0.24	-0.23	-0.237
		1998	3677	-3453	-5444	1984	-1991	-217	-0.059	-0.939	-0.542	0.54
	Minus	1998-1997	-7623	-742	-139	4663	603	3099				
Boom	Cumulative	1999-2000	25527	-7576	-8295	-11125	-719	-6107	-0.239	-0.297	-0.028	-0.436
		2000	16362	-3601	-6215	-9765	-2614	-383	-0.023	-0.22	-0.16	-0.597
		2001	-2588	-1887	-3521	3390	-1634	2718	-1.05	0.729	0.631	-1.31
	Minus	2001-2000	-18950	1714	2694	13155	980	3101				
Bust & after	Cumulative	2001-03	16790	-7888	-4385	-4900	3503	-7506	-0.447	-0.47	0.209	-0.292
	Cumulative	2002-03	19378	-6001	-864	-8290	5137	-10224	-0.528	-0.31	0.265	-0.428
Mexico												
	Cumulative	1980-89	72376	-20852	-42282	-27031	-21430	-3063	-0.042	-0.288	-0.296	-0.373

Table 1. (Continued)

		Years	NKI	NKO	NKOE	CA	EO	DR*	DR/NKI	NKO/NKI	EO/NKI	CA/NKI
	Cumulative	1990-2000	199409	-22604	-33388	-141091	-10784	-24929	-0.125	-0.113	-0.054	-0.708
Boom	Cumulative	1989-93	104636	-8917	-9443	-76006	-526	-19186	-0.183	-0.085	-0.005	-0.726
Bust & after	Cumulative	1994-96	53503	-19368	-26881	-33566	-7513	6944	0.13	-0.362	-0.14	-0.627
		1994	20258	-5670.1	-8994	-29662	-3324	18398	0.908	-0.28	-0.164	-1.464
		1995	22829	-7356.6	-11604	-1576	-4248	-9648	-0.423	-0.322	-0.186	-0.069
	Minus	1995-1994	2571	-1686.5	-2611	28086	-924	-28046				
South Korea												
	Cumulative	1980-89	12758	-12464	-16109							
	Cumulative	1980-93	52564	-33603	-37900	4916	-4297	-19580	-0.372	-0.639	-0.082	0.094
		1994-2002	134792	-82804	-99529	19888	-16725	-55151	-0.729	-0.614	-0.124	0.148
Boom	Cumulative	1994-96	109454	-58894	-60855	-35530	-1961	-13068	-0.119	-0.538	-0.018	-0.325
Bust & after	Cumulative	1997-1998	16770	-17904	-29132	31455	-11228	-19093	-1.139	-1.068	-0.67	1.876
		1996	48431	-25187	-24092	-22923	1095	-1416	-0.029	-0.52	0.023	-0.473
		1997	18956	-17566	-22575	-8256	-5010	11875	0.626	-0.927	-0.264	-0.436
	Minus	1997-1996	-29475	7621	1517	14667	-6104	13291				

Source: IMF, Balance of Payments Statistics (various years).

* Minus sign indicates increase.

c) Changes in the Reserves

While during the 1980-89 period reserve accumulation in Turkey amounted to 29.4 % of the net capital inflows by non-residents (DR/NKI), in the 1990s, it increased to 35.8 %. As for Mexico, these ratios were 0.04 % and 12.5 %, respectively. So, as revealed by the ratios, both countries were forced to accumulate much more reserves after the liberalization of capital accounts. Traditionally, when capital movements were controlled, reserve levels were required to offset temporary disequilibria in the current balance, to offset the gaps between the payments of import and export bills, usually equivalent to imports' bill of three or four months. However, with the liberalization of capital accounts, the precautionary reserve levels requirement increased radically, thus most developing countries were to be forced to accelerate the accumulation of reserves. And this meant an additional and "expensive" drain on non-resident inflows (Boratav and Yeldan, 2001:14). In contradistinction to the situation in Turkey and Mexico, in South Korea during the 1980s, the reserve accumulation exceeded the net capital inflows by non-residents. This difference displayed by South Korea in the 1980s may be understood by noting the fact that the current account indicated a surplus of $ 18.5 billion in the same period.

Even in countries with large reserve accumulations, financial crises result in serious erosions in reserves during the crisis periods. The 1994 crisis in Mexico has resulted in a decline that was almost equal to the amount of reserves accumulated in the 1989-93 period, and that was 90 % of the non-resident capital inflows; whereas for the South Korean financial crisis, the DR/NKI ratio betokened an erosion of 62 %. The ratio is irrelevant for Turkey, since the net capital inflows by non-residents displayed a negative value in 1994. An assessment of reserve movements in Mexico and Turkey reveals that they were clearly counter-cyclical in 1994. In Turkey, reserve accumulation seriously dropped off in 1993, in comparison with 1992, and a limited increase was recorded for the following year. In Mexico, similarly, following the serious erosion of 1994 came the reversal in 1995. Taking into consideration the increase in counter-cyclical net capital inflows by non-residents, this reversal may be explained by the large amount of the IMF funds received ($ 11.9 billion). As to South Korea, in 1997, the serious erosion in the reserves ($ 11.1 billion despite the IMF credits) proved a pro-cyclical change. In 1998, South Korea received an additional $ 5 billion IMF credit and piled reserves up to the level of $ 30.9 billion. Compared to the credits received by Mexico and South Korea, the credits received by Turkey from the IMF were limited: $ 344 millions in 1993, $ 347 millions in 1994; and despite the fact that the IMF provided Turkey with a fairly large credit ($ 10 billion) after the 2001 crisis, the erosion of reserves reached $ 2.7 billion (IMF, 2004).

ii) Arbitrage-seeking Short Term Capital Movements (Hot Money Flows):

The total assets item showing the "hot money" flows of residents reveals that in all three countries, the residents took hot money out of the country in the pre-crisis year. Then, the pro-cyclical outflows continued during the crisis year (in reduced amounts -in 2001- in Turkey and in Mexico, and increased amounts in South Korea) and some counter-cyclical inflows took place in Turkey in 1994. This might have stemmed from the fact that domestic banks struggling to pay their debts were forced to liquidate their external assets, because especially in the Turkish experience, the currency and banking crises went hand-in-hand (Boratav, 1999). An examination of total liabilities, in other words, non-resident hot money movements designates capital inflows in all three countries during the pre-crisis years, while this magnitude changes to negative during crisis years, in short, it moves in a pro-cyclical direction.

Table 2. "Hot Money" Inflows and Outflows

Turkey	Years	STI	STO	EO	STOE	NSF	NSFE
Cumulative	1980-89	2454	-2697	2910	213	-243	2667
Cumulative	1990-99	14630	-11375	-3284	-14659	3255	-29
Cumulative	1990-03	12698	-13045	-2395	-15440	-347	-2742
Cumulative	1989-93	9897	-9746	-1963	-11709	151	-1812
Cumulative	1990-93	9664	-9346	-2932	-12278	318	-2614
Cumulative	1994-96	-1374	2772	2339	5111	1398	3737
	1993	4478	-3242	-2222	-5464	1236	-986
	1994	-5913	2446	1766	4212	-3467	-1701
Minus	1994-1993	-10391	5688	3988	9676	-4703	-715
Cumulative	1995-97	5705	-1212	-2021	-3233	4493	2472
	1997	1166	-1538	-2594	-4132	-372	-2966
	1998	2267	-1083	-1991	-3074	1184	-807
Minus	1998-1997	1101	455	603	1058	1556	2159
Cumulative	1999-2000	7770	-4138	-719	-4857	3632	2913
	2000	4863	-1958	-2614	-4572	2905	292
	2001	-8516	-91	-1634	-1725	-8607	-10241
Minus	2001-2000	-13379	1867	980	2847	-11512	-10533
	2001-02	-10976	-9	-1718	-1727	-10985	-12703
Cumulative	2002-03	1721	379	5137	5516	2100	7237
Mexico		STI	STO	EO	STOE	NSF	NSFE
Cumulative	1980-89	6	-17631	-21430	-39061	-17625	-39055
Cumulative	1989-93	39805	-1251	-526	-1777	38554	38028
Cumulative	1990-2000	45039	-9094	-10784	-19878	35944	25161
Cumulative	1990-94	43356	-3560	-8353	-11913	39796	31442
Cumulative	1994-96	-6207	-12077	-7513	-19590	-18285	-25797
	1994	4001	-3198	-3324	-6522	803	-2521
	1995	-13622	-2825	-4248	-7073	-16447	-20695
Minus	1995-1994	-17622	373	-924	-551	-17249	-18174
South Korea		STI	STO	EO	STOE	NSF	NSFE
Cumulative	1980-89	2796	-1998	-3645	-5642	798	-2846
Cumulative	1980-93	21192	-11017	-4297	-15314	10176	5879
Cumulative	1994-02	30541	-21985.4	-16725.2	-38710.6	8555.6	-8169.56
Cumulative	1994-96	49420	-20831	-1961	-22792	28589	26627
Cumulative	1997-1998	-32389	-2585	-11228	-13813	-34973	-46201
	1996	20542	-9283	1095	-8188	11259	12354
	1997	-16081	-10434	-5010	-15443	-26514	-31524
Minus	1997-1996	-36623	-1151	-6104	-7255	-37774	-43878

Source: IMF, Balance of Payments Statistics (various years).

When we review the values associated with hot money movements by non-residents and residents within the framework of crisis and recovery, some interesting findings are to be arrived at. Both gross and net (NSF = STI+STO) hot money movements by residents and non-resident are shown in Table 2. The hot money inflows by non-residents (STI) show an important increase during the 1990s, in comparison with the 1980s (an increase from $ 2.5 billion to $ 14.5 billion). In the period between 1990-99, the share of hot money inflows within the inflows by non-residents (STI/NKI) increased by 10 %, over the 1980-93 period, and in the 1990-93 period, which was referred to above as the boom period, it reached 40 %.

In Mexico, while hot money flows by non-residents were negligible in the period of 1980-89, they reached $ 45 billion in the period 1990-2000. A similar development was observed in South Korea as well. Thus, after the liberalization of capital accounts, large scale increases in hot money inflows by non-residents are observed in the capital movements of all three countries.

The "hot money" components (STOE: short-term outflows, including unrecorded outflows) within the capital flows by residents are rather striking. While for Turkey, in the period 1980-89, we can speak of only a limited inflow of hot money, a value amounts to $ 14.6 billion, indicating 62% of the outflows by residents (STOE/NKOE[25]), was recorded[26] in the period of 1990-99. Unlike Turkey, in Mexico, the residents took large amounts of hot money out during the 1980s (important non-recorded outflows), and the ratio of STOE/NKOE preserved the high level of 60% in the 1990.

While, in South Korea, the ratio in question did not change between two periods, it climbed up to 68% in 1997. The significance of hot money flows by residents and non-residents during the crises augmented in Mexico and Turkey. In Turkey in 1994, there was the hot money component that exceeded capital inflows by residents (counter-cyclical) and hot money outflows that almost amounted to the total of the non-resident capital outflows (pro-cyclical). In Mexico, counter-cyclical[27] net capital inflows by non-residents and pro-cyclical hot money outflows took place simultaneously. Especially between 1994 and 1996, the "hot" money outflows by residents constituted a considerable portion of net capital outflows. The figures in South Korea, however, reveal that during the crisis, the size of hot money outflows by residents were almost equivalent to counter-cyclical inflows by non-resident. In the same period, the hot money component of outflows by residents is 47 %. It seems that although they have some different patterns of behavior, residents of all three countries have perceived the negative turn of events earlier than non-residents and brought about large amounts of hot money outflows during the pre-crisis year.

The net hot money flows by residents and non-residents hide some inclinations that are open with gross values mentioned above; however, it has been observed in many countries that the net value is not positive as expected by the liberalization of capital accounts. "It's noteworthy that the country whose hot money balance sheet produced the highest positive values after 1990 was India which continues to implement effective controls on capital accounts" (Boratav, 2003:29). In Turkey, after the 1989, at the time capital accounts were

[25] Net capital outflows by residents, including unrecorded outflows (see Table1).

[26] In Turkey, the hot money inflows-outflows of non-residents amount approximately to plus-minus 4-5 % of the GNP, while the hot money outflows of residents, amount to approximately plus-minus 3-4 % of the GNP.

[27] As mentioned earlier, IMF loans are among the most important factors behind this counter-cyclical value that emerged in both Mexico and South Korea during the financial crisis.

liberalized (1990-2003), net hot money flows by resident and non-residents (NSFE) produced an outflow of $ 2.7 billion. While similar net hot money outflows may be observed in South Korea after the liberalization of capital accounts, Mexico differed from this pattern due to the debt crisis and produced large amounts of hot money outflows during the 1980s. However, while the balance of hot money flows in Mexico was positive after 1990, residents engaged in considerable amounts of hot money outflows. It may be thought that in Mexico this becomes almost a permanent resident behavior.[28] In South Korea, despite the net hot money inflows in the period 1994-96, residents took out $ 22.7 billion of hot money. During the crisis and in its aftermath, pro-cyclical net hot money outflows may be observed. Thus, it is obvious that net flows will be misleading for an analysis of hot money inflows/outflows and their impact on the economy.

4. Conclusion

A comparison of the experiences of Turkey, South Korea, and Mexico discloses that the deregulation of financial markets and the removal of controls on capital movements result in financial instability and crises regardless of the fiscal balance. When Turkey experienced a financial crisis in 2000, she reduced inflation rate, increased growth rate and improved her financial position significantly as a result of a structural adjustment and stabilization program. Similarly, the Mexican crisis emerged at a time when Mexico, as a country that established financial discipline and reduced inflation substantially, was considered as "successful". And as for South Korea –a country that sustained stable growth for many years, with no public deficit and stable prices and a current account surplus– it could not avoid a boom-bust cycle, and was drawn into a crisis. In all three experiences, the rapid increase in capital –especially "hot money"- inflows caused by non-residents was an important factor of instability. Accordingly, when such inflows suddenly turn into outflows, they trigger off financial crises.

Thus, the findings of this study on the financial crises of Turkey (1994 and 2000-2001), Mexico (1994-95) and South Korea (1997) underline some similarities in the three experiences, despite the presence of their diffrentia specifica. A look at the capital movements that make the ground for this study reveals that the behaviors of actors who bring about these flows change from country to country, and from actor to actor within the country. For instance, a review of total assets shows that in all three countries, there were hot money outflows by residents during the pre-crisis years and pro-cyclical outflows continued during the crisis periods (they were reduced in Mexico and increased in South Korea) —but in Turkey there were some counter-cyclical inflows in 1994. Thus, even though these three countries display some different behavioral patterns, the residents perceived negative turns sooner than non-residents. When we look at total liabilities, in other words hot money movements by non-residents, we see that in all three countries, the substantial capital inflows of the pre-crisis years turned into negative values during the crisis years; in short, they moved in a pro-cyclical manner.

In our triad, hot money flows increased considerably both in absolute and relative terms during the 1990s. In the crisis years, the gross hot money inflows/outflows reached large

[28] In the period 1980-97, with the exceptions of 1986, 1989, 1992 and 1997, there is a constant outflow by resident.

magnitudes and became an important component of instability. Thus, we arrive at the conclusion that short term arbitrage-seeking speculative capital movements played a decisive role in all three financial crises. There is a broad agreement that the boom-bust cycle in capital flows needs to be moderated. Because of this, the reintroduction of capital controls and the reactivation of crucial policy tools in developing countries are essential. It is clear that capital controls (putting the monster back to sleep —bringing back traditional controls) are "necessary but insufficient" for preventing the crises. Otherwise, future crises are inevitable. As one observer has argued: "If Asia's people allow themselves to be persuaded that their politicians were the central problem and that they should cede control of their financial systems to international rules and institutions, they will be making a dramatic mistake, ensuring the 'Latin Americanization' of Asia" (Bienefeld, 2002:122). The domestic and foreign debt impasse of Turkey (monster's destructive activities —uncontrolled debt growth) is rapidly pulling the country towards a Latin-Americanization process. It may even be "convergence" that will take place by the Latin-Americanization of the developing countries.

APPENDIX

I. The Items of Capital Movements in the Standard Framework of Balance of Payments Statistics

	IMF codes		
Capital account	Credit: 2994	Debit: 3994	
Direct investment	4555		
Direct investment abroad	4505		
	IMF codes of residents	IMF codes of non-residents	Explanations
Portfolio investment	4602	4652	
Portfolio investment in equity securities	4610	4660	Portfolio investment in equity securities
Portfolio investment in money market instruments	4630	4680	Portfolio investment in treasury bonds
Other Investment	4703	4753	
Short-term loans: Banks	4724	4774	Short-term loans to domestic (foreign) banks
Short-term loans: Other sectors	4727	4777	Short-term loans to domestic (foreign) firms and household
Currency and deposits: Banks	4733	4783	Changes in currency and deposits in national (foreign) currency held by non-residents (residents)
Currency and deposits: Other sectors	4734	4784	
Other short-term assets and liabilities: Banks	4745	4795	Other sectors: Firms and households

APPENDIX (CONTINUED)

I. The Items of Capital Movements in the Standard Framework of Balance of Payments Statistics			
	IMF codes of residents	IMF codes of non-residents	Explanations
Other short-term assets and liabilities: Other sectors	4748	4798	
Net errors and omissions (EO)	4998		Non-recorded capital flows of residents

II. The Method of Calculation of Capital Flows:	
A. The Decomposition of Capital Flows	B. The Decomposition of "Hot" Short-term Capital Flows
Net capital inflows by non-residents (NKI) = 2994 + 4555 + 4652 + 4753	Short-term inflows by non-residents (STI) = Total liabilities = 4660 + 4680 + 4774 + 4777 + 4783 + 4784 + 4795 + 4798
Net capital outflows by residents (NKO) = 3994 + 4505 + 4602 + 4703	Short-term outflows by residents (STO) = Total assets = 4610 + 4630 + 4724 + 4727 + 4733 + 4734 + 4745 + 4748
Net capital outflows by residents, including unrecorded outflows (NKOE) = NKO + EO	Short- term outflows, including unrecorded outflows STOE = STO + EO
Current account (CA) = 4993	Net short-term flows (NSF) = STI + STO
Reserve changes: Negative (-) means the increase (DR) = 4800	Net short-term flows, including unrecorded flows (NSFE) = Total assets + Total liabilities + EO = 4660 + 4774 + 4783 + 4784 + 4795 + 4798 + 4610 + 4724 + 4733 + 4734 + 4745 + 4748 + 4998
Net errors and omissions EO = 4998	

Sources: Boratav (1999, 2003), UNCTAD (1999) and IMF Balance of Payments Statistics Yearbook (2003).

REFERENCES

Akyüz, Yılmaz (1993). "Financial Liberalization: The Key Issues" *UNCTAD Discussion Paper* No. 56, Geneva.

Akyüz, Yılmaz (1990). "Financial System and Policies in Turkey in the 1980s" in Tosun Arıcanlı and Dani Rodrik (eds.), *The Political Economy of Turkey: Debt, Adjustment and Sustainability, London: The Macmillan Press.*

Amsden, Alice. H. (1989). *Asia's Next Giant: South Korea and Late Industrialization*, New York, Oxford: Oxford University Press.

Aspe, Pedro (1993). *Economic Transformation the Mexican Way*, Cambridge, Massachusetts, London: The MIT Press.

In: Korea: Economic, Political and Social Issues
Editors: P. H. Elwood, J. B. Albertus

ISBN: 978-1-60456-513-3

Chapter 6

FILM, POSTMODERNISM AND THE SOCIOLOGICAL IMAGINATION: EXPLORING THE POWER OF LOCAL STORIES IN SOUTHERN KOREA AND NORTHERN ENGLAND

Sung Kyung Kim and Rob Stones
University of Essex, Wivenhoe Park, Colchester, UK

INTRODUCTION

In this chapter our primary starting point is the conviction that the post-modern turn in social theory unlocked and valorised the potential of the creative arts and humanities for the sociological imagination. This legitimised a broader rejection than hitherto of those kinds of 'scientifically' based analyses which flattened out the rich complexity of social life. Post-modernism played a highly fruitful and productive role in the social sciences in valorising or re-valorising a long list of dimensions whose legitimacy had been in question. After postmodernism it has been far more difficult to simply dismiss the relevance and powers of, *inter alia*, phenomenology, hermeneutics and interpretation, emotionality, sensuality, a sense of place, social bonds, aesthetics, textuality, narrative and story-telling, a consciousness of time and history, nostalgia, values, and morality. In addition to its role in liberating these many rich dimensions of being, of ontology and the ontic, which had been secreted away and ignored or left underdeveloped, postmodernism also embodied a healthy scepticism towards claims to objective knowledge. The latter, in retrospect, was closely linked to the former. It was inevitable that postmodernism's sensitivity to the greater complexity of being – which included the complicated relationship between being human and such things as meaning, embodiment, emotion and memory – would be mirrored by a greater sensitivity to the embeddedness of knowledge in this complexity, and thus to the ensuing partial and corrigible nature of all kinds of knowledge.

The two feature films through which we will pursue our argument here are the South Korean film *A Beautiful Time* (in English *Spring in My Hometown*), set in a small rural village during the Korean war – far from the battlefield but touched by the war in many ways - in the early 1950s (see Kim, 2006b, pp.321-34), and the English film *Spring and Port Wine* set in the early 1960s amongst the factories and mill chimneys of the Lancashire cotton town of Bolton. Our choice of films and our perspectives on these films have been clearly marked by our respective positions as 'insiders', at least in some respects, to each of these cultures, with Sung Kyung Kim in her early 20s and at University in Seoul when *Spring in My Hometown* was released, and Rob Stones a 12 year old schoolboy in Bolton when *Spring and Port Wine* was shown in the local cinemas. In analysing these two films, one from South Korea and the other from Northern England, we hope to emphasise the importance of stories, local settings, and situated phenomenological perspectives, and to note that these emphases follow seamlessly from the greater recognition of the rich complexity of social life mentioned above.

The resonance of local stories is closely related to the significance of specificity and context in, certainly, the causal unfolding of events, but also, just as importantly, in the existential anchoring and orientation of people's experiences. We believe that in the postmodern media age it is vital that we continue to make films which are rooted in local contexts, and that these are not just American contexts. We argue that in providing the chance to view, experience, and reflect upon these contexts film, as one part of civic culture, can offer moorings and co-ordinates to people who threaten to be be overwhelmed by the speed, ubiquity and seemingly arbitrary nature of change in current times. The films we analyse here, rooted in discernibly 'realistic' social contexts from the relatively recent past - the past of the previous generation and the early years of the present generation or the present generation's parents – and in, or on the borders of, the art film genre[1], have specific kinds of resources to offer in this respect, in the struggle to defer or allay post-modern anomie and loss of meaning (see Bauman, 2004; cf. Hall, 1990, p.59)[2].

The co-ordinates, or anchors, which are most immediately apparent in the kinds of films we will discuss here are those of geography, culture and biography. The weight and power of these dimensions within film can act as counterweights to postmodernity's pressure towards psychological disorientation through contributing to a valuable sense of security, familiarity and belonging. These dimensions, however, can be given further weight when audiences have the resources to situate them with respect to what C Wright Mills, in *The Sociological Imagination* (1959), referred to as the large forces of history and social structure. The greater the combination of these types of anchoring then, *ceteris paribus*, the greater the ability of the viewer to engage in *verstehen*-like identification with the characters in the stories and to reflect upon how they feel – their sensibilities, pleasures, sufferings and so on - how they cope, and how, ideally, they should act within those circumstances. In turn, we would argue that the development of the skills and dispositions required to engage in these kinds of judgements allows contemporary viewers to situate their own biographies and to make similar judgements with respect to the circumstances of their own lives.

In discussing both the textual representation in film of local settings and stories, and the likely effect of these representations on audiences, we will draw on several of the

---

[1] On the distinctive characteristics of the art film genre see Bordwell and Thompson, 1993, also see Stones 2002b, pp.230-1.

[2] For excellent general reviews of postmodernism see Turner ,1990, and Featherstone, 1988.

ontological/ontic[3] themes of the social which were rejuvenated and newly licensed by postmodernism, and we will also draw on postmodernism's embedded, partial, and tentative view of knowledge and understanding. This commitment to the strengths of postmodernism will be combined with a, suitably refined, ontological and epistemological commitment to the real, one which is also informed by broader trends in contemporary social theory which have themselves influenced and been influenced by the insights of postmodernism[4]. It is important not to jettison all engagement with issues of reality, or with the systematic style of argument required to make this engagement meaningful. We believe that the political and cultural power of postmodernism can, perhaps paradoxically, be that much greater if it dispenses with those more extreme and radical positions within its borders that reject[5] every kind of disciplined and systematic approach to knowledge construction. Of course there are dangers in the latter but ultimately it is possible to believe that real things happen to real people, and that all sorts of experiences can have real effects on the consciousness of people, without wanting in any way to oversimplify the complex nature of these things, to underestimate the obstacles in gaining access to them, or to underplay the many mediations involved in their representation (see Stones, 1996).

Both of our films, at least in their English language versions, have the word 'spring' in their titles. We choose to read this to indicate that the films deal with people attempting to cope with situations of change; change which is demanding and disruptive but which also heralds new possibilities, for both good and ill. In one of the films, shot soon after the times it portrayed, 'port wine' stands as a symbol of new forms of consumption, lifestyles and morality for the working classes, forms which unsettled the ways of the older generation. In the other film, shot nearly half a century after the time of its setting, the appeal of the 'hometown' in a time of war is as a reminder of what has been disrupted, a provocation to nostalgia about what still remained, and a promise of a better state that was longed for and might later return. The age of postmodernity is the age of an eternal spring. The perpetual nature of change within postmodernity, and the speed of change, places a special onus on the ability of people to adapt continually without losing their bearings, purpose and sense of coherence and meaning. It is not surprising that postmodern views of the subject never stray far from the threat of fragmentation and disorientation in the face of flux, speed, flows and the implosion of meanings and purpose as signifiers are unhinged from signifieds. Frederic Jameson's diagnosis of 'schizophrenic identities' in postmodernity combines this erasure of meaning with a parallel loss of a sense of history (Jameson, 1983, pp.117-9). The flip side of 'historical amnesia' in this account is the experience of living in an eternal present, without connections to the past, without co-ordinates that can help to situate the present: Jameson is pessimistic about the implications of this state of being for the fate of the self:

> schizophrenic experience is an experience of isolated, disconnected, discontinuous, material signifiers which fail to link up into a coherent sequence. The schizophrenic thus does not

---

[3] On the distinction between the ontological and the ontic, or ontology-in-situ, see Stones, 2005, pp. 7-8, and 76-81.

[4] In a previous work, Stones, 1996, labelled this approach past-modernism, indicating a combination of postmodernism with a broader approach to social theory underpinned by theoretical realism. Perhaps a better label would be *postmodern realism*, simply indicating the combination of postmodernism's richness and scepticism with a sustained but suitably chastened commitment to a complex and sophisticated form of realism.

[5] On a useful distinction between sceptical and affirmative postmodernists see Rosenau, 1992.

> know personal identity in our sense, since our feeling of identity depends on our sense of the persistence of the "I" and the "me" over time (Jameson, 1983: 119; see also Jameson, 1994).

There is an unexpected thematic convergence between this analysis and Alasdair MacIntyre's conviction expressed in *After Virtue* that the sense of a narrative unity of one's biography is a precondition for sustaining the sense of one's life as a moral quest that involves both self and community (MacIntyre, 1985, pp.204-25). MacIntyre's analysis is more explicitly moral and prescriptive, but it is clear that both writers are in agreement about the nihilistic effects of living in a discontinuous succession of presents, without co-ordinates or anchors to provide orientation and meaning. MacIntyre's emphasis on morality is relevant to the issue of anomie, as along with the threat to *meaning* presented by the structural dynamics of postmodernity there is also the ever present threat of a breakdown in shared expectations about *norms.* Anomie within postmodernity[6] results from the fluidities, disjunctions, and simulations which sever signifiers from signifieds and norms from even the most transient of legitimising traditions. Both meaning and norms are essential to social and mental health, and, we would argue, are closely connected to all the co-ordinates mentioned above.

Zygmunt Bauman (e.g. 1995, pp.63-5; 2000. p.7 and *passim*) seeks to make a virtue out of postmodern anomie as he argues that the ethical codes inherited from a less frenetic modernity cannot provide effective social norms in an age of Post or *Liquid Modernity.* Bauman's answer to the current state is to encourage us to rediscover a deeper moral impulse shorn of ethical codes, to open out to the *Other* in a selfless way which transcends, because it precedes, any thought of instrumentality or questions about 'what is to be done' (Bauman, 1995, pp.64-5). For Bauman, '(I)f the modern 'problem of identity' was how to construct an identity and keep it solid and stable, the postmodern 'problem of identity' is primarily how to avoid fixation and keep the options open'. (Bauman, 1995, p.18; cited in McCrone, 1998, p.31). However, this is to underestimate the importance of continuity and coherence, co-ordinates and anchoring, in the survival of the self. There is a need to find a middle way between the modern social self, which is 'stable, fixed and constructed', and the decentred or postmodern self that is so 'open, contradictory, unfinished, and fragmented' (Hall 1992, pp.274-291) that its experience is one of deracination, meaninglessness and schizophrenia.

---

[6] The sociological concept of anomie, of norm-lessness, as explicated most famously by Emile Durkheim (Durkheim, 1952/1897) and Robert Merton, can be usefully placed alongside the picture of individual experience painted by theorists of the postmodern era. According to Merton anomie involves a breakdown in the organized set of shared 'normative values governing behavior which is common to members of a designated society or group' (Merton, 1968, p.216). The specific form of breakdown focused on by Merton is that caused by a disjunction between the cultural norms and goals of a group or society 'and the socially structured capacities of members of the group to act in accord with them' (p.216). On this reading it is the social structure that 'strains' the cultural values and norms, as it makes it impossible for some individuals to act on them, to realistically achieve prescribed and desired goals. The greater the number of people who are frustrated and disappointed by this situation, and who consequently feel pressure to act in non-conforming ways of one kind or another, the greater the degree of anomie in a society. In the picture of postmodernity we have painted here there is indeed a sense of norm-lessness, a breakdown in mutually accepted proprieties, and there is also a close relationship between social structure and (the breakdown in) cultural norms. However, there are also profound differences. Postmodern anomie does not derive from frustration and disappointment caused by a socially structured inability to successfully pursue societal prescribed goals in a normatively acceptable manner. Rather, the postmodern breakdown in norms results from the fluidities, disjunctions, and simulations which sever signifiers from signifieds and norms from even the most transient of legitimising traditions.

The middle way can be constructed by building on a crucial analytical distinction between two aspects of what Pierre Bourdieu calls *the internalisation, within the agent, of social externality* (e.g. Bourdieu, 1977/72, p.72). Here, it is possible to recognise equally both Bourdieu's ontological notion of habitus, a concept that refers to a system of lasting transposable dispositions, skills and orientations within the agent which transcend any particular situation, and structuration theory's recent separation between this realm and an agent's internal appreciation and perception of the immediate situation or conjuncture (see Stones, 2005, pp.87-94). To these can be added the flexibility and improvisation required in the interaction process itself (cf. Mouzelis, 1991, pp.198, Plummer, 1991). Lodged in the enduring dispositions of habitus are so many of the human and social dimensions, mentioned at the outset, that have been valorised by postmodernism, from the phenomenological and hermeneutic capacities of the person to her embodied emotional, sensual, motor and aesthetic dispositions, her stock of stories and narratives, her values and perceptions of virtue and so on. The important point here is that the recognition of the centrality of habitus indicates that is not only possible but probably also inevitable that one retains dispositions and orientations that are inherited and learned from the past. The recognition of the further ontological category of situationally specific knowledge, and the requirement that dispositions and orientations be employed flexibly within unfolding interactions, indicates the possibility of a middle way in which agents are anchored in relatively enduring dispositions but are also able to combine this with reflective and practical responses to the changing present. The flexibility or transposability of habitus was at the centre of Bourdieu's conceptualisation from the outset. Macintyre takes this one step further into the realm not just of 'what is' but also of moral deliberation about what 'should be', based on a combination of inheritance and conjuncture. He invokes Aristotle's notion of *phronesis* and makes much of the ability of agents to apply their judgement wisely to completely new situations on the basis of a reflective but flexible relationship to their inherited traditions (Macintyre, 1985, pp.204-25; see also Bernstein, 1986, pp.94-114). This grouping of concepts, taken together, allows one to see that agents have always been adapting, more or less flexibly, to circumstances on the basis of a combination of more or less enduring inherited dispositions and of past, present and future orientations.[7] The capacities invoked by habitus have thus tended not only to provide communal and individual world-views, but also inner resources that are anchored and resilient enough to allow change to be confronted from a position of relative autonomy and self-containment.

The concepts themselves need to be fleshed out at the more contextual, ontic, level, in order to see whether or not capacities for, say, orientation and flexibility are retained or subverted. Our position on this is guided by a belief that: the discontinuities between modernity and postmodernity, whilst radical and significant, are often over-exaggerated; the changes and upheavals within modernity itself are often under-estimated; and that consequently there is an equivalent underestimation of the degree to which the inherited dispositions of previous generations were confronted with disorienting and deeply testing times. Whilst there are without doubt radical changes at the socio-structural and cultural levels which present current experience with particular kinds of pressures that are unprecedented in their intensity and capacity for the subversion of both individual and collective identities, it is important not to underestimate the resources we already have, and

[7] On the role of time in agency deliberation see Emirbayer and Mische, 1998.

which we can muster, in their defence. Films of the recent past can provide an anchor for habitus through the dimensions of geography, culture and biography, each situated at the junction with the great forces of history and social structure, and it is within such locations that we can, and should, think about norms, values and how life should be lived. These moorings can help, through radically changing times, to hold the signifiers and the signifieds together. This is especially so when, as in the case of the films we have chosen, they focus precisely on the attempts of people to come to terms with difficult and changing times which tested their own sense of security and identity.

STORIES, GEOGRAPHIES AND CULTURES: SOUTHERN KOREA AND NORTHERN ENGLAND

Spring in My Hometown (1997, Yi Kwangmo, dir. Entitled *A Beautiful Time* in Korean) was the winner of the Best Picture Prize at the 'Grand Bell Award', Korea's equivalent of the Academy Awards. It also received the Grand Prix at the Vancouver Film Festival in 1998 and at the 52nd Locarno Film Festival in 1999. The film is set during the Korean War of 1950 to 1953 in a small village settlement in South Korea.[8] The village nestles next to a river but spreading in its buildings and its activities into the woods and hills on its verges. It is probably quite close to the frontline, but not imminently so. Much of the village seems to have been destroyed, probably in fighting, although attempts are made at repair, and at least a segment of the population is made up of refugees. School is held in a makeshift quadrangle of dark green military canvas tents. The presence of the US military is continually apparent in the background. The film subtly conveys the disruptions and suffering that the war brings to those away from the immediate fighting. Its storylines encompass the everyday lives of ordinary people.

The film is narrated in the form of written inter-texts by a boy, Choi Sung-Min, whose family are refugees from Northern Korea. They are separated from their wider family and also from the eldest son, who had to stay behind. A small room in the house of Sung Min's family is rented out to the family of the boy's best friend, Chang-Hee, who lives with his mother and sister. The absence of Chang Hee's father is one of many traces of the war imprinted on the lives of the village. Mr Song is imprisoned in the infamous Gujae prison, his exact fate uncertain. The family has for a long time been unable to pay their rent. In contrast, Sung Min's father, Mr Choi, has a well paid job at the US military base, a job found for him through his daughter who is dating an American soldier, First Lieutenant Smith, and who also works at the base. Mr Choi clearly feels a weight of dependence on the Americans, mixed with admiration for the cultural artefacts of western consumer culture. This has something to do with his willingness to allow his daughter, Young Sook, to go to parties at the base and stay out late, against all the usual proprieties and whilst knowing that his wife strongly disapproves. The relative wealth and comfort brought to the Choi family by these jobs is expressed symbolically by objects which Mr Choi brings back with him from the base, from sausages and hams to a radio and gramophone. The latter become familiar fixtures amongst the more traditional objects in the *mise- en- scène* of the household. Some of these objects, we

[8] For a more extensive account of the film see Kim Sung Kyung, 2006b, pp.321-34.

begin to realise, have possibly been given as presents but, more likely, have been stolen by Mr Choi. Whilst Mr Choi is generous and decent in many ways, he ultimately places his role as material provider above all else, including the fortunes of others. Relative affluence is also conveyed by the family's subsequent move to a large traditional house, one that is said to have been the mayor's house before the war. Extensive work needs doing to the buildings but the family is able to call on the services of a group of labourers who immediately set to work on the restoration.

Cultural resonances[9] abound in the natural and social landscapes and social relations we encounter. The preparation of Korean pancakes in the ubiquitous wide pan (*bunchul*) owned then by all Koreans, and cooking soup in the back yard during the house warming party held by Sung Min's family, are very familiar images in Korean minds, as is the gathering of people together in the front yard, sitting on mats and taking in food and drink, on the day the family move into their new house. Nostalgic resonances are also conveyed through sound (cf. Powrie, 1997: 19). The song, 'Spring in My Hometown', accompanied by the simplified Korean organ, widely used in classrooms right up until the 1980s, would be irresistibly evocative for large numbers of Koreans, as would the accent and intonation of the anchorman on the radio news – the only radio station at a time before the advent of TV. Childhood games portrayed in the film would also melt away the years as we see the children playing hop scotch, rolling blazing cans in winter, and watching stag beetles wrestle.[10]

Images of a patriarchal hierarchy and division of labour are just as familiar, with Sung Min's mother[11] carrying most of the luggage to the new house and all mothers performing most of the physical and domestic work including cleaning, cooking, and washing. We see Sung Min's mother solicitously brushing the dust off Mr Choi's clothes. All of this is remarkably similar to the scenes we see in *Spring and Port Wine*. There can be a complex ambivalence in one's present reception of these and other images, and nostalgia mixed with a desire for critique. However, an anchoring in the memories and evocation of the embodied, lived, experience of the times, rather than a culturally schizophrenic inability to relate at all to those times is a precondition for any sort of meaningful critique.[12]

In a fateful development of the plot Mr Choi helps Chang Hee's mother to get work washing the underwear of the US soldiers, a task that occupies several of the people in the village, with the regimented washing lines and shapes of the drying garments creating striking geometric patterns across the landscape. When Chang Hee's mother loses the underwear entrusted to her for washing, soon after being told to hang it in a less intrusive place by Sung Min's mother, who shows little warmth to her poorer lodger, we enter into a narrative that reveals much more of the invidious power relations and attendant moral geography behind the calm and beauty of the landscape. Faced with a dilemma in which, we infer, Mr Choi needs to restore his own good name in the wake of this mishap, he arranges for Chang Hee's mother to have sex with a US soldier at a rice mill beyond the village as reparation for her failure. The

---

9 This central emphasis on cultural resonances in film is taken from Kim, 2006b, pp.65-79, and *passim*.

10 Rolling blazing cans is a traditional recreation during winter.. Children play it at night by rolling a blazing can with the intention of setting fire to the fields.

11 Korean women do not change their name after marriage, and we are not told the names of Chang Hee's and Sung Min's mothers, hence the necessity for this rather awkward locution throughout.

12 The kind of social and individual anchoring discussed here provides an important additional dimension to the exploration of *internal moral critique* made in Stones, 2006, and relevant to the final substantive section of this chapter.

soldier arrives at the mill in a jeep, along with the noise of the engine and a trail of dust. Most communities in the 1950s were heavily reliant on agriculture and every village would have a rice mill which went into relative disuse after newly harvested rice had been refined during the autumn. Mills were routinely familiar parts of the visual landscape and were also culturally associated with clandestine intimate liaisons of various kinds. As the influence of Confucianism on Korean society carries with it strict codes on sexual conduct (cf. Lee, 2000, pp.90-93) the mill has become imbricated with significations of darkness, guilt, secrecy and illicit sexuality in the background understandings of Koreans.

Earlier in the film we have seen another man in the role which is now taken by Mr Choi, waiting patiently and diffidently outside the mill, leaning on his bicycle – itself a symbol of relative wealth - acting as pimp for a girl who needed money to pay for medicine for her sick father. The man, drawing naturally on the Confucian inspired ideas of authority, obedience and piety in Korean relationships, tells the girl that she is a 'good daughter', using the word *hyonye*, which can be translated more accurately as a filial and dutiful daughter (cf. Lee, 2000, pp.135-7). On that occasion, as in this, the boys were secretly present. We are used to them, by now, in images of the times which are culturally familiar to all Koreans, playing in the woods and on the paths beyond the village, typically following the Americans when they see them, asking for chocolate (pronounced *jjoggoraet* by Koreans then as now, linked generically to the glamour of 'American Products') as they chase the jeeps, and looking for other exotic trophies left behind, such as a lighter found by Chang Hee in the straw covering the floor of the mill. They know why the US soldiers come to the mill. We have seen them on the previous occasion taking turns to watch, mischievously and voyeuristically, through a small hole in the wall of the mill. This time, looking back the other way through the hole in the wall, we watch Chang Hee's face in close up, – this is the only close-up sequence in the whole of the film – as he realises that the woman he can see is his mother. We then watch Sung Min's face as it replaces that of his friend. The camera then frames the emotions in both faces together and their mutual evasions of gaze as both confront what they have seen and what it might mean for them, and for each other. There is shock, and shame, of different kinds, on both sides.

Chang Hee takes revenge by setting fire to the mill, and then he disappears. We don't know how he would feel about facing his mother again, and we don't know how afraid he might be of being caught. In any case, he does not return. A year or so later the decomposed body of a child is discovered. Everybody believes the body must be that of Chang Hee. Unable to reclaim the body his friends prepare a coffin, enact traditional rituals and hold a funeral procession, in Indian file bearing the catafalque adorned with flags, before holding a mock cremation for the small, absent, body of their companion. At one point the procession is broken up, temporarily and fleetingly, by a jeep which doesn't slow at all and which a few of the children chase, as a reflex response, in search of *jjoggoraet*. They are chastised by one of the boys who has, respectfully, held his ground..

In another strand of the narrative it has transpired that Young Sook is expecting Lieutenant Smith's baby. What we see in the sjuzet-text[13] suggests the family accepts this

[13] The term *sjuzet*-text here references a distinction drawn by the Russian Formalists in which the *sjuzet* refers to the story as it is told within the text, whereas the *fabula* refers to a set of inferred real events in time and space. *Sjuzet*-text indicates not just the plot but all the textual content of a film, book or other form of representation. For more extensive discussion see Bal, 1997, and Genette, 1979, and, combined with a social theory dimension, Stones, 1996, pp.167-91, and 2002a.

seamlessly and we see Young Sook in various stages of pregnancy, her mother solicitous and Sung Min resting his head gently on his sister's tummy listening for the kicking she has told him she feels. We learn in one of the final intertexts that Young Sook was never to see Lieutenant Smith again. The final frames of the film are taken up with the shame and humiliation of both Sung Min and his father as the latter walks through the village after being daubed in red paint by the US authorities, a sign that he has been caught stealing and smuggling contraband goods. His romance with the Americans, it seems, had its limits. Now, it was over. He knew from local stories that his home was likely to be torched to the ground the following morning. At the break of dawn the family departs, probably northwards, with an oxcart laden with their possessions.

Spring and Port Wine (dir:Peter Hammond, 1970) is an adaptation by the playwright Bill Naughton – probably most well known for his screenplay for the film *Alfie* – of his 1967 play of the same name, itself a revised and re-written version of his 1957 drama *My Flesh, My Blood.* The film is set in the late 1950s or early 1960s amongst the mill chimneys and cobbled streets of the industrial town of Bolton, Lancashire where Naughton - whose family moved from County Mayo, Ireland in 1914 when he was four - grew up, married and had children before moving to London before the Second World War. In this film, as in the first, the sense of place is strong; our sense of who the characters are is very much bound up with the characteristics of where they live, so there is much more than the provision of an empty space in which the narrative unfolds. A significant difference, however, between the two films is that *Spring in My Hometown* is set in an unidentified South Korean village, so that the geographical and cultural motifs are systematically generic, whereas the setting here is determinedly and specifically Bolton, and by extension, Lancashire. There is a resulting use of precise linguistic or visual references which are extremely powerful culturally. Such references include: the moors, near Rivington Pike and Winter Hill, overlooking the town and familiar to all who live in the area; the nineteenth century Parish Church of St Peter's; Whitaker's department store on Deansgate with its distinctive black and white façade; the towpath by the canal; a scene in Queen's Park with the gas works_dominant in the background; a road sign to Trinity Street Station; 'the Wanderers', shorthand for the name of the local football team; Bolton Wanderers; one of Bolton's red and cream buses of the time, with number 36, Radcliffe, on its front; the *Bolton Evening News* clearly visible as it is read by one of the central characters as he puts his feet up after work; and a litany of idiomatic expressions.

But, it is not only those who have directly lived or passed-on associations with provincial north of England towns who will experience the evocation of roots and belonging from these and similar references. For, as Benedict Anderson's famous exposition of imagined communities implies, there is a fascination with the lives of those 'other' people who share our broader geographical and cultural space, most of whom we will never meet but with whom we will share many moments of civic ritual, or pass in cities, or hear about from afar, which means that the lived texture of their cultural dispositions, dreams and understandings will also play a significant part in our own feelings of orientation and belonging (see Anderson, 1991). These wider cultural associations are bolstered by a series of references that are less specific to Bolton, more generic with respect to a more broadly defined but still distinctive time or place, references that are closer in type to those we find in *Spring in My Hometown.* Thus, set amongst the cobbled streets and terraced houses, there is the Brooke Bond Tea advertising hoarding above the local shop, with its period colouring and typeface, and the bubble gum machine besides it, the women in headscarves with distinctive overcoats and bags, bottles of HP Brown sauce and Worcester sauce. There are also the fiercely graduated class distinctions between the herring on Friday or roast on Sunday at one house and the tripe and greasy egg in the other, places neatly set on a blue and white gingham tablecloth and boiled eggs in their own cups at a family breakfast, in one, and a breakfast with half empty milk bottles, an ashtray, magazines open, and a husband still dressed in his vest and hanging braces, hunched forward with elbows on the table, and slopping the dregs of his tea round and round his cup, in the other. There are men playing bowls, a mother knitting, men in poignantly styleless slippers and striped pyjamas, items of furniture redolent of the age, the saying of prayers kneeling by the bedside, the period formality of greetings, scout uniforms, a fish and chip van outside the factory gates, and the family singing by the piano.

The story of *Spring and Port Wine* revolves around the relationship within the Compton family, a self consciously respectable family from the skilled working classes of Bolton's army of labourers who live in a semi-detached house built on a piece of land raised, both physically and symbolically, just a little higher than the surrounding houses. It is approached up a stepped incline and unlike the neighbouring houses it has a decent sized garden, whose lawn – adorned with bird bath and spring flowers - provides virtually the only visible patch of green in some of the several iconic cinematographic scenes of the urban landscape. Domestic scenes in the film are typically preceded and introduced by 'That Long Shot of Our Town from That Hill' (Krish, 1963, p14, cited in Higson, 1996, p.133) before the camera closes in on smaller settings such as: the Compton's house; the interior of a house that Florence, the eldest daughter, and Arthur, her fiancée, are interested in moving to; or the bowling green. There are also scenes in which we follow characters on foot or in a car through urban and rural landscapes rich in the culturally resonant objects and associations mentioned above.

The opening scene sees the mother, Daisy Compton, struggling with the household accounts for that week, attempting to get everything straight so that she can show the books to her husband - an engine-shed worker in a cotton-mill - when he comes home. She asks her eldest daughter, Florence, a primary school teacher who is first back from work, to help her out. Her financial predicament is given an added twist when her neighbour, Betsy Jane, arrives in desperation to ask for a loan of five pounds to bring her payments up to date and stop the men already in her house from taking the TV away. One by one the family arrives home from their work in the factories. The narrative, as it begins to unfold, focuses on a battle of wills between the father, Rafe Compton, who insists on strict principles and norms, and his spirited and wilful teenage daughter, Hilda. As the family sits down to the traditional meal of fish on a Friday evening Hilda remarks that she doesn't feel like eating herring today. Her mother, Daisy, says not to worry and suggests an egg instead as she moves towards the kitchen. Rafe intervenes, 'just a minute, Mother', and asks Hilda what's wrong with the herring, a lovely fresh herring, done in best butter. He demands to know how she has the nerve to sit there and say she doesn't fancy it. He tells her to eat it like the rest of the family, '…this is a home, not a cafeteria'. Hilda can't or won't eat the herring and as she moves to leave the room Rafe orders her to return to the table, 'only pigs leave their troughs as it suits.' He tells Hilda that she'll eat nothing else at his table until she eats the herring. The next few days are punctuated by meal times in which Hilda is presented with the uneaten herring whilst the rest of the family eat freshly prepared meals. Rafe is determined that no child of his is going to get the better of him.

Just at the point where Hilda has resolved to eat 'that flamin' herring' to ease the strain in the household – 'I'll eat every damned morsel, skin, tail, fin, the lot, even if it makes me sick. I'll put him through it' - and Rafe has decided to relent as soon as Hilda shows the slightest sign of willingness to try the fish, any easy resolution of the predicament is inadvertently thwarted by the good intentions of Wilfred who secretly feeds the herring to the cat. An inquisition follows in which Rafe, holding the truth above all else, demands that his youngest son swears on the Bible that he didn't give the herring to the cat. The rest of the family look on in stunned amazement. A shocked and trembling Wilfred looks around for help: 'It'd be wrong, dad, to swear on the Bible over an' herring....wouldn't it mam?' Despite the protests, one after another, of the rest of the family (Hilda: 'No, mam, he can't do that...'), Rafe tells Wilfred to take this Holy Book high and say, 'I swear by Almighty God', and as he does so Harold uncharacteristically fails to hide his anger from his father, shouting 'alright, if you want to know, I took your bloody herring', and Arthur warns to look out as Wilfred is feinting, falling. As everybody, including Rafe, move quickly to get him air, and to make him comfortable, unfastening his collar and bringing water for him to sip, Hilda snatches the Bible and moves to strike her father with it, but is restrained by Florence who takes the Bible and replaces it on the piano.

The scene becomes quickly and strangely domesticated as it is agreed that Wilfred is 'having one of his turns'. But Rafe has gone too far this time. Hilda has run out of the room, slamming the door, and Arthur courageously refuses to return to the table to eat. He feels he has to speak his mind to Mr Compton even though he is breaking all the rules of propriety, being a guest in his home. He says that what Wilfred did for Hilda, and Hilda's defence of her brother, were done out of love, love for one another, and they showed some spirit, spirit that their father wanted to crush out of anyone who doesn't agree with him: 'I used to respect you, but now I see you're nothing but a tyrant.' He tells Rafe he'll never be able to stop doing harm as long as he rams his own way down everybody's throat. 'You used that Holy Bible for your own ends....My folk are nothing but they would never even dare to do a think like that...' He turns to Daisy, 'I'm sorry, Mother – I had to come out with it.'

Florence leaves with Arthur, in spite of Rafe forbidding it, and the boys soon also decide to pack their bags. Hilda goes to stay the night next door with Betsy Jane's family. The next day she returns once her father has left for work and tells her mother that she is 'getting out of it, going away', she is leaving for London that evening. We realise by now that she is probably pregnant, and – in parallel with Young Sook's situation - by a lover who has stopped contacting her. Desperate to give some money to her daughter to keep her safe in the strangeness of the city Daisy does the unthinkable and, with the help of Betsy Jane – who has still not returned her loan - breaks into Rafe's locked desk where a box with the household money is kept. Before they can open the box, however, Daisy comes to a sudden realization of what she is doing, puts it back in the desk and shuts the lid, although the lock remains open and visibly tampered with. Betsy Jane colludes in pawning Rafe's new coat, delivered amidst much awe, admiration and curiosity from everybody only the previous day; silk lined, hand-stitched, taped seams and costing thirty two guineas from Horsfall and Trott, Bespoke Tailors. Daisy intends it to be only for a day until she is paid back, but events conspire so that Rafe, on his way out to listen to the Huddersfield Choral Society sing Handel's *Messiah* in Manchester, looks for his coat and finds it missing.

When he comes back downstairs Daisy is gone and the door is wide open; he sees the desk has been broken into and there is an apologetic, distraught note scribbled by Daisy. She has headed for the canal, without a coat; we see her stumble and fall in the mud, get up again and continue. We sense Rafe's premonition of what is about to happen and he leaves the house urgently, looking for his wife. He catches up with her under a bridge on the towpath and there is an extended cathartic scene of emotional release and reconciliation in which Daisy rails against Rafe's rigid standards. An ashamed and chastened Rafe asks for forgiveness, seeming to understand for the first time that he has tried to do good by force and that force blinds a man as to what is truly important. For the first time, also, he tells Daisy how his childhood had been blighted by debt collectors, money lenders, shopkeepers and bailiffs, how he had come home one day to find bailiffs playing cards in the front room and his mother in the kitchen trying to gas herself at the stove. He'd vowed that nothing like all this would ever happen to him, but he realises now that he'd rather forfeit all the material things he has, all the savings, security and everything, rather than bring a moment's further worry to his wife or 'drive any one of our children from their own home.'

Social and Historical Contexts, Textual Style, and Moral Judgments

The force of the past in Rafe's current dispositions and trials are an indication that the understanding of both films can be deepened further by adding to the geographical and cultural contexts of the personal and family predicaments some appreciation of those social and historical forces and phenomenological inheritances emphasised by C. Wright Mills. The inherited dispositions, rigidities, pleasures, values, norms, fears and so on, that provide an anchor for habitus, are always themselves the product of prior specific social and historical settings. Thus, the characters of the people in *Spring in My Hometown* cannot be properly understood without an appreciation of the recent history of Japanese colonialism and concomitant degrees of collaboration, the division of the country at the 38th parallel in 1945 as the Soviet and American armies met and received the Japanese surrender, and the subsequent Korean war between 1950 and 53 which not only led to a great loss of life but also to the creation of hundreds of thousands of refugees, to hundreds of thousands of disrupted and fractured lives. South Koreans who lived through these times experienced an amalgam of their own 'suffering, the shame at their own weakness and their resentment against authority and big powers' and prime amongst these, the Americans (Breen, 2004, p.122). The conflicts, loyalties and feelings of the Comptons in *Spring and Port Wine* need to be placed within the very different historical context of the 1930s depression, when millions of people in Britain found themselves without a job and on the breadline, the Post War Keynesian settlement and the establishment of the welfare state, the near full employment of the late 1950s and 1960s and the attendant diffusion of commodification and the consumer society.

In both films one sees the marks of social, economic and cultural change through the power of commodities, and the typically greater readiness of the younger generations to embrace these. So, for example, the younger generation is more likely to be captivated by the objects of modern technology and disposable consumer capitalism, from 'American Products' such as the soft porn magazine the boys find in the old mill, the chocolate thrown to the boys by the GIs, their cigarette lighters, binoculars and the make-up Young Sook brings home from the base, and the sensationalist magazines and the collection of 45rpm records that occupy

Hilda's leisure time, through new forms of mass produced transport from the military jeeps in the Korean village to the scooters, Zephyrs, Ford Anglias and Arthur's striking yellow Land Rover in Bolton, to the pleasures of the gambling club that has moved into the old St Saviour's Hall where the older members of the Compton family used to attend concerts of classical music. The generational reaction to change is, however, complex. Mr Choi is enthralled by the radio he brings back from the US base, whilst Rafe sits contentedly by the fire listening to a record of *The Messiah* although he is ostentatious in his expression of disdain towards the television watched by Harold and Wilfred. It is clear that Mr Choi is more ready to compromise with his changing times than Rafe Compton is with those that confront him.

The personal histories of the two men, lived at the intersection of large historical forces and social structures, have naturally left their traces within the depth of their habitus. Both men confront their present circumstances of social change through the eyes of this inheritance. The two films have different ways of introducing us to the causal and formative traces of history and the wider society in the lives of these and other characters. For *Spring and Port Wine*, the traces are introduced most directly through personal anecdote. This is anecdote related in relative close up, usually with two or three people in frame, their facial expressions and emotional responses clear and defined. They are there in the story Rafe tells to Daisy on the towpath, of growing up in poverty, debt and shame. They are there also in a memory, one that is shared with Daisy from their days as newlyweds, that he relates to the rest of the family at the dining table after Hilda has first refused to eat the herring. It is told in an effort to make the children understand why an appreciation of food is so important to their parent's generation, and describes an occasion during the 30's depression when Rafe, Daisy and Harold, still a baby, walked to the end of the road and suddenly came on the Hunger Marchers from Clydeside in Scotland. These were men who had been out of work for years and had seen their wives and families go hungry. They were walking through Bolton on their way to the Houses of Parliament in London, a march of four hundred miles. Their feet were sore and bandaged up and, too weak to sing, they were whistling 'Loch Lomond'. Daisy had spontaneously given them the flour cakes and the bottle of cold tea intended for a family picnic in Queen's Park[14].

In *Spring in My Hometown* the traces of history and the wider society intruding on the lives of the villagers are more formally, and more extensively, indicated through the technique of the intertext, a regular punctuation of the visual narrative of the film with writing, in Korean script, which provides information in two registers. The first is some information from Sung Min which is about the events in the village and which serves to drive the narrative forward. Events are thus focalised in this way through Sung Min's point of view. The second, underneath in slightly smaller script, is a comment on the wider politics and proceedings of the war. So, in one, we first read: 'While our family prospered, Chang Hee's became poorer and poorer', and then, underneath, 'August 30, 1952 – Wartime Civilian Regulations. It is forbidden to wear foreign clothes'. And then, from another intertext later in the film, after we have witnessed a scene in the makeshift schoolroom where a boy is humiliated and beaten by

[14] It is interesting to note that more places are named in the play than in the film. Queen's Park, for example, is not mentioned in the film. We have left some of these further references in here as a compromise with respect to the written form of this chapter, providing a greater sense of place, something that the film compensates for by a richer array of visual cues and indices. Queen's Park, for example, is the very visible setting for a key scene in the film.

a female teacher for not doing his homework, we read: 'Sang Un, the "commie's son", quits school that day. His papa was responsible for the death of the teacher's family'. Underneath this is written: 'October 1st, 1952 - The UN agrees to a $200 million fiscal budget for Korea'. Further examples of the second, wider political, captions are: 'August 10, 1952 – Refugee Camp Riot Incident – mobs of refugees raid town hall offices' and 'October 2, 1952 – A freeze is ordered on relief aid to refugees'. We later hear an announcement on the radio telling us of the ceasefire: 'UN forces and North Korea came to a mutual agreement on the armistice. On the 27th October at 10.00 am, they will meet at Panmunjum to prepare the mutual agreement… .'

Both films rely on elements of realism to satisfy the sociological imagination, providing social and historical co-ordinates by which to situate and contextualise the people whose stories we find ourselves involved with. However, it is clear that the two films draw on such conventions in very different ways. In *Spring in My Hometown* one finds hardly any close ups on characters, their faces and emotional gestures. Very often the characters in the frame are shot from a long way off, with the surface texture of the film treated so that it has the almost sepia tinted grainy feel of newsreel film. Dialogue, also, is relatively spare and non-discursive, down to earth but sententious. This provides a sense of distance and perhaps objectivity, but it also places limits on how well we know the people in the story, especially their inner life. We see emotion and conflict, in the beating handed out to the communist in the opening scene, and the poignant protests and terms of endearment heard in the shouts of his wife, in the vehemence of the head teacher's anti-communist address to the children in school, in the anger of Mr Choi, unable to cope, as he forbids his wife to talk about the son they left behind when they fled from North Korea, and in the fire that burns down the mill where Chang Hee has watched his mother. But we mostly see from afar, without depth of characterisation. We are left with powerful but underdeveloped intimations.

When the director wishes to convey psychological intensity in the film's most climactic moments he does so not by a discursive and narrative exploration of the processes by which the external present enters into the internal experience of the film's characters, as happens in the Compton's story, but through a stylistic technique in which, as we have seen, the dominant long-shot is replaced by a close up for the only time in the film, of Chang Hee and then of the two boys together, and a close up whose duration is painfully extended for nearly 60 seconds of screen time. The emotion is quiet and subdued but clearly intense. This scene is followed by two more extended scenes, focusing on Chang Hee's mother now left alone in the mill, and then – followed from behind by the camera – walking very slowly and in silence back to the village with Mr Choi walking alongside, languidly wheeling his bicycle. In both these prolonged scenes we have returned to the film's dominant long-shot which gives to the scenery, the place and the social relations as large a role as the narrative, and which has returned us in some ways to a sense of objectivity and distance. However, this is combined with an intensification of the director's wilful exaggeration of the already relatively slow pace of the film, and as Chang Hee's mother sits and buttons her blouse, one by one, slowly, silently, and then walks alongside Mr Choi, the sun, the landscape and the unmade track insistently still, cruelly tranquil, this forces our attention to trauma we can only guess at on the inside.

The result is an unsettling sense of indeterminacy with respect to the characters, their values, worldviews, emotions and reasons for their responses to events, but it is a sense that has a familiar feel from our experience of everyday life. This mirrors the effect of the political intertexts which both provide co-ordinates of a kind at the very same time as they draw attention to the viewer's limited knowledge. There are many further questions contemporary viewers, Korean or non-Korean, might want to ask about the incidence and intensity of support for the Communists in the south during these years, about the status, perceptions, security and treatment of refugees, and about prevailing economic conditions. Again, the finite, partial and indeterminate quality of our knowledge of wider social and historical circumstanccs is familiar.

The existential weight of all these moorings - paradoxically reinforced by the indeterminacy we are used to living with - can be reinforced and deepened, finally, thorough a reflexive attention to questions of continuity and adaptation in the realm of norms and moral judgement. For norms and moral orientations, too, are never free floating, whatever the existentialist may say. They, too, have their own histories in which external and internal factors are closely related, and film can be a powerful tool reminding us of this. Bauman is surely right to warn against too much rigidity in the transmission and imposition of norms within a culture, but it would be equally wrong to be too dismissive of the powerful role that some accommodation with norms must continue to play in any adequate functioning of social relationships, or of the framework of meaning and purpose they give to everyday life. Films such as *Spring in My Hometown* and *Spring and Port Wine* are cultural forms which can help local audiences to think about the normative legacies they have inherited and about how they may be transposed and adapted, without gratuitous rigidity, to the current conjuncture. Whilst postmodernism tells us, rightly, that this information will always be partial and finite, the greater or lesser immersion in, and appreciation of, all the wider co-ordinates we have discussed provides the characters in the films with varying degrees of embodied understanding, knowledge and practical wisdom with which to make informed and meaningful judgements about how to act (*phronesis*). Audiences in the present conjuncture looking back on these films can draw sustenance from them in thinking about parallel co-ordinates for the present. Current reflections can be given sustenance through an appreciation of the situated normative judgements at work within these stories. The possibility of continuity of identity throughout a lifetime, and across generations, is enhanced through reference to the embodied sense of an inherited, but changing, moral community.

There are many examples of embedded and evolving normative rules in the two films, and of adherence and transgression with respect to them. We have seen that characters in both films are struggling, more or less, and with different degrees of suffering and success, to adapt to changing times. For the sake of expediency we will focus, briefly, just on Rafe and Mr Choi. The well meaning but overly rigid principles embedded within Rafe's moral dispositions are brought into confrontation with the rest of his family. He has long subjugated Daisy, but on her own she would have been unlikely to have ever challenged his regime. It is a relational combination of the actions of, primarily, Hilda, Florence, Daisy, Betsy Jane and Arthur which bring him to a profound reassessment of the ways in which he relates to both his children and his wife. The unfolding saga of the herring is a vehicle through which he eventually comes to see, through his sensitivity to the emotional reactions of those involved, that he cannot ignore the changed world in which his children are growing up.

The changing relations are subtle, and it is important to note that not everything alters overnight, but the authority relations he strives to maintain are increasingly experienced as oppressive. When, in his use of the Bible, his patriarchal traditionalism is combined with his transgression of a traditional line between the sacred and the profane, mutually acknowledged by everyone else, there is an open rebellion. The structure of this rebellion is not unusual as the boundaries of moral acceptability, secular as well as religious, are very often reinforced by an implicit feel for the boundaries of the sacred. There is outrage here as each intuitively understands that Rafe's actions insult a set of newly emerged and mutually intuited moral codes. When Rafe has to choose between continuing to have his way and keeping the family together, he chooses the latter. Unlike Torvald in Ibsen's *A Doll's House*, to whom he can be compared in many ways, Rafe reveals himself to be bigger than status and money. There is more to him than instrumental reason. He had always wanted the family to be able to hold their heads up high and to have freedom from all the threats that come with debt, but he is shaken out of his rigidity when he realises that what started out as protection has now transformed itself into bullying and domination. From the socio-historical and cultural cues of the text we know that this situation has been brought to a head not only by the imminent contingencies which figure as the plot but also by deeper trends which have been internalised, in differently layered times, as value-commitments within the dispositions of the various protagonists. Audiences can see that Rafe now changes and adapts the texture and formation of his own dispositions, but without losing the sense of continuity with the past. He gives the key to the desk to Daisy as a symbolic gesture and both owns and professes shame about his previous behaviour. His patriarchy will not change immediately, and may never change completely, but there is real and non-trivial change which will improve the lives of the Comptons.

There is also a transgression of the line between the sacred and the profane in *Spring in My Hometown*. Although the style of the film means that the exact chain of events is left ambiguous, it is probably in order to save his own face that Mr Choi arranges for Chang Hee's mother to have sex with the American GI. Whether Mr Choi himself would concede he was responsible for a transgression of such magnitude we don't know. It is possible that the form of masculinity moulded by the patriarchal culture of the times inured him to this. On the other hand, we are left in little doubt that both Chang Hee and his mother have experienced a transgression of the sacred. The mother's virtues of enduring strength, self-sacrifice and devotion are glorified in Confucian family life, but this respect can sometimes come into conflict with the authority and power afforded to the father in particular and to men in general. It is by now a not unfamiliar sentiment in indigenous feminist circles that many Korean men achieved their safety during the turbulent times of colonialism and war through the sacrifice of Korean women (see Choi, 1994). Mr Choi certainly falls short of Bauman's universalist injunctions about *the Other* in his treatment of Chang Hee's mother. Intrinsic to his masculinity is the belief that he should give priority to looking after his family economically and materially, and this is in tension with a responsibility to care for his family's broader needs. As he fails to protect his daughter from indiscretions and dangers we are reminded of *honye*, the filial piety a daughter is expected to show to her father, but can question what *phronesis* should tell us about the conditions under which this is appropriate and when a sacred line is transgressed. In the event, just as Mr Choi sacrifices Chang Hee's mother, so he sacrifices his daughter.

We can place Mr Choi's actions within the context of the refugee experience, deracinated, living amidst the fierce political cleavages which undermine trust in general and faith in economic security in particular, and we can ask what difference, if any, this makes to our judgement. Mr Choi's initial generosity to Chang Hee's mother, and the warm father and son relationship he has with Sung-Min, symbolised by the telescope he makes for him, are enough to signal the complexity of his character and its relation to circumstances. We have seen from the account of the film that he finds it difficult to face up to his emotions, that he can be ambivalent and that, at least sometimes, he can't reach out to his wife when she needs him. We also feel that he is quite probably too rigid in his idea of how he should cope, too instrumental and narrowly determined. It is unclear what he feels when he strikes his son in anger for apparently stealing a lighter, at the same time as he himself is stealing from the American base. There is no point of realisation and conversion as there is with Rafe. The climax of his moral career within the film remains patently ignominious, on the surface, as he is daubed with red paint and leaves the village in ostensible shame whilst others sleep. His family, accompanying him, are victims of circumstances, and of Mr Choi's agency within those circumstances. However, Korean relationships to the war and to the large powers are not straightforward, and the film's, male, director seems not to judge Mr Choi too harshly as he dedicates the film to his father and grandfather, who we take to be represented by Sung Min and Mr Choi. There is much to deliberate about here which involves morality but does so in the context of a complex relationship between a broadly drawn social externality and the internality of identity and agency.

Conclusion

We hope to have made a case for the potential of locally embedded narratives, specifically here those of film, in the anchoring and orientation of identities in the age of postmodernity. We have seen that local films can provide powerful reference points of geography, culture, biography, history, social structure and moral values to combat the forces of postmodern fragmentation and schizophrenia. They do so in different ways, depending on focus, genre, style and texture, conveying specific pasts in specific ways, and all this will make a difference to their impact on the future phenomenological outlooks and identities of audiences. Modes of representation can thus be powerful in and of themselves, but they have a particular kind of power when they retain their connections to social realities and experiences. We have argued that postmodernist approaches to both social issues and to textual representation were a major influence in unlocking the potential of the creative arts and humanities for the sociological imagination, allowing it to engage with the kinds of argument presented here. These new and revived sources of inspiration, it has been argued, are particularly potent once they are combined with other trends in contemporary social theory, including a systematic but modified, epistemologically cautious, commitment to issues of realism. They can be even more potent when it is shown, as we hope it has been, that their application to detailed cases can begin to open up hitherto neglected aspects of social life with far-reaching implications for individual existence.

References

Anderson, B. (1991) *Imagined Communities*, 2nd edition. London: Verso.

Bal, M. (1997) *Narratology: Introduction to the Theory of Narrative*, 2nd edn. Toronto: Toronto University Press.

Bauman, Z. (1995) *Life in Fragments: Towards a Postmodern Morality*. Oxford: Blackwell.

Bauman, Z. (2000) *Liquid Modernity*. Cambridge: Polity Press.

Bauman, Z. (2004) *Identity*. Cambridge: Polity Press.

Bernstein, R. (1986) *Philosophical Profiles: Essays in a Pragmatic Mode*. Cambridge: Polity Press.

Bourdieu, P. (1977/72) *Outline of a Theory of Practice*. Cambridge: Cambridge University Press. Trans. Richard Nice, 1977.

Bourdieu, P. (2000/1997) *Pascalian Meditations*. Cambridge: Polity Press. Trans. Richard Nice, 2000.

Bordwell, D. (1985) *Narration in the Fiction Film*. London: Routledge

Bordwell, D and Thompson, K. (1993) *Film Art*, 4th edn. New York: McGraw-Hill.

Breen, M. (2004) *The Koreans*. Thomas Dunne Books, St Martin's Press: New York.

Choi, C (1998) *Dangerous Women: Gender and Korean Nationalism*. New York and London: Routledge.

Durkheim, E (1952/1897) *Suicide: A Study In Sociology*. London: Routledge & Kegan Paul. Trans. and ed. J.A Spaulding and and G.Simpson.

Emirbayer, M. and Mische, A. (1998) 'What is Agency?' *American Journal of Sociology*, 103, 4, pp.962-1023.

Featherstone, M. (1988) 'In Pursuit of the Postmodern: An Introduction', *Theory, Culture and Society*, 5 (2-3), pp.195-216.

Featherstone, M. (1991) *Consumer Culture and Postmodernism*, London:Sage.

Genette, G. (1979) *Narrative Discourse*. Ithaca, NY: Cornell University Press.

Hall, S. (1990) 'Cultural Identity and Diaspora' in J. Rutherford (ed.) *Identity: Community, Culture and Difference*. London: Lawrence&Wishart.

Hall, S. (1992) 'The Question of Cultural Identity' in S. Hall, D. Held, and T. McGrew, *Modernity and Its Future*. Cambridge: Open University Press, pp 273-325

Higson, A. (1996) 'Space, Place, Spectacle: Landscape and Townscape in the "Kitchen Sink" Film', in A. Higson (ed.) *Dissolving Views: Key Writings on British Cinema.* Cassell: London, pp.133-56.

Jameson, F. (1984a) 'Postmodernism: or the Cultural Logic of Late Capitalism', *New Left Review*, 146, pp.53-92.

Jameson, F. (1984b) 'Postmodernism and the Consumer Society' in H. Foster (ed.) *Postmodern Culture*. London: Pluto Press.

Jameson, F. (1991) *Postmodernism, or, Cultural Logic of Late Capitalism*. Durham, NC, and London: Duke University Press

Kim, S. (2006a) 'The Renaissance of Korean National Cinema as a Terrain of Negotiation and Contention between the Local and the Global: Analysing Two Korean Blockbusters, *Shiri* (1999) and *JSA* (2000)', *The Essex Graduate Journal of Sociology*, vol.6, pp.75-88

Kim, S (2006b) *Globalisation, Film and Authenticity: The Renaissance of Korean National Cinema.* PhD thesis, Department of Sociology, University of Essex, UK.

Krish, 1963, 'The New Realism and British Films', *Society of Film and Television Arts Journal*, Spring.

Kvale, S.1996, 'Themes of Postmodernity', in W. T. Anderson (ed.) *The Fontana Postmodernism Reader*. London: Fontana Press, pp.18-33.

Lee, H. (2000) *Contemporary Korean Cinema: Identity, Culture, Politics*. Manchester: Manchester University Press.

Lyotard, J.F. (1984) *The Postmodern Condition: A Report Knowledge*. Tr. G. Bennington and B. Massumi, Minneapolis: University of Minnesota Press.

McCrone, D. (1998) *The Sociology of Nationalism: Tomorrow's Ancestors*. London: Routledge.

MacIntyre, Alasdair (1985) *After Virtue: A Study in Moral Theory*. London: Duckworth.

Merton, R. (1968) Social *Theory and Social Structure*, rev. and enl.edn. New York.: Free Press.

Mills, C.W. (1959) *The Sociological Imagination*. Oxford: Oxford University Press.

Mouzelis, N. (1991) *Back to Sociological Theory: The Construction of Social Orders*. London: Macmillan.

Mouzelis, N. (1995) *Sociological Theory: What Went Wrong? Diagnoses and Remedies*. London: Routledge.

Naughton, B. (1967) *Spring and Port Wine*. London: Samuel French.

Plummer, K (1991) (ed.) *Symbolic Interactionism: 2 volumes*. Aldershot: Edward Elgar.

Powrie. P. (1997) *French Cinema in the 1990s: Continuity and Difference*. Oxford: Oxford University Press.

Rimmon-Kenan, S. (1983) *Narrative Fiction: Contemporary Poetics*. London: Routledge.

Rosenau, P. (1992) *Postmodernism and the Social Sciences*. Princeton, New Jersey: Princeton University Press.

Stones, R. (1996) *Sociological Reasoning: Towards A Past-Modern Sociology*, London: Macmillan.

Stones, R. (2002a) 'Social Theory, the Civic Imagination and Documentary Film: A Past-modern Critique of the 'Bloody Bosnia' Season's *the Roots of War' Sociology*, 36(2), pp 355-375.

Stones, R. (2002b) 'Social Theory, Documentary Film and Distant Others: Simplicity and Subversion in *The Good Woman of Bangkok*', *European Journal of Cultural Studies*,.5 (2), pp 217-237.

Stones, R. (2005) *Structuration Theory*. London: Palgrave Macmillan.

Stones, R. (2006) 'Rights, Social Theory and Political Philosophy: A Framework for Case Study Research', in L. Morris (ed.) *Rights: Sociological Perspectives*. London: Routledge, pp.133-51.

Turner, B.S. (ed.) (1990) *Theories of Modernity and Postmodernity*, London: Sage.

In: Korea: Economic, Political and Social Issues
Editors: P. H. Elwood, J. B. Albertus
ISBN: 978-1-60456-513-3

Chapter 7

SUBSTANCE USE AND DELINQUENCY AMONG KOREAN ADOLESCENTS

Hun-Soo Kim
Department of Psychiatry,University of Ulsan, College of Medicine,
Asan Medical Center, Seoul, South Korea
Hyun-Sil Kim
Department of Nursing, Daegu Haany University, Daegu, South Korea

ABSTRACT

In this review of the literature on substance use, juvenile delinquency and criminal behavior, three specific themes are addressed: 1) the prevalence of substance use among Korean adolescents; 2) the risk factors associated with substance use; and 3) the relationship between substance use and delinquency. Studies have shown that the prevalence of substance use/abuse is steadily increasing among Korean adolescents and elsewhere in the world, and the types of frequently used substance have diversified. Familial, intrapersonal, social, and cultural factors all appear to contribute to a given individual's risk for substance use/abuse, and the preponderance of evidence indicates that substance (i.e., alcohol) use could play a causal role for delinquent and violent behavior. However, the relationship between substance use and violence is interactional and multi-factorial, and differs depending on the type of drug.

INTRODUCTION

Interpersonal violence and substance use are two of the greatest public health risks facing adolescents today. In particular, substance use and abuse in adolescents, which has become one of the most prevalent and serious social problems in South Korea as well as in many western countries, is a serious concern because these substances can affect health, quality of life, and life outcomes both during adolescence and later in life. Furthermore, substance use also can reduce academic achievement and may be closely related with a variety of problem behaviors among adolescents.

Numerous studies have sought to estimate the prevalence of substance use, identify risk and protective factors related to adolescent substance use, and explored the relationship between adolescent substance use and violence [Kim & Kim, 1998a, b; Centers for Disease Control and Prevention(CDC), 1998, 2004; Johnston, O'Malley, & Bachman, 2001; Kim & Kim, 2002; Kim & Kim, 2004]. However, school-based assessments of the prevalence of substance use among adolescents can lead to underestimation of these issues; thus the nature, risk factors of substance use and the relationship between substance use and violence have not yet been fully elucidated.

The major challenge facing researchers is figuring out how to develop an accurate view of the nature and extent of adolescent substance use and abuse, and how to determine the relationship between substance use and violence. In this paper, we will use data from previous studies to address the following three basic topics: (1) the prevalence of substance use; (2) the risk factors associated with substance use; and (3) the relationship between substance use and delinquency/violence among Korean adolescents, a long with cross-cultural comparisons thereof.

The Prevalence of Substance Use Among Korean Adolescents: Cross-Cultural Comparison

Substance use/abuse tends to bring serious negative consequences to individuals and the community at large, making it an important social and health problem among Korean adolescents, who are being increasing exposed to alcohol and other drugs. Although empirical data are rather sparse [Korea Ministry of Culture and Sport, 1996], we previously found that during the period from 1985 through 1987, 27.2% of Korean adolescents in middle and high school admitted to smoking, 57.3% reported drinking alcohol, 31.0% used stimulants, 26.2% used volatile solvents, and 25.0% used sedatives [Kim, Yoo, Na, Lee, & Min, 1988]. These data reflect that during this period, Korean adolescents found it relatively easy to acquire alcohol, cigarettes and some of drugs. In particular, amphetamines (e.g. the drug sold commercially under the brand name 'Timing'), which students preparing for the university entrance examination often used to reduce sleeping time, could be easily obtained in drug stores at this time.

In a subsequent study on the prevalence of the drug use among a representative sample of 971 Korean delinquent adolescents [Kim & Kim, 1998a], we found that the drugs used most frequently by delinquent adolescents were inhalants/solvents (glue) (82.5%), benzol (5.0%), philopon (5.0%), marihuana (2.5%), romilar (2.5%) and butane gas (2.5%). Glue was the most popular drug used by Korean delinquent adolescents because it was very cheap and easy to obtain. In contrast, the most widely used drugs in the United States at the same time were cocaine/crack and amphetamines [Friedman, 1998], which have been strongly associated with violent acts.

Our more recent study [Kim & Kim, 2002] showed that Korean delinquent adolescents had a much higher rate of substance use than did non-delinquent adolescents (Table 1). Our results revealed that the prevalence of smoking among Korean adolescents was 48.6%

(delinquents vs. non-delinquents; 96.0% vs. 25.7%). The prevalence of alcohol drinking among Korean adolescents was 44.5% (delinquents vs. non-delinquents; 79.2% vs. 21.2%) (Table 2). The type of drugs used were as follows: inhalants/solvents (47.1%: delinquents vs. non-delinquents: 47.1% vs. 1.1%); cold medicines (antitussives) (23.3%: delinquents vs. non-delinquents: 30.6% vs. 18.9%); butane gas(14.2%: delinquents vs. non-delinquents: 35.4% vs. 1.2%); sedatives (sleeping pills) (10.3%: delinquents vs. non-delinquents: 21.2% vs. 3.8%); stimulants (amphetamines) (8.3%: delinquents vs. non-delinquents: 11.5% vs. 6.5%); hallucinogens (LSD) (6.6%: delinquents vs. non-delinquents: 17.0% vs. 0.5%); marihuana (5.3%: delinquents vs. non-delinquents: 13.1% vs. 0.6%); cocaine (1.9%: delinquents vs. non-delinquents: 5.0% vs. 0.1%); heroin or opium (1.9%: delinquents vs. non-delinquents: 5.0% vs. 0.2%); philopon (1.8%: delinquents vs. non-delinquents: 4.8% vs. 0.1%); and anxiolytics (Valium) (1.1%: delinquents vs. non-delinquents: 2.6% vs. 0.3%) in the order named (Table 2). Thus, the frequency of inhalants/solvents (glue) use decreased from 82.5% in 1998 to 47.1% in 2002 among Korean delinquent adolescents, whereas, the use of marihuana increased from 2.5% in 1998 to 13.1% in 2002 [Kim & Kim, 1998a; Kim & Kim, 2002]. This may be related to the economic development (increase of GDP) in Korea during this time, in that adolescents had more free cash available for drug purchases, with the rapidly increase of studying abroad among Korean adolescents and international exchange among youth. However, the prevalence of stimulant use decreased from 31.0% in 1988 [Kim et al., 1988] to 8.3% in 2002 [Kim & Kim, 2002], likely as a result of the recent government enactment of stronger drug-related laws of Korea Food and Drug Administration focused on Korean adolescents.

As shown in Table 3, these studies also revealed that delinquent adolescents used substance more frequently [Kim & Kim, 1998b], and used polydrugs more often than non-delinquents [Kim & Kim, 1998b; Kim & Kim, 2002]. Delinquent adolescents also tended to use more serious drugs (e.g. philopon, heroine and cocaine) than did non-delinquent adolescents [Kim & Kim, 2002].

Cigarettes and alcohol were most frequently used by Korean adolescents [Kim & Kim, 1998 a,b; Kim & Kim, 2002]. This is noteworthy because cigarettes have been identified as a "gate-way" drug to other substances such as alcohol, inhalants, and other drugs. Consistent with this, we found that adolescents who frequently used cigarettes were also more likely to frequently use alcohol and other drugs [Kim & Kim, 1998 a,b; Kim & Kim, 2002]. Thus, cigarette smoking poses not only an immediate threat to adolescent health, but also functions as a significant risk factor to the onset of other substance use.

Table 1. Substance Use in Delinquents vs. Non-delinquents ( )=%

Group	Total	Substance user	Substance non-user	χ^2	df	P
Delinquent	506	218 (43.1)	288 (56.9)			
Non-delinquents	1,184	179 (15.1)	1,005 (84.9)	656.1	2	0.001
Total	1,690	397 (23.5)	1,293 (76.5)			

Table 2. Incidence of Drug Use in Korean Adolescents

Group Name of Drug	Drug use Among adolescents	Drug use among delinquents	Drug use among non-delinquents
Cigarettes	48.6%	96.0%	25.7%
Alcohol	44.5%	79.2%	21.2%
Cold medication	23.3%	30.6%	18.9%
Inhalants/Solvents	18.8%	47.1%	1.1%
Butane gas	14.2%	35.4%	1.2%
Sedative (Sleeping pills)	10.3%	21.2%	3.8%
Stimulants (Amphetamine)	8.3%	11.5%	6.5%
Hallucinogens (LSD)	6.6%	17.0%	0.5%
Marihuana	5.3%	13.1%	0.6%
Cocaine	1.9%	5.0%	0.1%
Heroine or Opium	1.9%	5.0%	0.2%
Philopone	1.8%	4.8%	0.1%
Anxiolytics (Valium)	1.1%	2.6%	0.3%

Our studies exploring the motives for substance use/abuse among Korean adolescents [Min, Kim, Lee, Suk, & Shin, 1990; Kim & Kim, 1998b; Kim & Kim 2002] showed that the most prevalent motives for cigarette smoking were curiosity (41.7%), maintaining friendships (39.3%), relieving tension (15.5%), recreation or diversion (9.4%) and others(0.1%) [Min et al., 1990], while our later study showed that the most prevalent motives for the use of substances (including smoking) were curiosity (53.8%), maintaining friendships (12.3%), relieving tension (11.4%), feeling powerful (8.5%), improving sexual relationships (4.7%), feeling transcendence (3.4%), aesthetics (1.7%) and religious fascination (1.7 %) [Kim & Kim, 1998b] (Table 4). Thus, curiosity was consistently the most prevalent motive for substance use among Korean adolescents, but their motives for substance use became much more diversified over time.

As mentioned above, estimated substance use among Korean adolescents was found to differ in delinquents versus non-delinquents [Kim & Kim, 2002]. Unfortunately, 81.9% of Korean delinquent adolescents (27.1% of the total delinquent adolescents) reported having tolerance, 90.1% (13.8% of the total delinquent adolescents) met the diagnostic criteria for alcoholism, using CAGE questionnaire [Ewing, 1984] (Table 5) [Kim & Kim, 2002], and 78.5% (14.0% of the total delinquent adolescents) showed some kinds of health problems related to their smoking, alcohol and drug use, including anorexia, sleep disturbances and weight loss [Kim & Kim, 2002]. These findings suggested that adolescents who use

Table 3. Chi-squared Comparison of Drug Use Frequency in Delinquents vs. Students ( )=%

Variables	Total	Delinquent	Student	X^2	df	p
Marihuana						
Never	1,702	584(34.3)	1,118(65.7)			
1~2times for the last year	67	60(89.6)	7(10.4)	131.6	2	0.001
Daily use for > 2wks	28	28(100.0)	0(0.0)			
Total	1,797	672	1,125			
Hallucinogens (LSD)						
Never	1,701	562(33.0)	1,139(67.0)			
1~2times for the last year	85	81(95.3)	4(4.9)	186.0	2	0.001
Daily use for > 2wks	36	34(94.4)	2(5.6)			
Total	1,822	677	1,145			
Stimulants (Amphetamine)						
Never	1,660	590(35.5)	1,070(64.5)			
1~2times for the last year	131	60(45.8)	71(54.2)	25.7	2	0.001
Daily use for > 2wks	20	17(85.0)	3(15.0)			
Total	1,811	667	1,144			
Philopon						
Never	1,772	630(35.6)	1,142(64.4)			
1~2times for the last year	21	20(95.2)	1(4.8)	52.7	2	0.001
Daily use for > 2wks	12	12(100.0)	0(0.0)			
Total	1,805	662	1,143			
Sedatives (Sleeping pills)						
Never	1,634	533(32.6)	1,101(67.4)			
1~2times for the last year	164	123(75.0)	41(25.0)	139.5	2	0.001
Daily use for > 2wks	23	20(87.0)	3(13.0)			
Total	1,821	676	1,145			
Anxiolytics(Valium)						
Never	1,787	645(36.1)	1,142(63.9)			
1~2times for the last year	8	5(62.5)	3(37.5)	23.3	2	0.001
Daily use for > 2wks	12	12(100.0)	0(0.0)			
Total	1,807	662	1,145			
Cocaine						
Never	1,775	632(35.6)	1,143(64.4)			
1~2times for the last year	22	21(95.5)	1(4.5)	54.3	2	0.001
Daily use for > 2wks	12	12(100.0)	0(0.0)			
Total	1,809	665	1,144			

Table 3. (Continued)

Variables	Total	Delinquent	Student	x^2	df	p
Heroin or Opium						
Never	1,772	630(35.6)	1,142(64.4)			
1~2times for the last year	21	21(100.0)	0(0.0)	51.7	2	0.001
Daily use for > 2wks	14	12(85.7)	2(14.3)			
Total	1,807	663	1,144			
Antitussives						
Never	1,399	471(33.7)	928(66.3)			
1~2times for the last year	353	149(42.2)	204(57.8)	75.3	2	0.001
Daily use for > 2wks	71	59(83.1)	12(16.9)			
Total	1,823	679	1,144			
Inhalants/Solvents						
Never	1,512	380(25.1)	1,132(74.9)			
1~2times for the last year	218	206(94.5)	12(5.5)	613.3	1	0.001
Daily use for > 2wks	132	132(100.0)	0(0.0)			
Total	1,862	718	1,144			
Butane gas						
Never	1,584	454(28.7)	1,130(71.3)			
1~2times for the last year	197	183(92.9)	14(7.1)	418.0	1	0.001
Daily use for > 2wks	66	66(100.0)	0(0.0)			
Total	1,847	703	1,144			

Table 4. Motives for substance abuse among Korean adolescents ( )=%

Curiosity	127(53.8)
Friendship	29(12.3)
Peace	27(11.4)
Power	20(8.5)
Sexual relation	11(4.7)
Transcendence	8(3.4)
Sex Companion-seeking	6(2.5)
Aesthetics	4(1.7)
Religious fascination	4(1.7)
Total	236

cigarettes, alcohol and other substances are urgently in need of health care, and should be screened by professional health personnel. Delinquent adolescents most frequently reported their alcohol use as "not currently using" and "more than 1 time/week", whereas the most common response of non-delinquent adolescents was "never use." The highest motive for alcohol and drug use among Korean delinquent adolescents was peer pressure (91.9%), followed by curiosity (89.3%), whereas that in non-delinquent adolescents was relieving physical strain (92.7%) (Table 5) [Kim & Kim, 2002]. In terms of cigarette smoking, delinquent adolescents most frequently reported smoking "more than one pack/day" or "10-20 cigarettes/day", whereas the most common responses in non-delinquent adolescents were "sometimes" and "never smoke"(Table 6). Korean delinquent adolescents reported that they smoked to relieve tension, maintain social relationships and as a diversion; these adolescents reported having a strong need for nicotine, suggesting dependence, but they rarely attempted to quit smoking. In contrast, almost all of the non-delinquent adolescents (96.8%) in this sample were non-smokers (Table 6).

Table 5. Chi-squared Comparison of Alcohol and Drug Use Frequency in Delinquents vs. Students ( )=%

Variables	Total	Delinquent	Student	X^2	df	P
Alcoholism diagnosis						
not alcoholic	1081	163 (15.1)	918 (84.9)			
moderate	756	461 (61.0)	295 (39.0)	656.1	2	0.001
alcoholic	111	100 (90.1)	11 (9.9)			
Total	1,948	724	1,224			
Tolerance						
Yes	226	185 (81.9)	41 (18.1)	85.5	1	0.001
No	1,035	497 (48.0)	538 (52.0)			
Total	1,261	682	579			
Health problems						
Yes	121	95 (78.5)	26 (21.5)	31.5	1	0.001
No	1,132	586 (51.8)	546 (48.2)			
Total	1,253	681	572			
Frequency						
>1 time/week	222	199 (89.6)	23 (10.4)			
1 time every 2-3weeks	58	47 (81.0)	11 (19.0)			
1 time every 6mths	153	76 (49.7)	77 (50.3)	549.3	4	0.001
Not currently using	86	81 (94.2)	5 (5.8)			
Never used	1,205	264 (21.9)	941 (78.1)			
Total	1,724	667	1,057			
Drug taking motivation						
Curiosity	289	258 (89.3)	31 (10.7)			
Power seeking	35	21 (60.0)	14 (40.0)			
Peace seeking	44	35 (80.0)	9 (20.0)			
Peer pressure	74	68 (91.9)	6 (8.1)	120.2	7	0.001
Sexual pleasure	18	16 (88.9)	2 (11.1)			
Meditation	21	15 (71.4)	6 (28.6)			
Physical strain	24	2 (8.3)	22 (92.7)			
Depression	26	16 (61.5)	10 (38.5)			
Total	531	431	100			

Table 6. Chi-square Test Comparison of Smoking Variables by Group (Delinquent/Student) ( )=%

Variables	Total	Delinquent	Student	X^2	df	p
Daily smoking						
> 1 pack/day	265	253 (95.5)	12 (4.5)			
10-20 cigs/day	450	385 (85.6)	65 (14.4)	2356.1	3	0.001
Sometimes	176	83 (47.2)	93 (52.8)			
Never smoke	944	30 (3.2)	914 (96.8)			
Total	1,835	751	1084			
Motives for smoking						
- Relieving tension						
Not at all	349	133 (38.1)	216 (61.9)			
A little	313	267 (85.3)	46 (14.7)			
Mostly	260	224 (86.2)	36 (13.8)	246.2	3	0.001
Exclusively	113	96 (85.0)	17 (15.0)			
Total	1,035	720	315			
- Social relationships						
Not at all	499	275 (55.1)	224 (44.9)			
A little	283	224 (79.1)	59 (20.9)	91.6	3	0.001
Mostly	184	160 (87.0)	24 (13.0)			
Exclusively	58	48 (82.8)	10 (17.2)			
Total	1,024	707	317			
- For diversion						
Not at all	472	236 (50.0)	236 (50.0)			
A little	263	214 (81.4)	49 (18.6)	152.2	3	0.001
Mostly	195	173 (88.7)	22 (11.3)			
Exclusively	94	84 (89.4)	10 (10.6)			
Total	1,024	707	317			
- Nicotine need						
Not at all	749	454 (60.6)	295 (39.4)			
A little	144	133 (92.4)	11 (7.6)	98.2	3	0.001
Mostly	97	89 (91.8)	8 (8.3)			
Exclusively	35	34 (97.1)	1 (2.9)			
Total	1,025	710	315			
Attempted to quit						
Not at all	67	64 (95.5)	3 (4.5)			
1-3 times in the past year	130	108 (83.1)	22 (16.9)			
4-6 times in the past year	223	185 (83.0)	38 (17.0)	16.6	4	0.002
7-9 times in the past year	184	147 (79.9)	37 (20.1)			
>10 times in the past year	218	162 (74.3)	56 (25.7)			
Total	822	666	156			

Similar to the situation in Korea, adolescent drug and alcohol use is widespread within the United States. In a nationwide survey in 1998, 79.1% of school-aged adolescents had reportedly tried alcohol, 70.2% had smoked cigarettes and 47.1% had tried marihuana, while a smaller percent (18%) reported having experimented with more illicit substances, such as cocaine, steroids and LSD [Centers for Disease Control and Prevention (CDC), 1998]. In 2000, Johnston, O'Malley, and Bachman [2001] estimated that more than half (57%) of all seniors in the U. S. had used illicit drugs at least once, and over 80% of all seniors had used alcohol or cigarettes during their high school years. Despite the well-known health risks of smoking, American adolescents continue to smoke at alarming rates. Over the past decade, the smoking rate in adolescents reached 36.4% (comparable to that found in Korean adolescents), and cigarette-related mortality was the most prevalent cause of premature death in the United States [Center for Disease Control and Prevention, 2004]. In Australia, data from the 2004 National Drug Strategy household survey revealed that about 3.4% of Australian adolescents consumed alcohol at a high-risk level which was defined as having 43 or more standard drinks per week [Australian Institute of Health and Welfare, 2005]. This is slightly higher than the proportion of the entire population over 14 years of age classified as high risk drinkers (2.8%) [Doran, Gascoigne, Shakeshaft, & Petrie, 2006].

In Iran, Ahmadi and Hasani [2003] reported that 30.23% of Iranian high school students reported substance use at least once during their lives; these substances included cigarettes (25.4%), alcohol (9.6%), opium (3.5%), hashish (2.8%), marihuana (1%), heroine (2%), LSD (0.5%), cocaine (1%) and morphine (0.8%). Only 13.86% of the students were currently using at the time of the survey, with the used substances including cigarettes (8.3%), heroine (1%), morphine (0.3%), alcohol (4.3%), opium (0.8%), LSD (0.3%), cocaine (0.5%), hashish (0.8%) and marihuana (0.8%). Similarly, this study showed that, among Iranian high school students, cigarettes and alcohol were the most commonly used substances, and it has been reported that substance use was significantly higher among males than females [Ahmadi & Hasani, 2003]. In Turkey, the substances used most commonly by Turkish youths included cannabis (10.8%), cocaine (10.8%), glue (6.6%) and heroin (4.3%) [Ozer, 1991]. Notably, the alcohol consumption rate was 10%, which was low compared to that in western countries [Aytaclar, Erkiran, Kirisci, & Tarter, 2003], and the rate of lifetime exposure to drugs in Turkey was generally lower than that in the United States [Johnston, O'Malley, & Bachman, 2000]. The prevalence of alcohol and cigarette use among Iranian and Turkish youths was significantly lower than among Korean adolescents. Thus, these findings seem to indicate that drug use levels and the types of commonly used drug may vary greatly among countries. Aso, we may think that these findings could differ depending on the research population and methods for the data collection.

Across all nations, the use of cigarettes, alcohol and illicit drugs is considered to be primarily a male problem [Kim & Kim, 2002; Thom, 2003]. Many studies of drug use in the general population have reinforced this assumption. Among European Union Member States, for example, males who had tried drugs outnumbered females who have tried drugs in all countries and all age groups [European Monitoring Centre for Drugs and Drug Addiction, 2002]. In the United States, males were found to be more likely than females to use, abuse and be dependent on alcohol or illicit drugs [Office of Applied Studies, 2004]. Other recent findings, however, suggest that the extent of gender differences among drug users may be less clear than previously thought. In a national survey in the United States, the same percentage (9 %) of females and males aged 12 to 17 were found to be dependent on or abusing alcohol or an illicit drug [Office of Applied Studies, 2004], while 12th grade girls and boys in the United States were found to have roughly the same rates of cigarette smoking [Johnston, O'Malley, Bachman, & Schulenberg, 2004]. Similarly, in Britain, 44% of girls and 42% of boys age 14-15 reported having at least one drink per week [Join Together Online, 2004]. A similar pattern was reported for binge drinking, with 29% of girls and 26% of boys age 15-16 reportedly engaging in this behavior [Global Internet News, 2004]. In Israel in 2006, the reported prevalence of cigarette use was comparable in boys and girls (77% and 69%, respectively) but, boys were significantly more inclined to drink alcoholic substances, such as beer (61% boys, 45% girls), wine (48% boys, 36% girls), and liquor (43% boys, 31% girls). A similar pattern of use was found for marihuana (8% boys, 3% girls) and hashish (7% boys, 2% girls). Analysis of drug-related behavior also showed that boys were more likely to binge drink during the last days (32% boys, 23% girls) [Isralowitz & Rawson, 2006].

Clearly, these studies indicate that alcohol and cigarettes are the most popular drugs among students by far, regardless of nationality or gender. However, drug use levels and the types of commonly used drug may vary greatly among countries. Therefore, some care should be taken when directly comparing these results, since the target population, definition of substance use and research methodologies differed amongst these studies.

Risk Factors Associated wth Substance Use During Adolescence

Numerous studies have sought to identify familial, intrapersonal, social, and cultural risk factors associated with alcohol, tobacco, and illicit drug use among adolescents [Grunbaum, Tortolero, Weller, & Gingiss, 2000; Chen, Sheth, Elliott, & Yeager, 2004]. The identified familial factors associated with substance use include having a substance using parent and dysfunctional family dynamics such as poor family adaptability, family cohesion, parent-child relationships and positive parental attitude toward drug use. Studies have shown that substance abusers report having substance-using parent (particularly fathers) significantly more often than the non-abusing control subjects [Wu & Kandel, 1995]. This cross-generational influence was usually understood to occur as a social learning process. In particular, numerous studies have demonstrated that children of parents with alcohol problems are at increased risk for early alcohol use and alcohol-related problems in adolescence, including automobile accidents, homicide and suicide [Loukas, Piejak, Bingham, Fitzgerald, & Zucker, 2001b]. Other reports have concluded that parental socialization practices and parenting are related to both delinquency and drug use [Wu & Kandel, 1995]. Delinquent participation and the use of drugs (including cigarettes) by children and adolescents appear to be related to lack of affection between parent and child, conflict, poor child identification with the parent, lack of supervision of the child's activities, explosive discipline, and inconsistent parenting.

From a study of family adaptability and cohesion, Friedman, Utada, Glickman, and Morrissey [1987] reported that families of adolescent drug abusers tended to describe themselves as having a family environment characterized by rigid parent-child relationships and disengaged family cohesion. In contrast to the notion found in mailstream literature [Kelly, Halford, & Young, 2001], some study suggested that family cohesion was not associated with alcohol use or family aggression [Kelly & Kowalyszyn, 2003]. In addition, the development of illicit drug use/abuse was found to be associated with childhood physical abuse by the parent [Dembo, Dertke, Border, Washburn, & Schmeidler, 1998]. For instance, alcohol and drug-abusing women were found to be more likely than other women to report having been both physically and emotionally abused by parents during childhood [Covington, 1983]. Compared to those without alcohol problems, individuals with alcohol problems tended to report more family conflict, and women with alcohol problems tended to report higher family independence.

In the specific context of smoking, a number of factors have appeared as being associated with adolescent smoking, including age [Breslau & Peterson, 1996], ethnicity [Gfellner, 1994], family structure [Covey & Tam, 1990], parental socioeconomic status and personal income [Stanton, Oei, & Silva., 1994], parental and peer smoking and attitudes [Pederson, Koval, McGrady, & Tyas, 1998], attachment to family and friends [Piko, 2000], school factors [Allison, 1992], lifestyle [Hawkins, 1992], stress [Byrne, Byrne, & Reinhart, 1995; Kim & Kim, 2002], self-esteem, and personality characteristics [Shedler & Block, 1990; Kim & Kim, 2002]. Other factors contributing to adolescent smoking, particularly in girls, included parents' disliking attitude to smoking, and father's level of education. Interestingly, several studies reported that parental level of education did not have a significant effect on adolescent smoking [e.g. Gfellner, 1994], whereas Chen, Pederson, and Lefcoe [1992] found that the paternal education level had a significant effect on adolescent smoking while the maternal education level did not. The latter result likely reflects the fact that paternal education level is traditionally a stronger determinant of household socioeconomic status (SES) than maternal education, suggesting the existence of a relationship between SES and problem behaviors like substance use/abuse among adolescents. Consistent with this association, a father's attitude toward smoking in general, and toward their own children's smoking in particular, has been related to adolescent smoking [Pederson et al., 1998].

Although the above familial dynamics act as risk factors for adolescent substance use, a number of parent and family factors have also been found to protect against adolescent substance use, including parental monitoring and family cohesion [Roth & Brooks-Gunn, 2000]. Theoretically, both parental monitoring and family competence are key protective factors because they meet an adolescent's need for structure, security and connection [Roth & Brooks-Gunn, 2000]. Adolescents who live in families where parents monitor their actions and provide a sense of family connectedness, may be less likely to use substances. Because these adolescents know that their behavior is limited by parentally-monitored boundaries, they may find fewer opportunities to use drugs and may have a lower likelihood of being exposed to violence. Furthermore, parental monitoring gives an adolescent a sense of parental concern and family connection, and this may help the individual manage the negative effects produced by exposure to violence [Kliewer, Murrelle, Prom, Ramirez, Obando, Sandi, & Karenkeris, 2006].

In terms of familial problems among Korean substance abuser, our study [Kim & Kim, 1998b] examining correlates of juvenile substance abuse among 1,690 Korean adolescents (1,184 student adolescents and 506 delinquent adolescents) showed that compared to family members of non-substance abusers, the family members of substance users had significantly higher levels of mental health problems, such as chronic disease, alcoholism, depression, suicide attempts and suicide as well as legal problems such as criminal acts (Table 7). This strongly suggests that the families of substance users tended to have multiple familial problems, potentially indicating that these dysfunctional families are unable to provide protective measures against adolescent substance use, such as parental monitoring and discipline.

Table 7. Problems among the Family Members of Korean Substance Abuser ( )=%

Variables	Total	Non-user	Abuser	x^2	df	p
Depression						
No	1,640	1,269 (76.9)	378 (23.1)	6.3	1	0.012
Yes	56	35 (62.5)	21(37.5)			
Suicide (or attempt)						
No	1,620	1,249 (77.1)	371 (22.9)	7.8	1	0.005
Yes	76	48 (63.2)	28 (36.8)			
Criminal behavior						
No	1,548	1,221 (78.9)	327 (21.1)	56.9	1	0.000
Yes	148	76 (51.4)	72 (48.6)			
Chronic illness						
No	1,510	1,169 (77.4)	341 (22.6)	6.8	1	0.009
Yes	186	128 (68.8)	58 (31.2)			
Alcoholism						
No	1,617	1,254 (77.6)	363 (22.4)	22.4	1	0.000
Yes	79	43 (54.4)	36 (45.6)			

Another group of potential risk factors for adolescents substance use includes personality and mental problems such as anxiety, depression, psychosomatic symptoms, antisocial personality, and the others. Because personality traits are enduring dispositions [McCrae & Costa, 2003], it is important to establish whether certain personalities increase the risk for substance use among adolescents. A given individual is characterized by a unique combination of personality traits that largely determines who he/she is and how he/she behaves [Robins, John, Caspi, Mofitt, & Stouthamer-Loeber, 1996], and these traits may have important consequences for a broad range of behavioral outcomes [Robins et al., 1996], including smoking and drug use [Terraciano & Costa, 2004].

In particular, smoking is addictive, harmful and may lead to fatal health problems [de Vries, Engels, Kremers, Wetzels, & Mudde, 2003]; therefore, there is need to understand which factors contribute to smoking onset. Because experimentation with cigarette smoking often starts during adolescence, some studies have explored whether personality plays a role in smoking initiation among adolescents, in the hopes of eventually designing more effective intervention and prevention programs, formulating specific public policies, and perhaps developing more personalized treatments to discourage or prevent adolescent smoking [Wijatkowski, Forgays, Wrzesniewski, & Gorski, 1990]. Among the personality traits examined to date, cross-sectional findings have indicated that extraversion, agreeableness, conscientiousness and emotional stability are related to onset of adolescent smoking [Harakeh, Scholte, de Vries, & Engels, 2006]. Adolescents scoring high on extraversion were more likely to smoke, whereas individuals scoring high on agreeableness, conscientiousness, and emotional stability tended to show less involvement in smoking. In addition, curiosity and susceptibility to smoking were independently associated with increased risk of future smoking in all individuals who reported never having smoked [Pierce, Distefan, Kaplan, & Gilpin, 2005]. Thus, curiosity may be a precursor to smoking, and future research on smoking initiation should examine curiosity and its influencing factors. Another personality trait, sensation seeking, has been linked adolescent alcohol use [Kim & Kim, 2002].

Sensation seeking is characterized by the tendency to seek out varied and novel sensations and experiences. These experiences may include participation in risky physical activities (e.g. mountain climbing, bungcc jumping, skydiving, ctc), an attraction to novel political and philosophical ideologies, or participation in activities that are potentially addictive such as gambling and substance use [Hittner & Swickert, 2006]. Sensation seeking is thought to be a normally distributed personality characteristic that is influenced by both biological and environmental factors [Zuckerman, 1994]. Although numerous articles and book chapters have been written on the cause, correlates and consequences of sensation seeking, few topics have received as much attention as the association between sensation seeking and alcohol use [Zukerman & Kuhlman, 2000]. Higher levels of sensation seeking have generally been shown to correlate with greater quantity and frequency of alcohol consumption [Zuckerman, 1994].

Moreover, empirical research in adults entering alcohol abuse treatment found a negative relationship between sensation seeking and both age at first use of alcohol and age of onset of alcohol abuse [Ball, Carroll, & Rounsaville, 1994], suggesting that high sensation seekers use and abuse alcohol at an earlier age than their lower-scoring counterparts. Relative to other measures of personality, sensation seeking has been shown to be a particularly strong predictor of initial substance use and abuse in adolescents across a variety of drug use categories [Andrucci, Archer, Pancoast, & Gordon, 1989].

Grinspoon [1989] noted that among substance abusers, “there seem to be two partially overlapping groups: people who are anxious or depressed, and people who are impulsive, rebellious and antisocial.” Studies of substance abusers applying for treatment have shown high rates of dual diagnosis, i.e. substance use plus a psychiatric disorder such as antisocial personality [Herz, Volicer, D’Angelo, & Gadish, 1990]. Indeed, studies have shown that 25% to 50% of individuals entering treatment for substance abuse have antisocial disorders [Herz, Volicer, D’Angelo, & Gadish, 1990]. Consistent with this, Hesselbrock, Meyer, and Keener [1985] found that of women hospitalized for alcohol abuse or dependence, 52% had concomitant major depression and 44% had antisocial personality disorders.

These findings are consistent with reports that psychological problems, emotional discomfort and psychiatric symptoms often precede drug use [Huba, Newcomb, & Bentler, 1986]. Pandina [1990] studied a representative sample of New Jersey (U.S.) adolescents and concluded that negative affectivity, which could result from any number of biological, psychological, and socio-environmental conditions, was common in intensive drug use. Consistent with this, Labouvie [1986] reported that illicit drug use was typically initiated for the purpose of relieving emotional distress, and Newcomb and Bentler [1989] found that drug use during adolescence was related to increased psychotic thinking in young adulthood and that hard drug use during adolescence was associated with increased suicide ideation in young adulthood. However, it is not entirely clear whether drug use/abuse is largely the cause or the effect of psychiatric problems.

Undoubtedly, negative affect, alcohol use and smoking have been positively associated with one another [Wills, Sandy, & Yeager, 2002]. Smoking is associated with depression, but the direction of this relationship remains unclear. Some researchers have proposed that the stimulant properties of nicotine are particularly attractive for self-medication by depressed individuals [Fergusson, Goodwin, & Horwood, 2003], but other studies have suggests that smoking may actually precede depression in many individuals [Martini, Wagner, & Anthony, 2002]. Typically, individuals who are high in negative affect consume more substances in their efforts to reduce negative states or increase positive states [Cooper, Frone, Russell, & Mudar, 1995]. For example, adolescents who are regular smokers report higher levels of depression and anxiety than occasional smokers [Patton et al., 1996], and negative affect has been related to increases in smoking over time [Wills et al., 2002]. Furthermore, students reporting more depressive symptoms tended to be more likely to use marihuana and cocaine, although these results showed borderline significance [Grunbaum, Tortolero, Weller, & Gingiss, 2000]. In contrast, conscientious and self-disciplined individuals who were low in impulsivity tended to report less alcohol use and smoking, decreasing their likelihood of illicit substance use.

In accordance with the theory of attitude-behavior relationship [Ajzen & Madden, 1986], antismoking attitude (dominated by belief in the harmful effects and social influences of smoking) has been shown to strongly correlate with not smoking. This supports the idea that while generalized attitudes are not good predictors of subsequent behavior, behavioral intentions (a set of predispositions to actually perform a certain behavior) tend to be good predictors. Thus, while positive attitudes toward smoking and smokers tend to be related to an increased likelihood of smoking [Meier, 1991], particularly among girls [Charlton & Blair, 1989], negative attitudes based on knowledge about its harmful effects can be protect against smoking [Tuakli, Smith, & Heaton, 1990].

In terms of Korean adolescents, we recently reported [Kim & Kim, 2002] that although cigarette smoking, alcohol and substance use all had great influences on delinquency among Korean adolescents, maladaptive personality traits such as antisocial personality, depression, and complaints of psychosomatic symptoms had a strong influence on the process by which substance use leads to delinquency. Moreover, substance abusers tended to show significantly depressed, unstable or fluctuating moods, impulsiveness, and resistance against authority figures more often than substance non-abusers. In terms of risk factors, substance users reported to commit a higher rate of delinquent behavior than non-users (Table 8) [Kim & Kim, 2002]. In particular, male gender was significant predictor of all categories of substance use in Korea [Kim & Kim, 2002], as well as in western countries [Grunbaum, Tortolero, Weller, & Gingiss, 2000].

It has been reported that adolescent substance use, particularly smoking and drinking, are influenced by a variety of social factors [Piko, 2006] ranging from social norms and expectations to more direct peer invitations and pressure [Simons-Morton, Haynie, Crump, Eitel, & Saylor, 2001]. The peer context is perhaps the most salient predictor of adolescent substance use [Hussong, 2002; Piko, 2001a]; social pressure from peers is one of the key factors in the initiation of smoking [Li, Unger, Schuster, Rohrbach, Howard-Pitney, & Norman., 2003] and drinking [Wild, 2002]. The smoking of an adolescent's friend, particularly his or her best friend, is often the strongest predictor of that adolescence taking up smoking [de Vries, Engels, Kremers, Wetzels, & Mudde, 2003; Piko, 2001a]. Not surprisingly, the number of smoking friends (i.e. peer influence) was also found to be significantly related to the frequency of smoking [Tyas & Pederson, 1998]. As a consequence of these social influences, experimentation with smoking and drinking increases dramatically during adolescence [Gilvarry, 2000; Poikolainen, 2002]. In addition, the co-occurrence of smoking and drinking in adolescence is very common, due to the similarities in the related background variables, including social influences [Johnson, Boles, Vaughan, & Kleber, 2000], which may positively reinforce smoking and drinking [Read, Wood, Kahler, Maddock, & Palfai, 2003].

Table 8. Personality Characteristics of Substance Users vs. Non-users ( )=%

Variables	Total	Non-user	User	X^2	df	P
Impulsive behavior						
Never	937	748 (79.8)	189 (20.2)			
Rarely	349	246 (70.5)	103 (29.5)	41.7	3	0.000
Sometimes	160	95 (59.4)	65 (40.6)			
Frequently	63	39 (61.9)	24 (38.1)			
Fluctuation of mood						
Never	882	699 (79.2)	183 (20.8)			
Rarely	364	258 (70.9)	106 (29.1)	30.9	3	0.000
Sometimes	193	123 (63.7)	70 (36.3)			
Frequently	67	41(61.2)	26 (38.8)			
Depressed mood						
Never	532	433 (81.4)	99 (18.6)			
Rarely	378	291 (77.0)	87 (23.0)	36.3	3	0.000
Sometimes	437	312 (71.4)	125 (28.6)			
Frequently	169	101 (59.8)	68 (40.2)			
Resistance against authority						
Never	515	412 (80.0)	103 (20.0)			
Rarely	449	348 (77.5)	101 (22.5)	24.4	3	0.000
Sometimes	384	272 (70.8)	112 (29.2)			
Frequently	159	100 (62.9)	59 (37.1)			
Delinquent behavior						
Never	1,029	858 (83.4)	171 (16.6)			
Rarely	205	136 (66.4)	69 (33.6)	143.3	3	0.000
Sometimes	192	103 (53.6)	89 (46.4)			
Frequently	110	50 (45.5)	60 (54.5)			

Considerable research suggests that there is an association between affiliation with delinquent peers and adolescent substance use [Hawkins, Catalano, & Miller, 1992], and two mechanisms, selection and socialization, have been found to account for this association. The literature on peer selection and socialization has focused almost exclusively on externalizing behavior problems, and these studies have shown that children exhibiting high levels of externalizing behavior problems tended to select into peer groups that support and encourage delinquent behavior and substance use. Furthermore, these peer affiliations were found to increase the risk for externalizing behavior problems, including substance use socialization [Curran, Stice, & Chassin, 1997]. Consistent with this, a recent study reported that delinquent peer affiliations were associated with increases in externalizing behavior and early initiation of alcohol use [Fite, Colder, & O'Conner, 2006]. However, this study also provided evidence suggesting that internalizing behavior served as a protective factor for delinquent peer affiliations and for early initiation of alcohol use. Children high in internalizing symptoms may be fearful of potentially negative consequences of affiliating with delinquent peers as well as early substance use, reducing the likelihood of affiliating with delinquent peers and using alcohol [Fite, Colder, & O'Conner, 2006].

Cultural variables associated with substance use/abuse include church attendance, educational achievement, and educational aspirations [Grunbaum, Tortolero, Weller, & Gingiss, 2000]. Adolescents who attended church at least once per month were significantly less likely to use marihuana and cocaine compared to students who infrequently or never attended church. Furthermore, students who reported having bad grades were significantly more likely to use cocaine than those achieving higher marks, and students who saw high school as their highest educational goal were more than two times more likely to use cocaine than those with higher educational aspirations [Grunbaum, Tortolero, Weller & Gingiss, 2000].

Throughout this review, we have speculated on the associations among various risk factors for the use/abuse of alcohol, cigarettes, and illicit drugs. Although many factors have been found to contribute to substance use/abuse, the cause-and-effect relationships have not yet been clearly defined. Next, we will briefly review a number of theoretical frameworks used to examine the relationship between substance use/abuse and delinquency.

Relationships Between Substance Use and Delinquency

The relationship between substance use and/or abuse and human interpersonal violence is profound, costly, and undeniable [Hoaken & Stewart, 2003]. Any discussion of the relationship between drugs and "aggression" or "violence" should start by defining these terms. Aggression is defined as the "intent to harm or create a noxious condition for the target [Fagan, 1990]", whereas violence is defined as "behaviors by individuals that intentionally threaten, attempt or inflict physical harm on others [Reiss & Roth, 1994]". Violent behaviors are considered a subset of aggressive behaviors, the use or threat of physical harm is a necessary ingredient in the definition of violence, but not necessary for aggression [White, 1997].

The relationship between drugs and aggression is believed to hinge on at least four different causes, none of which are mutually exclusive per se [Pihl & Hoaken, 1997]; violence may be used to gain access to drugs or the resources to purchase drugs; violence may be used to resolve disputes within the drug culture, which is an illegal and thus inherently unregulated situation; violence and drug use may co-exist in an individual as the result of the same factors (e.g. high sensation seeking); and/or certain drugs can increase the likelihood of violence through their direct effects on the individual. Hoaken and Stewart [2003] divided the latter direct effects into three categories: direct pharmacological effects (intoxication), neurotoxic effects (damage caused by prolonged use), and withdrawal effects (symptoms caused by abstinence after prolonged use). Pharmacological effects may be further divided into four types [Hoaken & Stewart, 2003]. First, some drugs alter the psychomotor system to enhance excitation and reward. Psychomotor stimulants potentiate motor behaviors, including approach, sensation seeking and/or attack behaviors that would not ordinarily be manifested, thus potentiating human violence by amplifying risky behaviors. Second, some drugs alter the anxiety and/or threat system. Typically, individuals learn as children that heightened aggression is linked with increased likelihood of punishment. Thus, the cues that signal the need to become aggressive typically elicit anxiety, which in turn decreases the likelihood of aggression. Some drugs, however, dampen these internal inhibiting mechanisms, leading to increased probability of an aggressive response. Third, some drugs alter the pain system. This mechanism is idiosyncratic, in that the likelihood of aggression appears to be increased by drugs that both increase and decrease pain sensitivity; drugs that diminish pain sensitivity may diminish the normally punishing aspects of pain one may experience during a provocative interaction, whereas drugs that increase pain sensitivity may sensitize individuals to provocative stimuli increasing the likelihood of defensive aggression. Fourth and last, some drugs may alter certain higher order cognitive capacities that normally modulate the general motivational state. This kind of drugs may interfere with the cognitive capacities that underlie planning, the formulation of behavioral strategies, and the initiation and maintenance of goal-directed behavior in response to external and internal regulatory cues.

Weiner, Sussman, Sun, and Dent [2005] found correlations between drug use and both the perpetration of and victimization by violence, but the strict temporal sequences of these behaviors are not entirely clear. One model that may explain relationships among violence, victimization and drug use is Goldstein's [1985] tripartite conceptual framework, which offers three explanations for the link between drug use and violence and victimization: (1) psychopharmacological paradigm, where violence or victimization results from the excitability or irrationality that may follow drug use; (2) economic compulsion paradigm, wherein drug users perpetrate violent crimes (e.g. robbery) to obtain money to buy drugs; and (3) systemic paradigm, wherein violence and victimization result from the inherent dangers of participation in the illegal drug trade. However, despite the intuitive appeal of this theory, no empirical study has yet tested whether these theoretical domains mediate the violence-drug use and victimization-drug use relationships, and/or whether their influence varies according to the whether the utilized substances are illegal (e.g., marihuana, cocaine) or legal (e.g., alcohol, cigarettes) [Weiner, Sussman, Sun, & Dent, 2005].

Of Goldstein's three paradigms linking violence and drug use, only the psychopharmacological paradigm appears to explain the observed link between illegal drug use in adolescence to later violence and victimization [Weiner, Sussman, Sun, & Dent, 2005]. It is reasonable to suppose that illegal drug use could lead to violent behavior arising from direct drug effects or irritability from drug withdrawal, and that it could also conversely lead to victimization arising from decreased vigilance of the user [Goldstein, 1985].

A somewhat more recent paper [Kaplan & Damphouse, 1995] offered at five ways to explain the empirical relationship between drug use and crime; (1) drug use leads to criminal involvement; (2) criminal activity leads to drug use; (3) both the first and second interpretations are correct; (4) delinquency and drug use are two aspects of an individual's general disposition toward deviance; and (5) drug use and delinquency are independent forms of deviance that share common antecedents, resulting in a spurious relationship. Overall, the preponderance of the research evidence supports the notion that abuse of certain types of illicit drugs predisposes individuals to subsequent violent behavior [Friedman, 1998]. Kaplan [1995] examined the relationships among substance abuse, theft and violent behavior and concluded that substance abuse patterns cause violence and theft by reducing inhibitions that would normally (i.e. in the absence of drugs) restrain the individual from acting on his or her violent and acquisitive impulses, or by motivating the acquisition of money to buy drugs to support a habit. Conversely, involvement in theft causes drug use by leading drug users to interact with other teenagers who get into trouble.

Numerous correlational studies have supported the notion that individuals are more aggressive and violent while under the influence of alcohol and other drugs. In particular, statistics indicate that alcoholics are overrepresented among persons convicted of violent crimes, and alcohol consumption is often reported immediately prior to violent offenses in both clinical and non-clinical populations [Collins, 1993]. Research in adolescents has suggested that involvement in delinquency often occurs prior to or simultaneous with the first drink [Elliott, 1994]. In the sequence of delinquency and drug use, Elliott and colleagues [1989] found that minor delinquency almost always came first with no individual reporting initiating marihuana or polydrug use prior to minor delinquency. However, while this study suggested that the onset of minor delinquency led to the onset of drug use and not vice versa [Elliott et. al., 1989], a more recent analysis by the same group [Elliott, 1994] indicated that minor delinquency and alcohol use occurred simultaneously in a substantial majority of the study population.

While the above studies indicated that conduct disorders and delinquency typically precede the initiation into drug and alcohol use, other studies have shown that increases in property crime and acquisitive violence occur subsequent to regular use of hard drugs among adolescents [Zucker, 1991]. In addition, Elliott and colleagues [1989] found that while minor delinquency is more likely to influence the onset of alcohol/drug use than the reverse, serious drug use (repeated polydrug use) is more likely to influence serious, sustained delinquency than the reverse [Elliott et al., 1989]. This may suggest that alcohol/drug use may influence delinquency by reducing the probability of an individual terminating delinquency rather than by increasing the probability of the individual initiating delinquent behavior. Collins [1986] also stated that while problem drinking may not be related to the onset of a criminal career, problem drinking may intensify or prolong serious involvement in criminal behavior in young adulthood.

Our previous study on juvenile drug use and criminal patterns in a representative sample of 877 Korean delinquent adolescents [Kim & Kim, 1998a] revealed that 230 (26.2%) of surveyed adolescents committed criminal behaviors while intoxicated with alcohol, whereas 647 (73.8%) were not under the influence of alcohol when committing criminal behavior.

Delinquent adolescents under the influence of alcohol showed a higher rate of person-oriented crimes such as physical assault and aggressive crimes, whereas delinquents not underthe influence of alcohol tended to commit object-oriented, property crimes such as stealing, theft and burglary, and relatively minor crimes such as violation of traffic regulations (Table 9). Here, aggressive crimes included more serious offense, such as armed robbery, vandalism, or manslaughter and assault crimes involved physical fighting with kicking or punching, sexual assault (or forcible rape) or gang fighting. Furthermore, delinquents who were in a drunken state while committing criminal behaviors tended to use knives, stones, or fist-kicking as weapons, whereas delinquents who were not in a drunken state tended not to use weapons(Table9).

We further found that most of the alcohol-related crimes among adolescents were committed between midnight and 4 AM on weekend, in dark, cloudy, and/or stormy whether,whereas non-alcohol-related crimes tended to occur on weekday afternoons in nice whether.

Table 9. Characteristics of Juvenile Criminal Activity in Alcohol Users vs. Non-users ( )=%

Variable	Drinking	Non-drinking	Total	X^2	df	p
Type of crime						
Property crimes	39 (17.6)	243 (38.9)	282 (33.3)			
Aggressive crimes	89 (40.1)	156 (25.0)	245 (28.9)	73.68	3	.001***
Assault crimes	72 (32.4)	92 (14.7)	164 (19.4)			
Violation of criminal special law	22 (9.9)	134 (21.4)	156 (18.4)			
Tools used by the criminal						
Knives	44 (20.5)	87 (15.6)	131 (16.9)			
Stones	42 (19.5)	95 (17.0)	137 (17.7)	17.76	4	.001***
Fist-kicking	30 (14.0)	44 (7.9)	74 (9.6)			
Drugs	11 (5.1)	68 (12.1)	79 (10.2)			
No weapons	88 (40.9)	265 (47.4)	353 (45.6)			
Accompanying person						
No other person	45 (20.1)	157 (24.9)	202 (23.6))			
Family member	10 (4.5)	7 (1.1)	17 (2.0)	17.91	3	.001***
Friend	140 (62.5)	422 (66.9)	562 (65.7)			
Peer group	29 (13.0)	45 (7.1)	74 (8.7)			

*** : p< .001

Crimes committed by alcohol-users tended to occur in streets or recreation spots (e.g. clubs, sports arenas), whereas crimes among non-users tended to more often occur in the victim's house, another person's house, or in a restaurant [Kim & Kim, 1998a]. The victims assaulted by offenders in both drunken and non-drunken states were most often passers-by (65.4%), followed by the offender's friends (25.1%). Among Korean delinquent adolescents, the reasons given for committing crimes included "to get money for amusements"(30.4%), "incidentally"(23.8%), "curiosity or heroism" (18.9%), "to get money for living"(8.3%), "domestic trouble"(4.6%), "sexual conflict"(4.3%), "rage" (3.6%), and others (6.1%). Among these respondents, alcohol-related crimes tended to occur accidentally or impulsively without any intention or concrete planning, whereas non-alcohol- related crimes tended to be purposeful, directed to make money, or motivated by curiosity or a desire to live heroically [Kim & Kim, 1998a]. When we compared the severity of the injuries to victims, we found that the more serious injuries (e.g. cerebral hemorrhage, intestinal rupture and even death) were committed by adolescents who reported using drugs, whereas the milder injuries (e.g. facial laceration or rupture of tympanic membrane) tended to be associated with the non-drug-using adolescents. In general, we found that drug-related juvenile crimes were more violent, aggressive and serious than non-drug-related juvenile crimes in our Korean study population [Kim & Kim, 1998a].

In a more recent study [Kim & Kim, 2004], we found that the most powerful contributing factors for delinquent behavior among Korean adolescents were as follows; antisocial personality tendency, alcohol and drug abuse, smoking, gender, psychosomatic symptoms, and parent-child relationships in the order named.

Thus, while substance abuse was found to be a relatively powerful contributing factor for delinquent behavior among Korean adolescents, the family dynamic environment and the adolescent's own personality were also critical factors. In particular, we found that personality characteristics such as antisocial personality tendency, aggressive impulsiveness, depressive trends, sociability, complaints of psychosomatic symptoms and frustrated needs were very closely related to drug use and deviance. These findings suggest that in order to address the problems of alcohol, drug abuse and delinquent behavior among adolescents, prevention efforts should take into account not only family, personality, social and cultural factors but the likelihood for substance use and abuse that may relate to involvement in antisocial acts and delinquent behavior.

Interestingly, although male adolescents always showed higher rates of alcohol and drug abuse than female adolescents, substance use among female adolescents has escalating significantly in Korea over the past decade [Kim & Kim, 2005]. In more recent study [Kim & Kim, 2005], we found that the strongest contributing variables affecting male delinquent behavior were age, antisocial personality and the parent-child relationship in that order, whereas those for female adolescents were alcohol and drug use, feelings of isolation, antisocial personality and the parent-child relationship in that order. Thus, although Korean male adolescents had much higher rates of alcohol and drug use than female adolescents, alcohol and drug use were more powerful contributing factors in explaining delinquent behavior among female adolescents. This may suggest that the initiation of female adolescents into delinquent and violent behavior is more highly related to the use of alcohol, cigarette or marihuana with a deviant peer group.

CONCLUSION

Substance use and abuse among adolescents is a pervasive and costly social problem for South Korea as well as many other industrialized countries. Thus, it is important to understand the prevalence and risk factors of adolescent substance use and abuse, as well as relationship between adolescent substance use and violence. Various studies have shown that the prevalence of substance use/abuse is steadily increasing among adolescents in Korea and elsewhere in the world, and the types of frequently-used substance have diversified. Interestingly, although male adolescents have a higher overall rate of substance use/abuse, the impact of substance use/abuse on delinquent behavior appears to be greater on female adolescents than their male counterparts.

Studies have shown that familial factors (parent-child relationships, parental monitoring and family cohesion), intrapersonal factors (personality, mental problems, attitudes and motives), social factors (peer pressure, social norm, or socialization etc), and cultural factors (religion, educational achievement and beliefs) all appear to contribute to a given individual's risk for substance use/abuse.

In addition, the preponderance of evidence indicates that there is a relationship between drug and violence and/or aggression. In particular, Korean delinquent adolescents under the influence of alcohol had a higher rate of more violent and aggressive crimes than delinquent adolescents who were not under the influence of alcohol. However, the relationship between substance use and violence is interactional and multifactorial, and differs depending on the classes of drug. While some drugs undeniably lead to heightened aggression (i.e. alcohol), other drugs do not appear to elicit aggression (i.e. depressants). If one thing can be said unequivocally about the relationship between drugs and aggression, it is that we do not yet know enough about this topic.

In recent years, the more highly-developed countries have made increasing efforts to reduce the prevalence of alcohol and drug use. Some of these efforts have been moderately successful; for example, the frequency of smoking among Korean male adolescents has decreased over the past few years due to strong antismoking initiatives. However, no such reduction has been reported in female adolescents and children in their early teens. Moreover, alcohol consumption among Korean adolescents has continued to increase, and the types of drugs in common use have become much more diversified over the past decade. Overall, empirical studies have demonstrated that strict abstinence programs have only limited success in reducing alcohol consumption and alcohol-related consequences. Recently, researchers have sought to develop more flexible moderation-oriented approaches may be more easily disseminated to and accepted by a larger number of problem drinker. This may offer a more pragmatic and compassionate approach for the prevention and treatment of problem drinking, thus shifting the focus of substance abuse problem away from alcohol use.

In summary, the literature on substance use, violence and delinquency in adolescence serves best to encourage researchers to perform additional studies, and to broaden their research methodologies. In addition, it would seem useful to train health professionals to recognize various environmental and developmental contexts for substance use/abuse in adolescents and apply interventions as appropriate, in an effort to avoid serious health consequences, delinquency and violence in this vulnerable population.

REFERENCES

Ahmadi, J., & Hasani, M. (2003). Prevalence of substance use among Iranian high school students. *Addictive Behaviors, 28*, 375-379.

Ajzen, I., & Madden, T. J. (1986). Prediction of goal-oriented behavior: attitudes, intentions, and perceived behavioral control. Journal *of Experimental Social Psychology, 22*, 453-474.

Allison, K. R. (1992). Academic stream and tobacco, alcohol, and cannabis use among Ontario high school students. *International Journal of the Addictions, 27*, 561-570.

Andrucci, G. L., Archer, R. P., Pancoast, D. L., & Gordon, R. A. (1989). The relationship of MMPI and sensation seeking scales to adolescent drug use. *Journal of Personality Assessment, 53*, 253-266.

Australian Institute of Health and Welfare (2005). 2004 National drug strategy household survey. *Canberra: AIHW Drug Statistics Series No. 13.*

Aytaclar, S., Erkiran, M., Kirisci, L., & Tarter, R. (2003). Substance abuse and associated psychosocial risk factors among Turkish male adolescents. *Addictive Behaviors, 28*, 1419-1429.

Ball, S. A., Carroll, K. M., & Rounsaville, B. J. (1994). Sensation seeking. Substance abuse, and psychopathology in treatment seeking and community cocaine abusers. *Journal of Consulting and Clinical Psychology, 62,* 1053-1057.

Breslau, N., & Peterson, E. L. (1996). Smoking cessation in young adults: age at initiation of cigarette smoking and other suspected influences. *American Journal of Public Health, 86*, 214-220.

Byrne, D. G., Byrne, A. E., & Reinhart, M. I. (1995). Personality, stress and the decision to commence cigarette smoking in adolescence. *Journal of Psychosomatic Research, 39*, 53-62.

Centers for Disease Control and Prevention (CDC). (1998). Youth risk behavior surveillance-United States, 1997. *Morbidity and Mortality Surveillance Summary: 47*, 1-90

Centers for Disease Control and Prevention. (2004). Cigarette use among high school students-United States, 1991-2003. *Morbidity and Mortality Weekly Report, 53*, 499-502.

Charlton, A, & Blair, V. (1989). Predicting the onset of smoking in boys and girls. *Social Science and Medicine, 29*, 813-818.

Chen, Y., Pederson, L. L., & Lefcoe, N. M. (1992). Father's educational level, adult's smoking status, and children's smoking behavior in Shanghai. *Health Values, 16*, 51-56.

Chen, K., Sheth, A. J., Elliott, D. K., & Yeager, A. (2004). Prevalence and correlates of past-year substance use, abuse, and dependence in a suburban community sample of high-school students. *Addictive Behaviors, 29*, 413-423.

Collins, J. J. (1986). The relationship of problem drinking to individual offending sequences. In Blumstein A, Cohen J, Ruth J, et al.(eds.). *Criminal Careers and "Career Criminals*". Washington DC, National Academic Press, vol 2, pp. 89-120.

Collins, J. J. (1993). Drinking and violence: an individual offender focus. In S. E. Martin (Ed.), *Alcohol and interpersonal violence: fostering multidisciplinary perspectives* (pp. 221-236). Rockville, MD: US Department of Health and Human Services, Public Health Service, National Institutes of Health, National Institute on Alcohol Abuse and Alcoholism.

Cooper. M. L., Frone, M. R., Russell, M., & Mudar, P. (1995). Drinking to regulate positive and negative emotions: A motivational model of alcohol use. *Journal of Personality and Social Psychology*, 69, 990-1005.

Covey, L. S., & Tam, D. (1990). Depressive mood, the single-parent home, and adolescent cigarette smoking. *American Journal of Public Health*, 80, 1330-1333.

Covington, S. S. (1983). Sexual experience. dysfunction, and abuse: A descriptive study of alcoholic and nonalcoholic women. *Dissertation*, The Union for Experimenting Colleges and Universities, Cincinnati. OH.

Curran, P. J., Stice, E., & Chassin, L.(1997). The relation between adolescent alcohol use and peer alcohol use: A longitudinal random coefficients model. *Journal of Consulting and Clinical Psychology, 65*, 130-140.

Dembo, R., Dertke, M., Border, S. Washburn, M., & Schmeidler, J. (1998). The relationship between physical and sexual abuse and tobacco, alcohol, and illicit drug use among youths in a juvenile detention center. *International Journal of Addictions*, 23, 351-378.

de Vries, H., Engels, R. C. M. E., Kremers, S. P. J., Wetzels, J. J. L., & Mudde, A. N. (2003). Parents' and friends' smoking status as predictors of smoking onset: Findings from six European Countries. *Health Education Research, 18*, 627-636.

Doran, C. M., Gascoigne, M. B., Shakeshaft, A. P., & Petrie, D. (2006). The consumption of alcohol by Australian adolescents: A comparison of revenue and expenditure. *Addictive Behavior, 31*, 1919-1928.

Elliott, D.S. (1994) *Youth Violence: An overview*. Boulder CO. The Center for the Study and Prevention of Violence.

Elliott, D.S., Huizinga, D., and Menard, S. (1989). *Multiple Problem Youth: Delinquency, Substance Use and Mental Health Problems*. New York: Springer-Verlag.

European Monitoring Centre for Drugs and Drug Addiction (2002). 2002 *Annual report on the state of the drugs problem in the European Union and Norway* (Retrieved Jannuary 26, 2005 from). http://ar2002.emcdda.eu.int/en/page23-en.html

Ewing, J. A. (1984). Detecting alcoholism: the CAGE questionnaire. *JAMA, 252*, 1905-1907.

Fagan, J. (1990). *Intoxication and aggression*. In Tonry, M. & Wilson, J. Q., eds. Crime and Justice. Vol. 13. Chicago: Univ. of Chicago Press, pp.241-320.

Fergusson, D. M., Goodwin, R. D., & Horwood, L. J. (2003). Major depression and cigarette smoking: Results of a 21-year longitudinal study. *Psychological Medicine, 33*, 1357-1367.

Fite, P. J., Colder, C. R., & O'Conner, R. M. (2006). Childhood behavior problems and peer selection and socialization: risk for adolescent alcohol use. *Addictive Behaviors, 31*, 1454-1459.

Friedman, A. S., Utada, A. T., Glickman, N. W., & Morrissey, M. R. (1987). Psychopathology an antecedent to, and as a "consequence" of, substance use, in adolescence. *Journal of Drug Education, 17*, 233-244.

Friedman, A. S. (1998). Substance use/abuse as a predictor to illegal and violent behavior: a review of the relevant literature. *Aggression and Violent Behavior, 3(4)*, 339-355.

Gfellner, B. M. (1994). A matched-group comparison of drug use and problem behavior among Canadian, Indian and White adolescents. *Journal of Early Adolescence, 14*, 24-48.

Gilvarry, E. (2000). Substance abuse in young people. *Journal of Child Psychology and Psychiatry, 41*, 55-80.

Global Internet News (BBC News) (2004*). "Ladette" binge drinkers outnumber males*, Dec. 15 (Retrieved January 15, 2005 from), http://www.dehavilland.co.uk

Goldstein, P. J. (1985). The drugs/violence nexus: A tripartite conceptual framework. *Journal of Drug Issues, 15(4),* 493-506.

Grinspoon, L. (1989). Drug abuse and dependence-Part II. *Harvard Medical School Mental Health Letter, 6,5*. Hendrin, H (1980). Psychosocial theories of drug abuse: A psychodynamic approach. In D. J. Lettieri, M. Sayers, & H. W. Pearson (Eds), Theories on drug abuse (pp. 195-200). *National Institute on Drug Abuse Research Monograph #30, DHHS Pub. No.*, (ADM) 80-967. Washington, DC: U.S. Government Printing Office.

Grunbaum, J. A., Tortolero, S., Weller, N., & Gingiss, P. (2000). Cultural, social, and intrapersonal factors associated with substance use among alternative high school students. *Addictive Behaviors, 25(1)*, 145-151.

Hawkins, W. E. (1992). Problem behaviors and health-enhancing practices of adolescents: a multivariate analysis. *Health Values, 16*, 46-54.

Hawkins, J. D., Catalano, R. F., & Miller, J. Y. (1992). Risk and protective factors for alcohol and other drug problems in adolescence and early adulthood: Implications for substance abuse prevention. *Psychological Bulletin, 112(1)*, 64-105.

Harakeh, Z., Scholte, R. H. J., de Vries, H., & Engels, R. C. M. E. (2006). Association between personality and adolescent smoking. *Addictive Behaviors, 31*, 232-245.

Herz. L. R., Volicer, L., D'Angelo, N., & Gadish, D. (1990). Additional psychiatric illness by diagnostic interview schedule in male alcoholics. *Comprehensive Psychiatry, 30*, 72-79.

Hesselbrock, M. N., Meyer, R. E., & Keener, J. J. (1985). Psychopathology in hospitalized alcoholics. *Archives of General Psychiatry, 42*, 1050-1055.

Hittner, J. B., & Swickert, R. (2006). Sensation seeking and alcohol use: A meta-analysis review. *Addictive Behaviors, 31*, 1383-1401.

Hoaken, P. N. S., & Stewart, S. H. (2003). Drugs of abuse and the elicitation of human aggressive behavior. *Addictive Behaviors, 28*, 1533-1554.

Huba, G. J., Newcomb, M. D., & Bentler, P. M. (1986). Adverse drug experiences and drug use behaviors: A one-year longitudinal study of adolescents. *Journal of Pediatric Psychology, 11*, 203-219.

Hussong, A. M. (2002). Differentiating peer context and risk for adolescent substance use. *Journal of Youth and Adolescence, 31*, 207-220.

Isralowitz, R. & Rawson, R. (2006). Gender differences in prevalence of drug use among high risk adolescents in Israel. *Addictive Behaviors, 31*, 355-358.

Johnson, P. B., Boles, S. M., Vaughan, R., & Kleber, H. D. (2000). The co-occurrence of smoking and binge drinking in adolescence. *Addictive Behaviors, 25*, 779-783.

Johnston, L. D., O'Malley, P. M., & Bachman, J. G. (2000). Monitoring the future: National survey results on drug use, 1975-1999. Washington, DC: *U.S. Department of Health and Human Services (NIDA), NIH Publication No.* 00-4802.

Johnston, L. D., O'Malley, P. M., & Bachman, J. G. (2001). National survey results on drug use from the monitoring the future study: 1975-2000. Rockville, MD: *National Institute on Drug Abuse*.

Johnston, L. D., O'Malley, P. M., Bachman, J. G., & Schulenberg, J. (2004). Monitoring the future: National results on adolescent drug use, overview of key findings 2003. (NIH Publication No. 04-5506). *Bethesda, MD: U.S. Department of Health and Human Services.*

Join Together Online (2004). UK girls drink more than boys (Retrieved August 18, 2004 from*). http://www.jointogether.org/sa/news/summaries/print*

Kaplan, H. B. (1995). Drugs, crime, and other deviant adaptations. *Drugs, crime, and other deviant adaptations: Longitudinal studies*. New York: Plenum Press.

Kaplan, H. B., & Damphouse, K. R. (1995). Self-attitudes and antisocial personality a moderators of the drug use-violence relationship. In K. B. Kaplan (Ed.), *Drugs, crime, and other deviant adaptations: Longitudinal studies* (pp.187-210). New York: Plenum Press.

Kelly, A. B., & Kowalyszyn, M. (2003). The association of alcohol and family problems in a remote indigenous Australian community. *Addictive Behaviors, 28*, 761-767.

Kelly, A. B., Halford, W. K., & Young, R. McD. (2001). Expectations of the effects of alcohol use on relationship functioning: an assessment of women who consume alcohol at harmful levels. *Addictive Behaviors, 26*, 1-14.

Kim, H. S., & Kim, H. S. (1998a). Correlates variables of juvenile substance abuse in Korea. *J Korean Academy of Addiction Psychiatry, 2(1)*, 76-81.

Kim, H. S., & Kim, H. S. (1998b). Correlation between juvenile drug problems and their criminal patterns in Korea. *J Korean Academy of Addiction Psychiatry, 2(1)*, 82-90.

Kim, H. S., & Kim, H. S. (2002). The influence of alcohol drinking and substance abuse on delinquent behavior among Korean adolescents. *J Korean Neuropsychiatr Assoc, 41(3)*, 472-485.

Kim, H. S., & Kim, H. S. (2004). Aggression in Korean adolescents: relevant variables and path diagram. *J Korean Neuropsychiatr Assoc, 43(1)*, 75-85.

Kim, H. S., & Kim, H. S. (2005). Gender differences in delinquent behavior among Korean adolescents. *Child Psychiatry and Human Development, 35(4)*, 325-345.

Kim, H. S., Yoo, Y. S., Na, C., Lee, C., & Min, B. K. (1988). Adolescent and drug problem. *Chung-Ang University Journal of Medicine, 13(3)*, 417-424.

Kliewer, W., Murrelle, L., Prom, E., Ramirez, M., Obando, P., Sandi, L., & Karenkeris, M. Del C. (2006). Violence exposure and drug use in Central American youth: Family cohesion and parental monitoring as protective factors. *Journal of Research on Adolescence, 16 (3)*, 455-478.

Labouvie, E. W. (1986). The coping function of adolescent alcohol and drug use. In R. K. Silbereisen, K. Eyferth, & G. Rudinger (Eds.), *Development as action in context: Problem behavior and normal youth development* (pp. 229-239). Berlin: Springer-Verlag.

Li. C., Unger, J. B., Schuster, D., Rohrbach, L. A., Howard-Pitney, B., & Norman, G. (2003). Youths' exposure to environmental tobacco smoke (ETS). Associations with health beliefs and social pressure. *Addictive Behaviors, 28*, 39-53.

Loukas, A., Piejak, L. A., Bingham, C. R., Fitzgerald, H. E., & Zucker, R. A. (2001b). Parental distress as a mediator of problem behaviors in sons of alcohol-involved families. *Family Relations: Interdisciplinary Journal of Applied Family Studies, 50*, 293-301.

Martini, S., Wagner, F. A., & Anthony, J. C. (2002). The association of tobacco smoking and depression in adolescence: Evidence from the United States. *Substance Use and Misuse, 37*, 1853-1867.

McCrae, R. R., & Costa Jr., P. T. (2003). *Personality in adulthood: A five-factor theory perspective.* New York: Guilford Press.

Meier, K. S. (1991). Tobacco truths: the impact of role models on children's toward smoking. *Health Education Quarterly, 18*, 173-182.

Ministry of Culture and Sport (1996). White paper for Korean adolescents. *Ministry of Culture and Sports*, Seoul, Republic of Korea.

Min, B. K., Kim, H. S., Lee, K. H., Suk, J. H., & Shin, H. S. (1990). Adolescent maladjustment behaviors in Korea (1975 through 1986). *Human Science, 14(7)*, 433-444.

Newcomb. M. D., & Bentler, P. M. (1989). *Consequences of adolescent drug use: Impact on the lives of young adults*. Beverly Hills, CA: Sage Publications, Inc.

Office of Applied Studies (2004). Results from the 2003 national survey on drug use and health: National findings, (DHHS publication No. SMA 04-3964, NSDUH Series h-25). Rockville, MD: *Substance Abuse Mental Health Services Administration.*

Ozer, A. K. (1991). Attitudes and sociodemographic characteristics of secondary school students to psychoactive substance use. Unpublished thesis. Istanbul, Turky: Bakirkoy State *Hospital for Neurological and Psychiatric Disease.*

Pandina, R. (1990). *The Journal of Health and Social Policy*, as reported in "Some negative feelings can fuel abuse of drug," by Tina Adler, The APA Monitor.

Patton, G. C., Hibbert, M., Rosier, M., Carlin, J. B., Caust, J., & Bowes, G. (1996). Is smoking associated with depression and anxiety in teenagers. *American Journal of Public Health, 86*, 225-230.

Pederson, L. L., Koval, J. J., McGrady, G. A., & Tyas, S. L. (1998). The degree and type of relationship between psychosocial variables and smoking status for students in Grade 8: is there a dose-response relationship? *Preventive Medicine, 27*, 337-347.

Pierce, J. P., Distefan, J. M., Kaplan, R. M., & Gilpin, E. A. (2005).The role of curiosity in smoking initiation. *Addictive Behaviors, 30*, 685-696.

Pihl, R. O., & Hoaken, P. N. S. (1997). Clinical correlates and predictors of violence in patients with substance use disorders. *Psychiatric Annals, 27(11)*, 735-740.

Piko, B. (2000). Perceived social support from parents and peers: which is the stronger predictor of adolescent substance use? *Substance Use and Misuse, 35*, 617-630.

Piko, B.(2001a). Smoking in adolescence: Do attitudes matter? *Addictive Behaviors, 26*, 201-217.

Piko, B. F. (2006). Adolescent smoking and drinking: The role of communal mastery and other social influences. *Addictive Behaviors, 31*, 102-114.

Poikolainen, K. (2002). Antecedents of substance use in adolescence. *Current Opinion in Psychiatry, 15*, 241-245.

Read, J. P., Wood, M. D., Kahler, C. W., Maddock, J. E., & Palfai, T. P. (2003). Examining the role of drinking motives in college student alcohol use and problem, *Psychology of Addictive Behaviors, 17*, 13-23.

Reiss, A. J., & Roth, J. A. (eds.) (1994). *Understanding and preventing violence*. Vol. 3. Washington, DC: National Academy of Press.

Robins, R. W., John, O. P., Caspi, A., Moffitt, T. E., & Stouthamer-Loeber, M. (1996). Resilient, overcontrolled, and undercontrolled boys: Three replicable personality types. *Journal of Personality and Social Psychology, 70*, 157-171.

Roth, J., & Brooks-Gunn, J. (2000) What do adolescents need for healthy development? Implications for youth policy. *Social Policy Report, 14*, 3-19

Shedler, J., & Block, J. (1990). Adolescent drug use and psychological health: a longitudinal inquiry. *American Psychologist. 45*, 612-630.

Simons-Morton, B., Haynie, D. L., Crump, A. D., Eitel, P., & Saylor, K. E. (2001). Peer and parent influences on smoking and drinking among early adolescents. *Health and Behavior, 28*, 95-107.

Stanton, W. R., Oei, T. P. S., & Silva, P. A. (1994). Sociodemographic characteristics of adolescents smokers. *International Journal of the Addictions, 24*, 913-925.

Terraciano, A., & Costa Jr., P. T. (2004). Smoking and the Five-Factor model of personality. *Addiction, 99*, 472-481.

Thom, B. (2003). Risk-taking behavior in men: Substance use and gender. London: *Health Development Agency.*

Tuakli, N., Smith, M. A., & Heaton, C. (1990). Smoking in adolescence: methods for health education and smoking cessation. A MIRNET study. *Journal of Family Practice, 31*, 369-374.

Tyas, S. L., & Pederson, L. L. (1998). Psychosocial factors related to adolescent smoking: a critical review of the literature. *Tobacco Control, 7*, 409-420.

Weiner, M. D., Sussman, S., Sun, P., & Dent, C. (2005). Explaining the link between violence perpetration, victimization and drug use. *Addictive Behaviors, 30*, 1261-1266.

White, H. R. (1997). *Longitudinal perspectives on alcohol use and aggression during adolescence.* In Galanter, M., ed. Recent development in alcoholism. Vol. 13. New York: Plenum Press. pp.81-103.

Wijatkowski, S., Forgays, D. G., Wrzesniewski, K., & Gorski, T. (1990). Smoking behavior and personality characteristics in Polish adolescents. *The International Journal of the Addictions, 25*, 363-373.

Wild, C. T.(2002). Personal drinking and sociocultural drinking norms: A representative population study. *Journal of Studies on Alcohol, 63*, 469-475.

Wills, T. A., Sandy, J. M., & Yeager, A. M. (2002). Stress and smoking in adolescence: A test of directional hypotheses. *Health Psychology, 21*, 122-130.

Wu, P., & Kandel, D. B. (1995). The roles of mother and fathers in intergenerational behavioral transmission: The case of smoking and delinquency. In H. B. Kaplan (Ed.), *Drugs, crime, and other deviant adaptations: Longitudinal studies* (pp. 41-81). New York: Plenum Press.

Zucker, R. A.(1991). The concept of risk and the etiology of alcoholism: A probabilistic-developmental perspective. In Pittman, D. J., White, H. R. (eds). Society, Cultural, and Drinking patterns Reexamined. New Brunswick. NJ, Rutgers, *Center of Alcohol Studies*, pp. 513-532.

Zuckerman, M. (1994). Behavioral expressions and biosocial bases of sensation seeking. Cambridge: *Cambridge University Press*.

Zuckerman, M., & Kuhlman, D. M. (2000). Personality and risk-taking: Common biosocial factors. *Journal of Personality, 68*, 999-1029.

In: Korea: Economic, Political and Social Issues
Editors: P. H. Elwood, J. B. Albertus
ISBN: 978-1-60456-513-3

Chapter 8

CIVIL SOCIETY AND POLITICAL CHANGE IN SOUTH KOREA, INDONESIA, AND MALAYSIA

*Amy L. Freedman**
Department of Government
PO Box 3003, Lancaster, PA 17604

ABSTRACT

As a result of the economic crisis that rocketed through Asia in 1997-1998, several countries went through political transitions. In South Korea and Thailand, democratic elections resulted in opposition parties coming to power. In Indonesia, President Suharto was forced out of office after more than 30 years in power. In Malaysia, Prime Minister Mahathir's ruling coalition won only 56% of the popular vote (down from 70% in 1995) in 1999 elections, and, for a brief window (from 1997-2001), there was mounting political opposition to Mahathir's regime. This paper asks what the connection is between civil society and political change, and, how might we understand the variation in political transformations that occurred. Research for this project shows that several independent variables are useful in explaining the variation in political transitions: IMF involvement, popular protests, the nature of opposition groups and civil society, and elite coalition formation/dissolution at the highest levels of government.

In 1997 and 1998 Asia was hit with a severe economic crisis. Most countries in the region (from South Korea through Southeast Asia) were faced with massive currency fluctuations, banking crises, and plummeting stock markets. These economic problems were compounded by political turmoil. Given the experience in Asia of massive financial difficulties coupled with political upheaval (specifically in Thailand, South Korea, Indonesia,

* I would like to thank Rachel Ellenport for her assistance with this project. Rachel contributed substantially to the research for this paper and worked on a draft of the material for the Indonesia and South Korea case studies. Without her help this paper would not have gotten off the ground. All errors and omissions are my responsibility. Portions of this paper are taken from an earlier work, "After the Crash: Political Transformation in Asia after 1998" currently under review at *Democratization* E-mail:. amy.freedman@fandm.edu, Telephone: (717) 291-3963.

and Malaysia), this article begins with a broad question: what is the relationship between economic crises, civil society, and political change, specifically democratization?

In Thailand and South Korea democratic elections were held and opposition parties came to power for the first time since political liberalization. In Indonesia, Suharto's long period of authoritarian rule came to a crashing close when riots and demonstrations forced Suharto to become more and more politically isolated, finally compelling him to resign. In Malaysia the ruling coalition was able to maintain power but a new sense of political activism developed in the wake of Prime Minister Mahathir's firing of his popular deputy Anwar Ibrahim. When parliamentary elections were held in Malaysia in the fall of 1999 the ruling party faced two challenges: a new political party was formed based on the call for greater social justice, and more significantly the Islamic party PAS won an unprecedented number of seats at the state and national level.

Economic turmoil and political change present an opportunity to further our understanding of democratization and the key actors involved in bringing about political change. In much of the literature on transitions to democracy there is an implicit or explicit role for civil society to play in helping to bring about political change. Did civil society have an impact on the political transformations that occurred in South Korea and Indonesia? And, if so, how did the economic crisis impact the organization and goals of civil society? In order to answer these more specific questions we will look at the conditions leading up to the political transformations. We will look at institutional differences like elite coalitions and the party structure, the nature of political protests (from whom were calls for change coming, and were demonstrations peaceful), and the conditions imposed by the IMF to try and understand what impact these had on political changes.

There is a great deal of literature both on economic crisis and political change, and on democratization and civil society. This paper attempts to bridge the gap between the two. Earlier literature on economic crises and political change seems to fall into two distinct camps. Some scholars have found that economic problems lead to political instability and an end to democracy, while other studies have shown that fiscal crises can help consolidate democracy. What can the turmoil in Asia tell us about the link between economic conditions and political change, and what does this tell us about the larger theoretical debate? This paper argues that overall, the economic crisis in Asia seems to have strengthened democracy. Where our research departs from earlier work on crises and political change is that we found that political change comes as much from shifts in political elites' preferences and coalitions, rather than just from popular demands from a frustrated citizenry. This finding supports earlier literature on the role of civil society in helping advocate for democracy, but the paper argues that civil society is strongly impacted by other factors. The paper begins with a review of the relevant literature and then moves on to look more closely at what happened in Indonesia, South Korea, and Malaysia.

Literature Review

There is much scholarly literature that argues that economic turmoil threatens democratic regimes, particularly new democracies, and that democracies are less able to implement policies that will effectively ameliorate economic crises. For example, Przeworski (1991) argues that because of the political risk involved in adhering to fiscal austerity programs, democratic regimes would be less likely to "do the right thing". Likewise, Huntington (1968:41) argues that "modernity breeds stability, but modernization breeds instability". As an elaboration on this point, Londregan and Pool (1990) find economic "backwardness" is a necessary condition for coups to occur, but that the process of modernizing (if it involves economic growth) may inhibit coups. Londregan and Pool would, however, agree that if economic crisis occurs and economic growth turns into stagnation or decline, then a change in the executive (a coup) is more likely to transpire.

In contrast to the arguments above, much recent scholarship has actually found that economic crises can help consolidate democracy. Raymond Duch looked at former Communist regimes in Eastern Europe and found that regardless of "civic culture" (elements of which include levels of education and access to information) citizens were not likely to give up on democratic institutions and capitalism because of economic problems. He finds that citizens will not abandon democracy and capitalism because they have negative memories of authoritarian regimes, and because they value having a political choice. People understand the difference between institutions and politicians. Therefore, they may vote out incumbents and replace them with new leaders, but most citizens do not favor an end to the democratic political order. (Duch 1995:126)

Similarly, Karen Remmer looks at the effect of economic crises on electoral outcomes in Latin America from 1982-1990. Unlike Diamond and Linz (1989), Remmer finds that during the debt crisis in Latin American in the 1980s, economic woes were bad news for incumbents, but people did not turn to extremism and there were few breakdowns of democracy (Remmer 1991:777). In fact, instead of the disintegration of democracy during the economic crisis of the 1980s, democracy appears to have been consolidated or strengthened.

In most of the literature reviewed above there is an assumption of political mobilization or participation from a fired-up citizenry. That is, democracy is either consolidated or undermined because popular discontent about the economic situation fuels politicization, either in a destructive way when democratic institutions are flung aside, or in a manner in which entrenched political elites are swept out of power. While much of this scholarship is useful as a starting point for understanding the relationship between economic crisis and political change, it does not seem to provide a complete picture of what happened in Asia from 1997-1999. On first glance it appears that one could argue that the economic crisis of 1997 brought about greater democracy in Asia: opposition parties won elections for the first time in South Korea and Thailand, new signs of social unrest and political activism appeared in Malaysia, and President Suharto was forced to resign after 30 years of authoritarian rule in Indonesia. However, it is far too simple to say that a causal chain of events took place: economic crisis > popular politicization > greater democratization. On closer inspection the events do not exactly conform to this model.

It is relatively rare that "people power" alone brings down a regime. While it is convenient and perhaps idealistic to say that citizen anger can end authoritarian regimes, it often seems that there are intervening variables at work. If citizen are to act as key agents of change, they will be more effective if they are organized in some manner. Literature on civil society argues that groups express preferences and that their input effects the nature of policy making and regime change. People power works best when it is channeled into more organized forms of resistance and mobilizing institutions. In other words, if there are labor unions or business associations that can funnel demands to either those within power or those opposition players poised to take power, then mass political movements will be more effective.

Civil Society Approach

The term "civil society" is used by political scientists in many ways. The two most common ways that it appears are first as a descriptive term to highlight the decency (civility) of organizational life among citizen. Secondly, civil society is viewed in relation to the state. Schmitter (1995) and Diamond (1994) theorize the role of groups or associations in society as contributing to or articulating the demands and interests of various sectors of the population. In such a position civil society is poised to play a significant role in encouraging greater accountability and perhaps democratization. In fact, Diamond (1994:7-11) outlines the ten democratic functions of civil society:

1. setting the limit on state power;
2. supplementing the role of political parties;
3. developing democratic attributes;
4. creating channels for the articulation, aggregation, and representation of interst, and generating opportunities for participation and influence at all levels of governance;
5. mitigating the principal polarities of political conflicts;
6. recruiting and training new political leaders;
7. monitoring elections;
8. disseminating information and aiding citizens;
9. supporting economic reform;
10. strengthening the democratic state.

One particular question that has generated a great deal of scholarly literature has been the autonomy of civil society from the state. While this paper does not weigh in explicitly on this debate, we have assumed that in order for civil society to have an impact on democratization that it must be at least somewhat free from state domination.

When scholars first envisioned transitions from authoritarian rule, they looked at the processes that Europe and the United States went through over 200 years ago. What many argued was that economic development would lead to the creation of a middle class. This middle class would be more likely to form associations and groups to protect and promote their interests. Eventually, these groups would play a larger role in demanding accountability, protection of private economic interests, and responsiveness from the government. These demands would evolve into greater political openness and ultimately democracy. In democratic states interest articulation comes from a variety of sources in society, but the preferences that are best able to be heard are those coming from well organized, well funded, and well connected groups; civil society rather than just mass mobilization or participation. During times of crisis, does civil society play an important role in demanding accountability and change, or does the impetus for change come from elsewhere?

In Indonesia the economic crisis hit in the summer of 1997 and there were periodic demonstrations and acts of violence throughout the rest of 1997 and 1998. It is not until May of 1998 that Suharto finally steps down. In South Korea economic turmoil begins in late fall of 1997, just as the Presidential campaign was getting underway. Political activism from students and workers in South Korea is quite common, yet the economic crisis neither brought on extra-ordinary protests, nor did the Presidential candidates attempt to effectively use the crisis to their advantage. Opposition candidate Kim Dae-jung won the election in part because people were disappointed with Kim Young Sam and his party because of corruption scandals and multiple candidates split the vote. While Kim Young Sam was not running for re-election (the Constitution bars him from doing so), the candidate from his party was tainted by the corruption charges against Kim's friends and family.

In Malaysia, it was less the economic crisis that brought people into the streets to demonstrate against Mahathir than it was a sense of injustice about the way the Prime Minister drove out and allowed judicial proceedings to be taken against Anwar Ibrahim. By the time Mahathir called for parliamentary elections at the end of 1999 the economy had rebounded somewhat and the ruling coalition returned to power albeit loosing a number of seats in parliament and an additional state government.

Alone, mass mobilization as a result of economic turmoil cannot explain political change. The missing element is that certain political elites are able to take advantage of the economic crisis and are able to position themselves to either retain their position (like Mahathir) or are able out maneuver entrenched leaders and help bring about political change. Only by looking at internal political dynamics and coalitions and elite actors in civil society can we explain when and why political change and democratization occurs and why it might not. This statement is not particularly surprising. As Keohane and Milner (1996) explain, one can no longer understand domestic politics without understanding the world economy and the links between the two. Internationalization affects the opportunities and constraints facing social, political, and economic actors (1996:4). For Keohane and Milner the dependent variables are policy preferences of key actors and the national polices and policy institutions themselves. This argument expands on the "2nd image reversed"[1] literature of Gourevitch (1978) and Katzenstein (1978). Writing before the economic crisis hits Asia, Keohane and Milner seem almost to predict the region's events. Economic shocks from abroad can thus trigger political crisis that can reshape domestic politics (p. 16-17). Domestic politics changes not because of mobilization from below but because of realignments and shifting political coalitions among elite players.

Bienen and Gersovitz (1985) also point to the centrality of elite coalitions in understanding political stability. Their work directly addresses the impact of coming under an IMF program for domestic politics. Bienen and Gersovitz argue, "Economic and political concerns work in opposite directions. Politics calls for bargaining and incremental change...; economics often argues for rapid adjustments (747). "A regime that has lost legitimacy for other reasons becomes especially vulnerable to its opponents during negotiations with the IMF and during the implementation of an IMF package" (Bienen and Gersovitz 735). Since political elites might be divided on the question about whether to accept IMF conditions and/or how to implement necessary changes, it is logical that political instability, derived from a lack of elite unity, may result from IMF involvement.

[1] The notable contribution of "second image reversed" thinking is that international factors (institutions, agreements, laws, etc.) impact domestic decision making, rather than second image explanations, which find that domestic politics effects how a country behaves in the international arena.

The literature reviewed above offers various perspectives on the broad question about the relationship between economic crises, civil society and political change. In addition, this paper seeks to explain the variation in political transformations connected to the economic meltdown in Asia in 1997. Based on recent research, this paper will demonstrate the following arguments: Economic crises lead to democratization when a leader looses internal and external political allies. Variation in this process is attributable to the following:

1. The easier it is for opponents to challenge the policies of an incumbent government, (and the more autonomous civil society is) the more responsive the system will be to societal pressures. Thus, political change will be faster and easier (i.e. fewer protests and violence) in stable democracies than in authoritarian regimes (Garrett and Lange 1995:632). This was the case in South Korea.
2. Where there is credible opposition (in the form of an organized party with clear leadership in place), those who are disgruntled will look to them for support and assistance meeting their demands. Where there is no viable alternate group already in a position to gain politically, those who are angry about the economic crisis will seek regime change from outside the system. (Indonesia)
3. IMF prescriptions can "make or break" the regime in power based on weather or not their policy recommendations instill domestic confidence or further the sense of panic and uncertainty. And, IMF prescriptions can change elite coalitions based on who supports and who opposes IMF policies. In part this accounts for the difference between Malaysia, and South Korea and Indonesia.
4. The Political impact of popular protests: Popular protests will have greater impact if they are from an easily identified political constituency group (labor, or the military for example), if the protestors are well organized, and if they connect themselves to a coalition in or outside of power that broadens their base of appeal (South Korea and Indonesia).

The first and fourth scenarios are where civil society has the most power and influence.

Case Studies

We look at South Korea, Indonesia and Malaysia to gain a better understanding of the relationship between economic crisis and political change. For each country we look at the political and economic climate at the time the financial crises begins. Then we examine the incumbent regime's reaction to the economic crisis, and if there is popular support or opposition to official government policy. Next we detail the IMF's intervention (or lack there of in Malaysia) efforts and how this affected particular elites in power and public opinion of the masses and of crucial groups in society about the crisis. Overall, we try to explain the internal political dynamics as they shift in confronting the economic crisis. Finally, the political changes that occurred in all three countries will be explained. Particular attention will be paid to changing levels of support for various leaders (incumbents and challengers) and how the financial crisis impacted the political outcome of so much change. The account of events in Indonesia is more detailed than that of South Korea and Malaysia. The later two countries are simply used as comparisons to events and outcomes in Indonesia.

Indonesia

"An economic shock of the dimension of the financial crisis in East Asia places huge strain on political systems, and has unpredictable economic effects through resulting political changes. The deep recession in Indonesia broke the back of the decades-old Suharto administration, leading to a period of policy incoherence and political instability" (Garnaut 27). On July 8, 1997, Indonesia faced a currency crisis that badly devalued the rupiah. Throughout the summer Indonesia tried to cope with the falling rupiah on its own. Suharto and his closest allies were unable to decide if they wanted to accept the terms offered by the IMF for assistance in stopping the economy's free fall. Finally in November of 1997, in an effort to calm domestic and international fears of inaction, Suharto's government closed 16 insolvent banks and announced additional austerity measures. Instead of increasing confidence in those financial institutions that were sound, financial panic occurred and mass demonstrations erupted across the archipelago. Although it was announced that $33 billion in loans would be made available to Indonesia, Suharto was still unable to agree to terms of a bailout from the IMF. Finally in January of1998 Suharto agreed to a package of economic prescriptions from the IMF. Some of the requirements included curbs on official favoritism for companies controlled by his children and his closet allies, and reductions in subsidies.

In January 1998 Suharto announced that he would seek reelection later that year, it would be his seventh term as President of Indonesia. He also hinted that he would choose B.J. Habibie as his next vice President. Suharto's actions only served to further weaken investor confidence about reforms in Indonesia's economy, and, public disapproval over how Suharto was handling the economic crisis was growing alarmingly. Mass demonstrations increased throughout Indonesia in early 1998. On February 14th they turn violent. Rioters in Jakarta, Medan and other cities burned and looted shops. Churches were vandalized and burnt. Protests continued in major cities during February, although police sometimes tried to break them up, often police and military units stood by while protestors destroyed private property and even attacked other people, mostly ethnic Chinese. On March 10, 1998 Suharto was reelected by the legislature and was given significant new power to confront the economic crisis. His reelection triggered some of the largest and most fiery antigovernment demonstrations in 30 years. Adding to the pile of criticism against Suharto, he appointed several controversial figures to his new cabinet, including his eldest daughter and Bob Hasan.[2] Protests continued into the spring.

May began with violent riots in Medan and other cities over price increases resulting from reductions in government subsidies for cooking oil and other necessities. Thousands of students continued protesting against the regime. Some very notable and high profile individuals began calling for Suharto to step down. Muslim leader Abdurrahman Wahid called for Suharto's resignation and he pled with the nation to put an end to the hostility

---

[2] The choice of Bob Hasan for a cabinet position was highly controversial. Hasan was a close friend of Suharto's (and is ethnically Chinese) and has significant business holdings in industries like rattan and clove production. In his new post Hasan would be in a position to police and oversee the industrial sectors in which he a leader.

toward the Chinese community. Wahid's outspokenness against the government gave encouragement to the students to continue their protests and to take them outside the campus gates to the streets. On May 13, 1998, Jakarta police opened fire on thousands of student protestors at Trisakti University. Six were killed and dozens wounded. The next day protests turned horrifically violent. Hundreds of stores, vehicles, offices and homes were burned and looted. Most of the anger and damage was directed at Indonesia's ethnic Chinese minority because of perceived business ties to Suharto. Hundreds of Chinese women and girls told gruesome stories of being assaulted, raped, and tortured. Graphic tales of the violence have been widely documented.[3]

There are four factors that contribute to pushing Suharto out of office in May of 1998, the economic crisis, the protests and riots, the miscalculations of the IMF, and the internal and external pressures from elites.

A. The Role of Civil Society and Electoral Change

To what extent did civil society exist in Indonesia prior to 1997? There is no simple answer to this question. While Suharto certainly ruled autocratically, there were signs of autonomous organizational life, there were a multitude of business and professional associations and the press was moderately independent[4], These elements did have some impact on policy making. However, it would not be correct to say that civil society was independent of the state. This began to change in the late 1990s and came to a climax in 1997/98.

On May 21, 1998, after thirty plus years in office, Suharto resigned as President of Indonesia. B.J. Habibie became president and announced that he would stay in office only a year while the country planned for new elections. The most free and open elections since the 1950s were held in Indonesia on June 7, 1999. Forty-eight parties competed for seats in Parliament. The parties that won the most seats in the legislature were Megawati Sukarnoputri's party: PDI-P, the Indonesian Democratic Party in Struggle, capturing 34% of the popular vote; Golkar, Habibie's party that was still strong because of dense organizational networks established under Suharto, received 20% of the vote, Abdurrahman Wahid's (aka Gus Dur) party the National Awakening Party (PKB) and Amien Rais of the National Mandate Party (PAN) also received large number of votes. The President was to be chosen by an electoral college mechanism in October of 1999. Despite winning the most seats in the legislature, Megawati refused to network and build up a base of support with others in power. When Habibie withdrew from contention at the last minute, Wahid was chosen by the People's Consultative Assembly to be President. Although only in office 19 months before being impeached because of his inability to address continuing corruption at the highest levels, economic disorder, and separatist movements, Wahid's presidency was seen as the first democratic transfer of power in Indonesia's history.

---

[3] For a more detailed account of the violence against the Chinese see Freedman 2000.

[4] Freedom of the press varied tremendously under Suharto. At times newspapers were very outspoken and independent, however such papers risked loosing their permit and being shut down. For example, *Tempo* closed and reopened several times in the 1990s before Suharto silenced it for good. In addition, some professional organizations (mostly business associations) had significant influence in narrow areas of policy making. See Freedman 2000 for more information on this.

B. IMF Recommendations

On October 8, 1997, Indonesia formally turned to the IMF for aid with managing the economic crisis. After much negotiation with Suharto, the first IMF loan was made on October 31st for $43 billion (McBeth 1997A:79.) The first loan was to last for three years and the Indonesian government was to follow contractionary economic policies. The government was suppose to reduce expenditures and close insolvent banks. The goal behind these prescriptions was to restore investor (and domestic) confidence. The program also attempted to stabilize exchange conditions and oversee the restructuring of the external current account. These recommendations were to lay the foundation for the resumption of economic growth.

In addition to the fiscal requirements of the IMF, the Indonesian government was also suppose to further liberalize and deregulate their markets, for example, Indonesia was encouraged to remove many of the country's protective trade barriers over the three year period of the loan (IMF June 1, 2001). The IMF sought to persuade the Indonesian government to dissolve monopolies and allow for greater transparency in business decision-making. The IMF actually got involved outside its normal parameters by creating policy to dissolve the clove and plywood monopolies in Indonesia (ibid). None of these reforms were able to curb inflation, or slow the further decrease in the value of the rupiah, or halt skyrocketing unemployment (Susanto1997:32). Instead the economy slowed even further. On January 15, 1998 Indonesia negotiated a second IMF program. Among other requirements this loan called for the removal of subsidies on food and energy.

On April 8, 1998 the IMF and the Indonesian government agreed on a revised program since Suharto had failed to fulfill the first and second IMF accords. Again, the IMF pressed for greater liberalization of the economy in exchange for the $43 billion. To what extent did Suharto abide by these prescriptions? For the most part, Suharto acted to protect the wealth and power of his family and close friends (Mydans 1998). Food and fuel subsidies were removed but monopolies and corruption continued (Watson 1998). Examples of Suharto's inconsistencies included closing 16 banks, as per the IMF's request in November 1997, and then letting the banks reopen under new names. The 70% increases in petrol prices and 60% increase in electricity rates that were enacted were part of what drove protestors to the streets. The pain was not shared equally in Indonesia, the general population felt that they were being squeezed while Suharto's family and allies were able to escape censure. While the demonstrations began in February as a plea to do something about inflation and unemployment, by April and May protests escalated into bold demands for Suharto's ouster. While the protests were significant in and of themselves, as a bold criticism of authoritarian rule, they were also crucial because of the increasingly wide public support offered to the students.

> A 53-year-old farmer, Ansuwolo, proudly recounts his efforts to dissuade his son, a Yogyakarta policeman, from beating up protesters. He says many of his neighbors are also rooting for the students as they watch scenes of the demonstrations broadcast on the nightly television news. (Cohen 1998C).

The other significant element of the protests was that they provided opportunities for religious and secular activists to work together. "In Yogyakarta, young Muslim women in headscarves have joined flower-waving nuns at campus rallies" (ibid). Likewise, on May 1 representatives of 30 workers' groups in Greater Jakarta met with student leaders and the next day several workers addressed the student rally. Student-worker links were also made in Bandung and Surabaya.

C. Elite Pressure

Initially, powerful business interests stood behind Suharto because he attempted to shield them from IMF strictures. However, with increasing turmoil and financial disarray, even middle class and business interests (the backbone of civil society) began to agree that Suharto would have to be pushed aside. The violence and the damage from the riots caused even some of Suharto's staunchest allies to start questioning his leadership. After months of turmoil, House Speaker Harmoko on May 18, 1998 publicly offered Suharto three options: he could reshuffle his cabinet, resign, or face a special session of Parliament in which he might be impeached (Vatikiotis and Schwarz 1998). The military still seemed squarely behind the President at this point. On May 20th all 14 economic ministers resigned under pressure from Akbar Tanjung and Ginandjar Kartasasmita (lead economic ministers) (ibid). Suharto sent his vice president to convince the ministers to rescind their resignations, instead Habibie asked them to give him their support. House Speaker Harmoko threatened to go ahead with impeachment proceedings. Finally, on May 20th the military signaled that it too had lost faith in Suharto, General Wiranto met the President on May 20th and told him that he could not guarantee security in Jakarta, although there were 17,000 troops in the city, the General did not feel that they would be able to keep the peace when faced with further demonstrations. Although none of his close allies were able to directly tell Suharto to step down, many well-respected Islamic figures had spoken publicly about replacing the President, other leaders close to him hinted at their shifting views. Suharto resigned on May 21, 1998 after 32 years in office.

There is no question that the demonstrations, sparked by the economic crisis and the perception that the IMF conditions were implemented in such a way to protect Suharto's allies while the rest of the country was suffering, contributed to Suharto's abandonment by his closest advisors and the ultimately the military. However, it was not simply that democratization evolved because of demands from below. Only when Suharto lost internal and external elite support did he agree to step down, paving the way for elections to be held a year later.

South Korea

In the fall of 1997 South Korea was in the midst of a hotly contested presidential election. Then President Kim Young Sam was prevented by term limits from running again so the race was essentially between long-time political dissident Kim Dae-jung and the ruling New Korea Party (NKP) candidate Lee Hoi Change. Kim Dae-jung's victory in December was heralded as the first true democratic transfer of power in South Korea and the economic crisis was credited for giving people incentive to vote out the incumbent party.

As the Asian financial crisis hit one Southeast Asian nation after another, South Korea seemed as if it would be immune from similar ills. An article in the *Christian Science Monitor* in August 1997 describes how the students in South Koreas were less and less likely to mount large protests. There were fewer and fewer students joining political organizations on campus, and the number of radical student activists had fallen significantly. Political apathy seemed more the norm than political engagement by 1997.[5]

Into the fall of 1997 Kim Young Sam and his party were promising a reform package to help clean up debt-ridden banks. Thousands of Central Bank employees threatened to go on strike because the proposal would strengthen the Ministry of Finance's power by giving them supervisory authority over local banks (Choe 1997). There did not seem to be a larger public discussion about weaknesses in the economy and threats to economic stability. Activism came largely from Kia motors workers who went on strike repeatedly in October in protests of the government decision to turn the company into a state-controlled company through receivership.[6]

The banking sector had already been severely stressed by continued lending to struggling firms when in late October Hong Kong was beset by problems. As pressure was put on the Hong Kong dollar, financial authorities were forced to push up interest rates to defend the peg to the (US) dollar. This resulted in a severe sell-off in the Hong Kong stock market. This directly impacted South Korea. The country faced a liquidity crisis and Foreign banks refused to roll over short-term foreign credits to Korean financial institutions; on November 21, 1997 Korea was forced to give up supporting the won. On December 3rd South Korea agreed to a huge IMF program of $57 billion (with additional resources from the World Bank, the Asian Development Bank and other countries in the region). The package proved insufficient and at the end of December a new program was announced with additional resources and new conditions and terms with foreign banks to restructure short-term debt (Haggard 2000: 4).

On December 13, 1997 South Korean students and workers held a rally to protest against the IMF agreement. They carried signs and chanted slogans like "Arrest Kim Young Sam for ruining the economy" and "because the government and rich chaebol owners ruined the economy, workers will suffer the pain" (Choe 1997). After Kim Dae-jung won the election a few days later, commentators and the media generally credited the economic crisis for Kim's victory. While there is no doubt that the financial turmoil and uncertainly impacted the election results, it is too simplistic to say that the opposition party only won the Presidency because the crisis caused people to vote the incumbent party out of office. There were many reasons for South Korean voters to be displeased with Kim Young Sam and Lee Hoi Chang's party.

Resentment towards Kim Young Sam dates back to 1987. Roh Tae Woo won that election largely because the opposition was divided when Kim Young Sam split from his

---

[5] The logical explanation for the decrease in student activism in South Korea by 1997 is simply that the goals of the student movement dating from Syngman Rhee's rule in the 1960s and continuing through the 1980s had largely been met. Once seen as the champions of democracy and greater social justice, after successful political transformation of the late 1980s and early 1990s, there was a sense that the major goals of previous demonstrations had been met. Without a moderate cause to draw many supporters, students still active on campus in the mid and late 1990s tended to be more radical and called for reunification with the North under the North's framework. (WuDunn 1997:1)

[6] The Kia controversy came after a year of problems within some of South Korea's largest firms (chaebol). Hanbo was the first company in early 1997 to face significant problems, the government made no effort to save the firm's management, instead they contributed a flood of new money to the company, and effectively nationalized it. Later in the spring of 1997 when other large conglomerates faced similar problem (Sammi in March and Jinro in April) the government encouraged state and private banks to announce "anti-bankruptcy" policies which would allow them to continue to lend money to failing firms. The government contributed to the program by pumping money (liquidity) into the banking system (Hagggard 2000:56-57). Still it was not yet perceived as a dire crisis.

cooperation with Kim Dae-jung. Kim Young Sam formed the Reunification Democratic Party but with opposition forces in two camps RDP wasn't strong enough to wrest power from Roh. When Kim Young Sam won election in 1992 some Koreans viewed him as a sell-out. In the run up to that election Kim had joined Roh Tae Woo's Democratic Justice Party. Those who had worked or hoped for democracy in South Korea saw this party switch as a legitimation of an old order they wish to see changed. Kim took office in 1992/3 promising political and economic reforms. To this end he did initiate several high profile anti-corruption campaigns and both former Presidents Chun and Roh were brought to trial and convicted for corruption (their sentences were later commuted). However, throughout his administration new scandals arose about personal connections and favoritism. In particular, Kim Young Sam's second son, Kim Hyun Chul was implicated in the Hanbo kickbacks-for-loans scandal. So, at the outset people were disenchanted with Kim Young Sam's success. Party politics in South Korea are largely based on the personality and power of the party's leader. With Kim Young Sam's reputation diminished even before the economic crisis of October 1997, it was going to be a tight race in the Presidential contest.

In addition to Kim's diminished image, Lee Hoi Chang faced his own scandals. Lee was hurt by accusations that his son had avoided military service, and after a bruising primary Lee's party challenger Rhee In Je broke off from the NKP and ran again against Lee in the final election. Even with out competition from Kim Dae-jung, voters had many concerns about Lee's candidacy. As the election neared, all four candidates promised to uphold the agreement with the IMF. This was a somewhat surprising move on Kim Dae-jung's part. Kim's core support had always come from the left, from labor unions, and from his home region of Cholla. Initially, Kim had criticized the IMF agreement and his remarks implied that if he won election he would renegotiate the deal. This statement caused dismay in the financial community both within South Korea and internationally. Kim was forced to moderate his remarks and then he chose to agree with the other candidates in a rare show of public agreement among the contenders. One other significant move that Kim made as the election neared was that he announced a coalition with the conservative politician Kim Jong Pil and his United Liberal Democrats (ULD). Kim Dae-jung announced that he would appoint Kim Jong Pil as Prime Minister if elected. This pulled some conservative voters away from Lee Hoi Chang and the ruling party. This political alliance, and the competition from several challengers may have decided the outcome: Kim's margin of victory against Lee Hoi Chang was miniscule (40.3 vs. 38.7 percent).[7]

Over the years in South Korea, the most active areas of civil society have been students and labor activists. Until the 1980s middle and business class interests seemed more complacent about democratic values and input. Instead they tended to favor stability and economic development priorities. Such anti-democratic attitudes began to change with the Kwangju massacre in 1980. Student and labor groups began to be seen more sympathetically, as advocating greater social justice and democracy, rather than just being a radical tool of the left. The shift in middle class orientation helped nudge South Korea towards democracy in the late 1980s. Again in 1997/98 it was increased, if moderate, support from more conservative voters that may have given Kim Dae-jung the edge that helped him win the election.

[7] Ironically, the legislature did not approve Kim Jong Pil's appointment as Prime Minister.

Malaysia

Like Indonesia and South Korea, Malaysia faced an economic crisis in 1997/98. However, instead of turning to the IMF for help, Malaysia decided to address their financial difficulties without international assistance. Mahathir's regime in Malaysia, like Kim Young Sam's and Suharto's, faced large protest movements and internal dissent among political elites. Mahathir alone of these three leaders was able to hang on to power and in the fall of 1999 his party's coalition again won a large majority in parliament and he still serves as Prime Minister. How might we explain the lack of political change in Malaysia when so many of the independent variables there were similar to the conditions in Indonesia and South Korea? I believe that it is because Mahathir was able to outmaneuver more reform-minded leaders (both in the economic and political senses) within the government, and to thwart increased activism from a new reform movement (civil society). He is able to do this in part because the IMF was not requiring Malaysia to make changes in their political economy. Thus, there is no external incentive or backing for possible challengers to Mahathir's power, and UMNO leadership is able to protect economic elites with close ties to the party. In order to understand this, this paper will now take a closer look at the crisis in Malaysia in 1997/98.

Like neighboring countries, Malaysia too faced currency devaluations during the summer of 1997. The ringgit fell precipitously and the central bank tried to prop it up. While Thailand, Indonesia and South Korea opted for a bailout package from the IMF, Mahathir blamed currency traders and foreign financial forces for Malaysia's economic ills. While the Prime Minister denounced the likes of George Soros and other fund manages, his deputy Prime Minister Anwar Ibrahim was the one who quietly reassured investors that Malaysia would not invoke some of the proposed (by Mahathir) restrictions on currency trading. There were many rumors that Anwar and Mahathir were not getting along and that one would have to triumph over the other. In October of 1997 Mahathir returned from a trip to Latin America and at a press conference the following exchange occurred:

> Mahathir: "The press is asking questions. I'm answering and tomorrow the currency traders will try and push down the ringgit just because Dr. Mahathir opened his mouth."
>
> Anwar's laughing reply: "Then I will clarify and they will say we're quarrelling". (Jayasankaran October 9, 1997a)

In December of 1997 Anwar seemed to be in full control of economic policy, at Mahathir's request. On December 5th, the Deputy Prime Minister announced a series of austerity measures. This was viewed by many as a rebuke of, or at least and end to, the aggressive spending that Mahathir had led for over ten years. Over the next few months Mahathir became more assertive about saving large, high profile companies such as Malaysia Airlines. On June 24, 1998 Daim Zainuddin was appointed Special Functions Minister and given the task of overseeing economic policy. Most political analysts believed that Diam would also serve as a check on Anwar's power. On September 1, 1998, Mahathir announced that the country was imposing capital controls, the currency was fixed at 3.80 ringgit to the US dollar. The next day Anwar was fired from his posts as Deputy Prime Minister and Minister of Finance. Later he was expelled from the party and arrested on charges of corruption and sodomy (Freedman 2000:51-52). His ouster triggered demonstrations and calls for political reform.

> Malaysians are perfecting a new form of protest: the "shop-and-shout" technique. For the second Saturday in a row, a crowd of what looked like ordinary shoppers on October 17 transformed a main street in central Kuala Lumpur into a massive demonstration calling for Prime Minister Mahathir Mohamad to resign. As police looked on, several thousand people, mostly Malays, some Indians-pumped the air with their firsts and chanted slogans calling for the abolition of the Internal Security Act and demanding justice for former Deputy Prime Minister Anwar Ibrahim. (Hiebert and Jayasankaran October 29, 1998)

Protests continued into the fall as Anwar's trial began. The police used harsh tactics to break up the demonstrations, water canons and tear gas were both used. Although there seemed to be a huge outpouring of support for Anwar, and young people claimed to be politicized as never before, Mahathir's power never really seemed threatened. Even the creation of a new political party, the National Justice Party, led by Anwar's wife Wan Azizah, did not pose a significant challenge to the ruling apparatus. Mahathir called for elections in November of 1999 and although the Islamic opposition party (PAS) did increase their number of seats at the state and national level, the ruling coalition (the Barisan Nasional) was again able to maintain their hold over 60% of the seats in parliament.

The Role of Civil Society

The presence of autonomous civil society in Malaysia is questionable. A series of internal security acts are still on the books and are used to detain activists who try to mobilize citizen support, and they are used to break up demonstrations that the regime feels threatened by. Most media outlets are partially or wholly owned by companies connected to the dominant party coalition. Independent associations and not-for-profit groups are allowed to form but the government has been skeptical of such organizations and has curtailed their activities from time to time. The role of civil society is further complicated by ethnic relations. Malaysian Chinese have tended to be politically quiescent and they constitute a sizable proportion of the urban middle class. For a brief period in 1998 it looked as if oppositional political mobilization and organization might take root. However, many Chinese stayed away from the new activism and actually supported Mahathir in even greater numbers than before. Many business interests felt that their concerns were best addressed by the regime, not by the reform movement.

Lack of IMF Involvement

By not going to the IMF Mahathir did not have to implement structural reforms to the economy. Cozy relations were thus maintained between the BN coalition elites and business leaders. And, more liberal (economically speaking) forces in the government (namely Anwar) were left without external incentives for others to make changes in the political economy. Neither independent civil society advocates, nor Wan Aziz's National Justice Party, (or the long-standing opposition party the Democratic Action Party (DAP)) were able to capitalize on the new mood of discontent in Malaysia for several reasons:

1. The political system, particularly the electoral system, is highly gerrymandered in favor of the ruling coalition.
2. Chinese (who equal somewhat less than 30% of the population) became more supportive of the BN parties. In light of the violence in Indonesia, Chinese Malaysians seemed to feel that stability would be best maintained by the current regime. Additionally, many Chinese are among the economic elite. For them it was (and is) essential to nurture ties to politically powerful Malays.
3. Many of the newly politicized young people were kept off the voting rolls by lengthy and cumbersome voter registration requirements.

Ultimately, Mahathir was able to promote those who supported his policy preferences ad to push aside the most legitimate threat to his position. Popular protests did not translate into political change because the opposition parties are highly diverse in their constituent appeals, and because Malaysian political institutions make it significantly challenging to unseat the current elites. Likewise, Mahathir was able to avoid going to the IMF so Malaysia was not forced to restructure the close ties between business and political elites. Finally, Malaysian Chinese supported the ruling coalition in unprecedented numbers.

CONCLUSION

As the beginning of the paper explains, there are several reasons one can account for different political outcomes in Asia despite (roughly) similar economic woes in 1997/98. The case studies highlight the importance of political relations at the highest levels of power, and the relations between groups in society (civil society) and those in positions of power. Those leaders who were able to link support from some key element of society to the country's economic predicament were best able to hold power. So, Kim Dae-jung endorsed the IMF's plan and made an alliance with the more conservative Kim Jong Pil and so he did not alienate too large a section of the middle and business class. But, because of historical ties to labor activists and support for more left-wing causes, he appealed to a wide variety of voters. Since the elections were already scheduled and since South Korea already had fairly open and free elections, it was easier for a political opponent like Kim Dae-jung to challenge the incumbent government.

This is unlike the situation in Malaysia and Indonesia where opposition parties were either too narrow in their appeal (Malaysia) or emasculated (Indonesia under Suharto). Likewise, protestors in South Korea were able to look to Kim as a credible alternative to the ruling party. In 1998 in Indonesia, there was no opposition leader that protestors could look to for advocacy or power. Thus, toppling the regime was the only option. As for Malaysia, as popular a figure as Anwar was in 1999, he was in jail and his wife was unable to coordinate a large enough effort to challenge the system.

IMF prescriptions limited the maneuverability of Suharto and Kim Young Sam and opposition was able to capitalize on this weakness. The IMF programs empowered more 'liberal' leaders in Indonesia, thus increasing the number of top leaders who gradually withdrew their support from Suharto. Without IMF involvement in Malaysia, Mahathir was able to discredit and push Anwar aside.

Lastly, popular protests seemed effective in Indonesia and South Korea, but not in Malaysia. This is in part due to the size and intensity of the protests (particularly in Indonesia) but also because of who the protestors were and who supported them. In Indonesia business interests finally realized that Suharto's favoritism would cost them in terms of domestic stability and international economic imperatives. Additionally, the army was ultimately unwilling to ensure order. In South Korea students and labor groups were well organized and had already established links to Kim Dae-jung. When some middle class business interests also supported Kim, he was able to squeak out a victory. Neither of these elements was true in Malaysia.

Clearly, more research needs to be done on this link between economic crises, civil society and political change. Additional variables should be examined and more cases added to the sample.

REFERENCES

Agence France Presse. "South Korean President Warns of Stern Action Against Striking Kia Workers" October 27, 1997.

Baker, Michael. "Tear Gas and Protests Waft Away As South Korean Students Go Quiet." *Christian Science Mo*nitor August 20, 1989.

Bello, Walden. "Neither Market nor State: The Development Debate in South East Asia" *Ecologist* (London, England) July/August 1996:167-175.

Bienen, Henry S. and Mark Gersovitz. "Economic Stabilization, Conditionality, and Political Stability" in *International Organization*, Vol. 39, Issue 4, 1985, p. 729-754.

Choe, Sang-Hun. "South Korean Students, Workers Protest IMF Deal." *Associated Press* December 13, 1997.

-------------------. "South Korean Party Vows to Pass Bank Reform Bill" *Associated Press* November 14, 1997.

Cohen, Margot. "Divided They Stand" in *Far Eastern Economic Review*. March 12,1998A. p. 22-25.

Cohen, Margot. "Campus Crusaders: Students raise temperature of their protests" in *Far Eastern Economic Review*. March 26,1998B. p. 22-23.

Cohen, Margot. "To the Barricades" in *Far Eastern Economic Review*. May 14, 1998C. p. 21-24.

Cohen, Margot and John McBeth. "Unlikely Victor" in *Far Eastern Economic Review*. October 28, 1999, p.12-13.

Cohen, Margot; John McBeth and Michael Vatikiotis. "Into the Void" in *Far Eastern Economic Review*. June 4, 1998. P. 16-18.

Diamond, Larry. 1994. "Rethinking Civil Society: Toward Democratic Consolidation". *Journal of Democracy*, vol. 5, no. 3.

Diamond, Larry, and Juan J. Linz. "Politics, Society, and Democracy in Latin America." In Latin America, vol. 4 of *Democracy in Developing Countries*, ed. Larry Diamond, Juan J. Linz, and Seymour Martin Lipset (Boulder: Lynne Rienner. 1989.

Duch, Raymond. "Economic Chaos and the Fragility of Democratic Transitions in Former Communist Regimes" *Journal of Politics*, Vol. 57, No. 1 Feb. 1995:121-158.

Emmerson, Donald K. "A Take of Three Countries" in *Journal of Democracy* vol. 10 Issue 4. 1999, pp. 35-53.

Farley, Maggie. "Foes Push Indonesia's Suharto to Act or Quit" in *Los Angeles Times.* Times Mirror Company. January 11, 1998.

Fischer, Stanley. "Asia and the IMF". Speech delivered at the Institute of Policy Studies, Singapore. June 1, 2001.

Freedman, Amy L. *Political Participation and Ethnic Minorities* (NY: Routledge) 2000.

Frieden, Jeffrey A. *Debt, Development and Democracy Modern Political Economy and Latin America 1965-1985* (Princeton, NJ: Princeton University Press) 1991.

Garrett, Geoffrey and Peter Lange. "Internationalization, Institutions, and Political Change". *International Organization* Vol. 49, no. 4. 1995:627-655.

Garnaut, Ross. "East Asia after the financial crisis" in *Reform and Recovery in East Asia: The role of the state and economic enterprise* by Peter Drysdale. London, New York: Routledge, 2000.

Gasiorowski, Mark J. "Economic Crisis and Political Change: An Event History Analysis" *American Political Science Review* vol. 89, no. 4 December 1995.

Goldstein, Avery. "China's New Economic Scenario, Political Implications of a Slowdown" *Orbis* September 1999:203-221.

Gourevitch, Peter. "The Second Image Reversed: The International Sources of Domestic Politics." *International Organization* 32,4 (Autumn): 881-912.

Henderson, Jeffrey. "Uneven Crises: Institutional Foundations of East Asian Economic Turmoil" in *Economy and Society* Vol 28, no. 3. 1999:327-368.

Heo, Uk. "South Korea: Democratization, Financial Crisis, and the Decline of the Developmental State" in Horowitz, Shale and Uk Heo (eds.) *The Political Economy of International Financial Crisis* (NY: Rowman and Littlefield) 2001.

Hiebert, Murray, and S. Jayasankaran. "Consummate Insider" *Far Eastern Economic Review* (February 19, 1998a.

--------------------. "Mixed Signals*."* *Far Eastern Economic Review* (May 21, 1998b).

--------------------. "After the Fall" *Far Eastern Economic Review* (September 17, 1998c).

-------------------. "Bruised but Unbowed." *Far Eastern Economic Review* (October 8, 1998d).

Higgott, Richard. "The Asian Economic Crisis: A Study in the Politics of Resentment" *New Political Economy* Vol. 3, No. 3 1998.

Horowitz, Shale and Uk Heo "Explaining Precrisis Policies and Post Crisis Responses: Coalitions and Institutions in East Asia, Latin America and Eastern Europe." In Horowitz and Heo (eds.) *The Political Economy of International Financial Crisis* (NY: Rowman and Littlefield) 2001.

Huntington, Samuel. *Political Order and Changing Societies* (New Haven, CT: Yale University Press) 1968.

IMF Approves Stand-By Credit for Indonesia: Press Release Number 97/50. International Monetary Fund. November 5, 1997.

"Indonesian money crisis fuels student protests" in *The Toronto Star*. The Toronto Star Newspapers, Ltd. March 6, 1998.

"Indonesian President Suharto Resigns; Protests, Riots End President's 32-year Rule" in *Facts on File World News Digest*. Facts on File, Inc. May 21, 1998.

Japan Economic Newswire. "Kyonggi Gov. Announces bid for Presidential Nomination" March 24, 1997.

Jayasankaran, S. "High Wire Act" *Far Eastern Economic Review* (October 9, 1997a).

-------------------. "Eye of the Storm." *Far Eastern Economic Review* (October 16, 1997b).

-------------------. "Hit the Brakes." *Far Eastern Economic Review* (December 17, 1997c).

-------------------. "Malaysia: Surprise Attack." *Far Eastern Economic Review* (November 18, 1999).

Jeon, Jei Guk. "The Political Economy of Crisis Management in the Third World: A Comparative Study of South Korea and Taiwan in the 1970s" *Pacific Affairs* Vol. 67, Issue 4, Winter 1994-95.

Johnson, Tim. "Students protest on eve of Suharto reelection" in *Japan Economic Newswire.* Kyodo News Service. March 9, 1998.

Jordan, Mary. "Opposition Leader Wins South Korean Vote, New President Confronts Economic Crisis." *Washington Post* December 19, 1997:A1.

Katzenstein, Peter J. ed. *Between Power and Plenty: Foreign Economic Policies of Advanced Industrial Countries*. (Madison: University of Wisconsin Press) 1978.

Keohane, Robert O. and Helen V. Milner(eds.) *Internationalization and Domestic Politics* (NY: Cambridge University Press) 1996.

Lamb, David and Ron Tempest. "Suharto Resigns in Indonesia, Hands Power to Vice President" in *Los Angeles Times.* Times Mirror Company, May 21, 1998.

Londregan, John B. and Keith T. Poole. "Poverty, the Coup Trap and the Seizure of Executive Power" *World Politics*, Jan. 1990.

MacIntyre, Andrew. "Institutions and Investors: The Politics of the Economic Crisis in South East Asia." *International Organization* Vol. 55, no. 1 Winter 2001.

Manthorpe, Johnathan. "Confidence in Suharto nears breaking point: Indonesia, no stranger to violence, is facing food shortages and spiraling prices" in *The Vancouver Sun.* Pacific Press Ltd. February 20, 1998.

McBeth, John. "Family and Friends: Suharto unveils an inner-circle cabinet" in *Far Eastern Economic Review.* March 26, 1998A. P. 20-22.

McBeth, John. "Power Reversal: Electricity awards in Indonesia hark back to the old ways" in *Far Eastern Economic Review*. December 4, 1997. Vol. 160, No. 49, p. 79-80.

McBeth, John and Dan Murphy. "Balancing Act" in *Far Eastern Economic Review.* November 4, 1999, p. 18-19.

McBeth, John and Dan Murphy. "Double Whammy" in *Far Eastern Economic Review.* September 23, 1999, p. 8-10.

McBeth John and Henry Sender. "Default Options: Indonesia and the IMF count the cost of the rupiah's slide" in *Far Eastern Economic Review*. October 23, 1997. Vol. 160, No. 43, p. 88-92.

McBeth, John and Michael Vatikiotis. "Guess Again:Early signs cloud Megawati's presidential chances" in *Far Eastern Economic Review*. October 14, 1999. p.20.

McBeth, John and Michael Vatikiotis. "The Endgame" *Far Eastern Economic Review.* May 28, 1998, p. 12-15.

Mydans, Seth. "Suharto Is Still Weighing a Drastic Economic Move" in *The New York Times.* The New York Times Company. March 2, 1998.

Niles, Kimberly J. "Indonesia: Cronyism, Economic Meltdown, and Political Stalemate" in *The Political Economy of International Financial Crisis: Interest Groups, Ideologies, and Institutions* by Shale Horowitz and Uk Heo. New York, Oxford: Rowman and Littlefield Publishers, Inc: 2001.

Pastor, Manuel Jr. "The Effects of IMF Programs in the Third World: Debate and Evidence from Latin America" *World Development* Vol. 15, No. 2 1987:249-262.

Polglaze, Karen. "Crisis Encourages Democracy Leader To Take on Suharto" in *AAP Newsfeed*. AAP Information Services Pty. Ltd. May 14, 1998.

Przeworski, Adam. *Democracy and the Market: Political and Economic Reforms in Eastern Europe and Latin America.* (Cambridge: Cambridge University Press) 1991.

Remmer, Karen L. "The Political Impact of Economic Crisis in Latin America in the 1980s" *American Political Science Review* Vol. 85, No. 3 September 1991.

---------------------. "Democracy and Economic Crisis: The Latin American Experience" *World Politics* April 1999.

"Riots Hit Indonesian Capital for Third Day" in *AAP Newsfeed*. AAP Information Services Pty. Ltd. May 14, 1998.

Sakakibara, Eisuke. "IMF's Indonesia Reforms Too Severe" in *The Daily Yomiuri*. Global News Wire, December 10, 1999.

Schmitter, Philippe C. 1995. "On Civil Society and the Consolidation of Democracy: Ten General Propositions and Nine Speculations about their Relation in Asian Societies". Paper presented at an International Conference on Consolidating the Third Wave Democracies: Trends and Challenges, Taipei, August 27-30.

Schwarz, Adam and Michael Vatikiotis. "A Nation Awakes" *in Far Eastern Economic Review*. June 6, 1998. P. 21-26.

Susanto, Steven. "Indonesia and the IMF pill" in *Far Eastern Economic Review*. December 11, 1997. Vol. 160 No. 50 p. 32.

Torchia, Christopher. "Thousands of students stage anti-government protests in Indonesia" in *The Associated Press*. April 15, 1998.

Toyoda, Maria A. "Malaysia: Ethnic Cleavages and Controlled Liberalization" in Horowitz, Shale and Uk Heo (eds.) *The Political Economy of International Financial Crisis* (NY: Rowman and Littlefield) 2001.

Tripathi, Salil. "Stand-Off in Jakarta" in *Far Eastern Economic Review*. March 19, 1998. p. 18-19.

Vatikiotis, Michael. "Man the Pumps: IMF signals it may make stability the priority in Indonesia" in *Far Eastern Economic Review*. June 11, 1998, p.53.

--------------------- and Adam Schwarz. "A Nation Awakes." *Far Eastern Economic Review* June 4, 1998.

Watson, Paul. "Violence flares in Java" in *The Toronto Star*. Toronto Star Newspapers, February 1, 1998.

WuDunn, Sheryl. "Student Passion in Korea: What's the Point?" *New York Times* June 21, 1997:A1.

In: Korea: Economic, Political and Social Issues
Editors: P. H. Elwood, J. B. Albertus
ISBN: 978-1-60456-513-3

Chapter 9

THE DILEMMAS OF CHINA'S POLICIES FACING THE NORTH KOREAN CRISIS

Ting Wai

INTRODUCTION

The current relationship between the People's Republic of China (PRC) and the Democratic People's Republic of Korea (DPRK) is more than friendly, but it can hardly be called an alliance relationship. The two countries signed the Treaty of Friendship, Cooperation and Mutual Assistance in July 1961, and the "treaty cannot be revised or abrogated without prior mutual agreement (Article 7)".[1] However, despite the treaty, after the death of Kim Il Sung in 1994, China has not been able to exert strong influence upon North Korea. The leader of DPRK, Kim Jong Il, has been pursuing adventurous and brinkmanship activities independently for the national interests of North Korea, irrespective of the perceptions and national policies of China. Beijing always aspires to have a stable and peaceful security environment, so as to concentrate her efforts towards the modernization of the country. Paradoxically, China does never explicitly express her dissatisfaction of the misbehaviour of her neighbour, though by all means she is very much annoyed by those adventurous activities of North Korea that eventually drag the other powers, including Russia and Japan, into this crucial adjacent area of China. The alliance relationship could not be maintained as it was during the Kim Il Sung period, when Beijing was able to master the external behaviour of Kim, while also serving as a kind of intermediary in North Korea's relationship with the West. A hypothetical scenario could further test the so-called alliance relationship. If North Korea were attacked by the United States, would China assist in rescuing the North Korean regime and nation by sending army, similar to the Korean War in early fifties? Nobody would think that this is a possible scenario, and no serious scholars would also consider that the PRC would send an army to rescue her neighbour.

[1] See Samuel S. Kim, "China and the Future of the Korean Peninsula", in Tsuneo Akaha, *The Future of North Korea*, London: Routledge, 2002, p. 122.

This paper aims at investigating the dilemmas that China has to face in formulating and elaborating her policies vis-à-vis North Korea, especially after the September 11th incident in New York which causes a serious dislocation of power constellation in the international political order. Washington has been trying very hard, and not without success, to construct a worldwide "united front" in order to counter-attack terrorism. Beijing supports anti-terrorism, since it is burdened with fighting against the terrorist activities caused by the Xinjiang separtists who seek to establish the so-called East Turkistan. China aspires to establish a peaceful and stable external environment, especially in Northeast Asia, Central Asia, as well as South Asia, so that she could concentrate her energies on Taiwan problem and the South China Sea issues. The brinkmanship activities of North Korea have long been a matter of serious concern among Chinese leaders and analysts. Hopefully, with the "sunshine policy" of President Kim Dae Jung of South Korea which resulted in his visit in Pyongyang in June 2000, and the apparent amelioration of relationship between Pyongyang and Washington in the same year, it seems that China could feel secure and stable regarding her northeast border. However, with the advent of power of President Bush in 2001, who characterizes North Korea as a member of "axis of evil" after Iraq and Iran, Kim Jong Il gain uses the nuclear instrument in exchange for concrete benefits from the United States. He has especially sought for the guarantee of not attacking North Korea, through the establishment of a pact of non-aggression with the United States. Through the vicissitudes of Pyongyang's actions against the Bush administration since 2001, China has to face a series of dilemmas. It is aimed in this paper to reveal these dilemma and to analyze what efforts China has to make in order to resolve the problems caused by these dilemmas.

Dilemma 1: Decreasing Influence of China in Solving the North Korean Crisis

It is quite evident that Beijing has been frustrated by its decreasing role in solving the crisis launched by the North Korean regime. China always plays a significant intermediary role in North Korea's relationship with the outside world especially with the West, owing to Pyongyang's self-imposed isolation and its adoption of the *juche* ideology, which means self-reliance and independence. However, since the advent of power of Kim Jong Il, the situation has largely changed, as Kim is keen of directly dealing with the West, especially with the United States. The North Korean leaders seek for their own national interests, irrespective of Chinese leader's perceptions as well as Chinese political-strategic interests. China seemingly is gradually losing its role as the most significant intermediary between North Korea and the West. But on the other hand, China wants to have stability in Northeast Asia, which is a crucial part in the security environment of China. Beijing seeks to achieve a stable and peaceful security environment, so that she could concentrate her energy on the Taiwan issue. After the end of cold war, China should have paid more attention to the situation of Northeast Asia, especially the increasing divergence of perceptions of China and North Korea regarding the road of modernization. The former has virtually abolished the socialist economic system, while the latter is bemused by any modification of its socialist model. Indeed, China has not really tried to elaborate a policy on Northeast Asia after the cold war. However, she is now "dragged" upon by the instability in Northeast Asia, which is a result of the brinkmanship activities and adventurous actions of Kim Jong Il. Not only is China unable to "control" the activities of her dear neighbour, she is in return affected by the unilateral actions of Kim which causes instability in the northeast border region of China. This is indeed contrary to the situation when Kim Il Sung was in power, when Chinese leaders were confident of obtaining full support and cooperation from Kim Il Sung, due to the "friendship" built up as heritage of the Korean War. By all means one should not forget that Kim Il Sung was basically a Cold War figure. He did succeed in milking full support from both China and the Soviet Union.

In short, during the Kim Il Sung era, to a large extent China was able to "master" the situation in Northeast Asia, due to her capability to monitor the behaviour of the North Korean leaders. During the Kim Jong Il era however, even though North Korea has been at the brink of bankruptcy and China has been providing much assistance that her neighbour is in need, China's ability to influence the situation in Northeast Asia has in reality diminished. Yet, Beijing cannot disrupt her relationship with North Korea by adopting a harsher attitude, or providing less help as promulgated by many American analysts so as press the Pyongyang regime to abide by the requirements imposed by the West. A tougher attitude of China, longtime ally of the DPRK, might even result in a worse scenario in the eyes of Chinese leaders and analysts, as the Pyongyang regime might have no choice but implementing an even more adventurous position. So, though China has been trying very hard to monitor the situation in her northeast border, she feels rather frustrated by the reality that her influence towards her neighbour has diminished, thus augmenting the uncertainties and unpredictability in Northeast Asia that China has to face.

Dilemma 2: Stagnation in North Korean Economy and Its Staggering Economic Reform

China hopes to see economic reform in North Korea, base on the Chinese model that economic liberalization and the development of market economy can be proceeded under the one-party dictatorship. The leadership exercised by the Chinese Communist Party (CCP) in forging ahead economic reform, which results in better livelihood of the general masses, might even help to legitimize thus consolidate the rule of the CCP. However, the North Korean reactions have always been lukewarm. Despite the enactment of various laws and the plans of setting up special economic zones, what North Korea has achieved is extremely limited. The North Korean leaders have mixed feelings about economic reforms, fearing that the market economy is against socialism and would eventually disrupt the regime. They are not experienced and the measures adopted are ineffective. China has a lot of experiences to share with the North Korean leaders, and according to the Chinese analysts, the Chinese model of development is the best suitable model to liberate North Korea from its stalemate of economic crisis. But the slow progress in North Korea does not help the nation to categorically improve the situation, and a poorer North Korea would only add the sense of insecurity and danger among its leaders. Her resulting adventurous reactions would merely create a situation in Northeast Asia which is obviously not favourable to Beijing.

A South Korean scholar proclaims that Kim Jong Il "attempted to save the socialist system in North Korea by transforming socialism with the *juche* ideology while considering economic reform and open-door policy".[2] Back to the early 80s, the then North Korean leader Kim Il Sung enacted a "joint venture law" and also started a policy of foreign investment and trade. Accordingly, the Rajin-Sonbong Special Economic Zone in the northeast part of North Korea was created, and more than 130 joint ventured enterprises, including 40 Chinese investments and 70 investments of Korean residents in Japan, were established.[3] However, in comparison to two decades of rapid economic growth in China, what these foreign investments have contributed to the DPRK economy is minimal and questionable.

In fact, since the South Korean former President Kim Dae Jung proclaimed the "sunshine policy" in 2000, Pyongyang did establish two new Special Economic Zones in Shinijiu and Gaeseong. The former city is opposite to the Chinese border city of Dandong, just across the Yalu River. It is aimed to attract the investments of Chinese entrepreneurs. Gaeseong is an industrial city just north of the Demilitarized Zone (DMZ), thus very near to the border with South Korea, and it is hoped that South Korean investors will be attracted to set up manufacturing there. However, the fate of these two Special Economic Zones are different. Indeed, the development of Shinijiu was put to a halt, virtually by the Chinese authorities, since they arrested Yang Bin, the Dutch-nationality Chinese citizen who was appointed Chief Executive of Shinijiu by the North Korean regime. Eventually Yang was sentenced to 18 years in prison. Though apparently Yang was arrested due to his economic crimes committed in China, Beijing was in fact very irritated by the establishment and opening up of Shinijiu, and appointing Yang Bin as the official leader, without informing Beijing beforehand. If Shinijiu were opened up, which means that foreigners could enter this Special Economic Region freely, this would pose tremendous problems to the border city of China, Dandong. Gaeseong seems to have progress, with 10 pilot companies from South Korea selected in May 2004 that would start their operation by the end of the year.[4]

Since summer 2002, Pyongyang started to launch its economic reform program. The salaries of workers were raised by 18 times, while the prices of many commodities, including rice, skyrocketed many times. The price of rice has been raised 550 times.[5] The Pyongyang regime wants the price to reflect the market situation, as well as to balance the supply and demand of various products. The Korean People's Won, the currency of North Korea, was very much devaluated. Its exchange rate to US dollar was changed from 2.16 to 150, which is still quite far away from the black market rate of 900 or even 1500. The results of this reform remain unclear, but according to some independent analysts, the situation inside North Korea is not so bad. The GDP growth in the year 2002 has reached 1.2%, while the agricultural sector, including fisheries and forestry, recorded a growth of 4.2%.[6] According to Chinese sources, the scarce resources which were originally allocated mainly to the heavy industry, have now been diverted to the light industries in order to produce more consumer goods. Moreover, the liberalization of domestic and international trade can help to "have reduced

[2] See Ilpyong J. Kim, "China in North Korean Foreign Policy", in S. S. Kim ed., *North Korea Foreign Relations in the Post-Cold War Era*, Hong Kong: Oxford University Press, 1999, p. 97.

[3] Ibid., p. 107.

[4] Bertil Lintner "Shop Till You Drop", *Far Eastern Economic Review,* 13 May 2004, p. 16.

[5] See Dominique Dwor-Frécaut, "Korea" Long-term Decline in the North Korea premium", *Asian Rates and Credit Research*, Singapore: Barclays Capital, 27 February 2004, p. 2

[6] See Li Dunqiu, "Nuclear Crisis, Economic Reform in the North, Turmoils in the South", *Shijie Zhishi (World Affairs),* No. 1, 2004, 1 January 2004, p. 35. For the latest report on North Korean economy, see Bertil Lintner "Shop Till You Drop", *Far Eastern Economic Review,* 13 May 2004, pp. 14-20.

wastage and increased actual goods availability".[7] While all these are positive signs, analysts do not predict a fast and relatively healthy growth as in the case of China. Since the North Korean leaders are still heavily burdened with their ideology against capitalism, and have been skeptical with the possible negative effects arisen from economic reform and open-door policy, it is implausible that North Korea would progress vastly from its cautious economic reform. The Chinese authorities still need more patience in exporting its model of development.

DILEMMA 3: NORTH KOREAN POSSESSION OF NUCLEAR WEAPONS

China has long promoted a policy of non-nuclear Korean peninsula, thus she aligns with the United States in this difficult and yet crucial issue. Washington always emphasizes that the two countries have common interests regarding the stability of Korean Peninsula, and urges China to play a more active role in pressing against Pyongyang in accepting the conditions imposed by the West. China never wants to give the impression to Pyongyang leaders that they are standing besides Western particularly American leaders in forcing DPRK to accept the terms. But it is crystal clear that it is a nightmare to China if North Korea is equipped with nuclear weapons, even if it may mean a small amount of nuclear weapons.

Before the September 11th incident, North Korea had been using plutonium, which was created by the processing of uranium-238 by its heavy-water reactors, as a political instrument to exchange for concrete benefits from the United States, since the plutonium after reprocessing could be used to fabricate nuclear bombs. The 1994 crisis was solved with Washington agreeing to provide a light-water reactor by 2003, while the heavy-water reactors had to be shut down. During the interval, Washington agreed to give 500,000 tons of heavy fuel oil per year. In August 1998, North Korea launched the Tae Po Dong-I missile over Japan. In short, during the 1990s, Pyongyang was enthusiastic in provoking crises for its neighbours through using the missiles and the plutonium as a kind of bargaining chips, in order to exchange for material benefits, including heavy fuel oil, food and other financial assistance, from the United States, Japan and South Korea.

Nevertheless, after the September 11th, North Korea was named as a member of the "axis of evil" by the Bush administration, which even considers attacking "preemptively" these countries in order to enforce "regime change".[8] The "axis of evil" concept is quite awkward, as it is ludicrous to put Iraq, Iran and North Korea in the same basket. Facing the danger of being attacked by Washington, as in the cases of Afghanistan and Iraq, it is not impossible that North Korean leaders might envisage the possibility of fabricating nuclear weapons. Given the fact that United States main agenda item in its foreign policies is to prevent the proliferation of weapons of mass destruction, "provoking" the crisis of fabricating nuclear weapons may be useful in deriving a "higher prize" from the United States. In other words, promoting the idea of making nuclear weapons and dissipating the fear among its neighbours may again be used as bargaining chips to extract the maximum benefits from the United States. Moreover, developing nuclear weapons is less costly than developing conventional

[7] Ibid., p. 4.

[8] This is revealed by the "Nuclear Posture Review" prepared by the Department of Defense, United States, and disclosed by the *Los Angeles Times* in January 2002.

army. The one-million strong North Korean army is a heavy burden to the national economy of DPRK as the military expenditure reaches 25 % of the GDP.[9] Nuclear weapons can also help to stimulate national sentiments among the people, who have been suffering in the last decade due to economic downturn that resulted even in starvation. The nuclear weapons also produces the so-called "equalizer" effect, thus enables the weak North Korea to balance against the much stronger Japan and South Korea.

Even though the Chinese government does not know whether North Korea got nuclear weapons or not, it is obvious that Pyongyang, which is apt at launching crises in order to extract the maximum benefits, would use the pretext of already possessing nuclear weapons in exchange for a security guarantee from Washington. This is the source of crisis starting from October 2002. When the United States Assistant Secretary of State James Kelly asked whether North Korea has a plan to fabricate "enriched uranium" with the assistance of Pakistan, the DPRK officials hinted that they possessed nuclear weapons. Washington has been very consistent in requesting a "complete, verifiable, irreversible dismantlement" of North Korea's nuclear program. In order to apply the pressure to Pyongyang, the Bush administration decided to stop the export of 500,000 tons of heavy-fuel oil to North Korea in December 2002. In retaliation, North Korea in November 2002 declared that the "Agreed Framework" signed in 1994 was no longer valid, and reopened the heavy-water reactors at Yongbyon in December 2002. The IAEA inspectors were expulsed from the country, and Pyongyang declared that it would start to process the 8000 spent fuel rods from the nuclear reactors in order to extract the weapon-grade plutonium. Though perhaps only some of it would be reprocessed, the plutonium obtained could be used directly for the fabrication of nuclear weapons, so it is particularly alarming. United States intelligence officials agree that "the reprocessing is incomplete, but that the North probably made enough fuel last year for two or three more weapons".[10] In January 2003, the DPRK regime decided to quit the Nuclear Non-proliferation Treaty (NPT). The divergence between North Korea and United States has led to hot debates and diplomatic maneuvers. What North Korea wants is by all means security guarantee from the United States, in addition of economic aid including food, oil and other resources. What the Bush administration wants to achieve is not only to stop Pyongyang's nuclear program, but also "regime transformation" if not "regime change". The Director of Policy Planning of the State Department of the United States, Mitchell Reiss, hence declares, "our objectives are more encompassing. We do not simply seek a DPRK without WMD, but the transformation of the DPRK into a 'normal' state."[11]

China is again caught in a dilemma. On the one hand, she does not want to have a nuclearized Korean Peninsula, but she has no means to press the North Korean regime to stop its nuclear plan. On the other hand, she is not willing to join the United States in imposing sanctions against the regime, due to the past alliance relationship, as well as due to its own understanding that implosion of North Korea would be even worse than the current situation. What is more, if North Korea possesses nuclear weapons, that would certainly provoke Japan and South Korea to follow. Japan has been accumulating plutonium and she is able to fabricate nuclear weapons within a very short period of time. Strategic analysts call this "recessed deterrence". The deterrence effects are already there; even if Japan has no nuclear

[9] See *Military Balance: 2003-2004,* London: International Institute for Strategic Studies, 2003, p. 337.

[10] See "U. S. experts visit Korea nuclear site", *International Herald Tribune*, 12 January 2004, p. 6

[11] Mitchell Reiss, "North Korea's legacy of Missed Opportunities", *The DPRK Briefing Book: US Policy*, The Nautilus Institute, 12 March 2004, p. 5.

armaments now, she could have it almost immediately. The famous right-wing Japanese politician, Ichiro Ozawa has announced in a high-profile manner that Japanese nuclear plants have sufficient amount of plutonium to produce as much as three to four thousand warheads. Japanese scientists can fabricate a thousand warheads overnight. The former Chief Cabinet Secretary of Japanese government, Yasuo Fukuda, even hinted that Japan might consider abandoning the "Non-nuclear Three Principles", that is, no procession, no fabrication and no importation.[12] South Korea might also have the technological expertise to fabricate nuclear weapons. If the two Koreas plus Japan possess nuclear weapons, that would constitute a nightmare for the security environment of China, especially that she has already been very irritated by the possession of nuclear weapons as well as delivery vehicles, ballistic missiles, by her two southern neighbours, India and Pakistan, since 1998. However, one crucial question remains. It seems that both United States and China have eventually learned to accept India and Pakistan as nuclear powers. Why couldn't they accept North Korea as well?

DILEMMA 4: REUNIFICATION OF KOREA

China does not welcome the reality of a collapse of the DPRK regime. The disintegration of the country would pose tremendous problems to her neighbours, including China and South Korea. The continual economic crisis and food shortage in North Korea has pushed many North Koreans to leave the country, and become refugees or defectors in China. There have been estimates of between 100,000 and 300,000 illegal immigrants,[13] who hide themselves in the northeast region of China, with the assistance of Chinese-Koreans who reside in that area. Hundreds of thousands of illegal immigrants have created a lot of social and economic problems. China does not want to treat these people as refugees, thus disallows those humanitarian organizations from providing greatly needed assistance to them, causing a series of problems between these NGOs and the Chinese authorities.[14] Beijing does not recognize these people as refugees, but only as "economic migrants". As a consequence, they are repatriated back to North Korea and the people suffer from detention, forced labour, discrimination or even execution. Some of these "immigrants" manage to arrive at Beijing and try to get into the foreign embassies in order to acquire the protection of those nations as "political refugees". Eventually they manage to settle down in South Korea.

On the one hand, China does not want these North Korean illegal immigrants to become a burden for the development of the neighbouring regions of China, which have already been suffering from the bankruptcy of many state-owned entreprises. On the other hand, China is reluctant to let these immigrants become a source of conflicts between Beijing and Pyongyang. Apart from arresting them and sending them back, the best way in the mind of Chinese leaders is to stop these North Korean people from entering. It has been reported in

---

[12] See *Ta Kung Pao*, 9 April 2002, p. A3, quoted from Ting Wai, "Situational Dynamics of Korean Peninsula and the Chinese Security Environment", *The Korean Journal of International Studies*, Vol. 30, No. 1, Spring/Summer 2003, p. 114.

[13] See David Shambaugh, "China and the Korean Peninsula: Playing for the Long Term", *The Washington Quarterly*, Spring 2003, pp. 43-56. See also Ming Liu, "China and the North Korean Crisis: Facing Test and Transition", *Pacific Affairs*, Vol. 76, No. 3, Fall 2003, pp. 347-373.

[14] See "The Plight of North Korean Migrants in China: A Current Assessment", Congressional-Executive Commission on China, Washington D. C.,19 April 2004.

September 2003 that the border police was replaced by 150,000 soldiers.[15] Though it is specified in the Chinese press that it streamlines thc operations, since border police and border soldiers perform different functions and in the past they always overlapped, it is quite obvious that the border control executed by the soldiers thereafter has been much tighter. This aims to prevent cross-border crimes and illegal migration. Less illegal immigrants would relieve the pressure on Beijing regarding its relationship with the West, particularly the negative comments made by the humanitarian organizations on the mistreatment of those refugees by China, and on its relationship with the North Korean regime.

China continues to supply heavy fuel oil and food to North Korea. It is estimated that about "one million tons of wheat and rice and 500,000 tons of heavy fuel oil per annum" were supplied to North Korea since 1994. Mutual visits of Chinese and North Korean leaders are always marked by agreements on providing economic assistance. During the visit of a high-level North Korean delegation in May 1996, the two sides signed an agreement on economic and technical assistance, with an emergency shipment of half million tons of food grain to North Korea.[16] It was also promised that the food aid would continue until 2000. During former Chinese President Jiang Zemin's visit to Pyongyang in September 2001, North Korean government obtained "grant-in-aid" of 30,000 tons of diesel fuel and 200,000 tons of food.[17] China again supplied 200,000 tons of grains to DPRK during Kim Jong Il's visit to China in April 2004. It is estimated that 200,000 tons of grains is enough for the DPRK population to live for slightly more that a month. The continual supplies of food and oil did help to sustain the regime and prevent the implosion of the country, but China did not succeed greatly in instigating massive and effective reforms within North Korea. Albeit no collapse, negative growth constitutes already a source of crisis in North Korea. Facing a neighbour that is at the brink of collapse. what are the Chinese perceptions of the reunification of Korea?

According to Chinese leaders and analysts, reunification of Korea should be done peacefully, in phases, and the two sides must be equal during the process of negotiation. China does not want to see a reunification process with the "absorption" of North Korea by South Korea. This would yield another great democratic power in Northeast Asia that allies with the United States and Japan, resulting in China's disadvantage in the regional balance of power. Already the United States-Japan alliance is almost the only power clusters that is able to check and balance the rising power of China. Chinese analysts are not receptive to the idea of adding a unified and democratic Korea to this alliance. As a consequence, Beijing leaders seek to strengthen economic and political linkages with Seoul. Relationship has been healthily developed since the two established their diplomatic relations in 1992. On the other hand, South Korea is always very cautious of not to antagonize Beijing.

In early June 2004, the militaries of North and South Korea convened their second talk at the level of General. They arrived at an agreement to stop their propaganda at the DMZ, and to prevent military conflict at the western sea of the Korean Peninsula.[18] They also agreed to exchange information on illegal fishing of third country. In fact, just ten days later, on the 15

---

[15] See Tang Tian, "The Reality of Relieving Garrison of Chinese Army at the Sino-North Korean Border", *Jing Bao (Mirror) Monthly,* November 2003, pp. 52-54

[16] See Ilpyong J. Kim, "China in North Korean Foreign Policy", pp. 108-112.

[17] See Samuel S. Kim & Tai Kwan Lee, "Chinese-North Korean Relations: Managing Asymmetrical Interdependence", in Samuel S. Kim & Tai Hwan Lee eds., *North Korea and Northeast Asia*, Lanham: Towman & Littlefield, 2002, p. 116.

[18] See the report in *Ta Kung Pao*, 5 June 2004, p. A7.

June 2004 the two sides exchanged information on the alleged "illegal" fishing of Chinese fishermen at the sea between China and the Korean Peninsula.[19] This reflects the subtle nationalist feelings of the two Koreas though they are still hostile to each other.

Thus, though China does not want to see the collapse of North Korea, she is not prepared to see a unified Korea with South Korea incorporating North Korea. She would like to see effective reform of the North Korean systems, but so far the progress is slow and not obvious. The continual supply of aid by China would only sustain the stalemate, but not powerful enough to instigate changes. China cannot even monitor the North Korean leaders from provoking crises, and at the same time does not want to ally with the Western powers in adopting strong and hostile actions like sanctions. By providing only carrots without sticks, would China maintain a harmonious relationship with North Korea, and gradually convince the latter to accept a policy of reforms?

Prospects of the Six-party Talk: China's Role and Contributions

China does not want implosion of the country North Korea, or explosion of the situation. For the future of Six-party talk, China wants an incremental approach, but quick and forceful actions, in order to defend the principles of denuclearization of the Korean Peninsula and the peaceful resolution of the Korean crisis.

Following the crisis initiated in autumn/winter 2002, the United States and North Korea agreed to meet in Beijing in April 2003 for a preliminary discussion. Washington wants to have a multilateral setting to carry on the discussion, while Pyongyang wants to have a bilateral negotiation. Washington thinks that bilateral agreement is "useless", as in the case of the "Agreed Framework" signed in October 1994. The North Korean regime cannot be trusted. However, for Pyongyang, the crisis is a problem between the United States and DPRK, and it seeks to discuss on an equal status on a bilateral basis with Washington in order to breakthrough the diplomatic imbroglio and isolation imposed by the Bush administration. Pyongyang also trusts that bilateral talk would raise the status and influence of the nation, and that it could avoid the isolation in a multilateral setting. Eventually with China playing a subtle but crucial intermediary role, the United States and North Korea representatives succeed of sitting on the negotiation table, with the participation of other powers, including China, Japan, Russia and South Korea. The first Six-party talk was held in August 2003, and the second round in February 2004, and the third round in June 2004.

Being labeled as a member of the "axis of evil" since 2002, Pyongyang could not believe that the international community could hinter the development of American unilateralism and possible pre-emptive attack against these "rogue" states. North Korean leaders truly believe that the hawkish Bush administration strives to apply pressure, sanctions and containment policy against North Korea in order to incur the breakdown of the regime. The American actions can be illustrated by the following four possible steps. First, the United States government seeks to halt North Korea's nuclear program. Second, it would consider setting up a multilateral framework to contain and control the actions of North Korea in the future,

[19] See the report in a South Korean newspaper, *Chosun Ilbo*, 16 June 2004 (Internet edition).

through a series of multilateral negotiation. Third, it would also envisage applying economic and political sanctions in order to constrain the freedom of maneuver of the DPRK regime. Lastly, if effective actions are failed, it is estimated that the Bush administration may even consider launching pre-emptive attack, as in the case of Iraq. These strong actions of the United States are regarded as possible scenarios. As a consequence, following its habitual practice, Pyongyang also adopts strong actions, by escalating the conflicts to a level unacceptable to Washington. This time the North Korean regime uses the possible fabrication of nuclear weapons, not only through possessing the plutonium into weapon-grade, but also through enriched uranium, a technology that had been supplied by Pakistan's leading nuclear scientist, Abdul Qadeer Khan.[20] Again, the nuclear weapons are used as bargaining chips simply because the United States always regard the proliferation of weapons of mass destruction as the primary problem in East Asian security.

During the first multilateral negotiation in August 2003, North Korea proposed a "road map" that seeks to solve the problems "simultaneously in a basket". There should be four stages. During the first stage, the United States should restore the supply of heavy fuel oil and increase the food assistance, while North Korea would explicitly express that she would "freeze" her nuclear program. Entering into the next stage, the United States should sign with North Korea a pact of non-aggression, while North Korea would freeze her nuclear program, and allowing American investigators to make a verification once per year. The third stage would be characterized by the establishment of diplomatic relationship by the DPRK with United States and Japan, while the former would stop its testing and export of ballistic missiles. During the fourth and final stage, the Korean Peninsula Energy Development Organization (KEDO), under the leadership of Washington, should finish the construction of the two light-water reactors as stipulated in the "Agreed Framework" signed in 1994, while North Korea would remove all the other nuclear facilities.[21]

The American government categorically rejected this "road map". Starting from November 2003, the DPRK has tried to make the first stage more concrete. It is specified that during this first round of actions, the United States should remove the name of North Korea from the list of 'countries that support terrorism", and abolish all kinds of political, economic and military sanctions and containment measures. Washington and its allies should continue to provide energy assistance, such as supplies of heavy fuel oil and electricity. In exchange, the Pyongyang regime promises not to test or produce nuclear weapons, and even stop the peaceful use of nuclear facilities such as the production of nuclear energy.

However, what the Bush administration wants is persistently the "complete, verifiable and irreversible" dismantlement of all the nuclear facilities of North Korea. During the second round of Six-party talk, neither side has made any concession, though all the parties concerned agreed that the denuclearization of the Korean Peninsula should be the ultimate goal. In December 2003, the North Korean Foreign Ministry spokesman declared that all the nuclear programs, including the peaceful use of nuclear energy, could be stopped provided as some conditions are fulfilled. But during the 6-party talk, this position was retreated to stopping only the nuclear weapon program but not the civilian-use program. Thereafter, the DPRK only uses the term "freeze" in referring to its nuclear weapons program. Moreover,

---

[20] See Paul B. Stares & Banning Garrett, "Why North Korea might be ready for a deal", *International Herald Tribune*, 24 February 2004, p. 8.

[21] See Zhang Lianhuai, "A Test of Political Wisdom: the End of the Second Round of Six-party Talk concerning the Korean Nuclear Issue", *Shijie Zhishi (World Affairs)*, No. 6, 2004, 16 March 2004, p. 31.

North Korean representative at the talk simply denied the existence of enriched uranium inside the country. All these are considered as unacceptable by the United States, which urges for the complete destruction of all the nuclear facilities, before any assistance and normalization process could be started. In short, North Korea wants to have compensation in terms of economic assistance and security guarantee, in exchange for its "freezing" of nuclear program.[22]

Another major divergence between United States and North Korea is the meaning of denuclearization of the Korean Peninsula. Though both sides agree that this should be the final goal, what Pyongyang implies is the complete withdrawal of American nuclear weapons from South Korea, while Washington's understanding of denuclearization of the Peninsula merely means the abandonment of nuclear facilities by Pyongyang.

It is often emphasized by Chinese analysts that China has been playing a very significant role in bringing success to the Six-party talk. Fulfilling the conditions of both United States and North Korea to sit on the negotiation table is already regarded as a diplomatic success. Despite the three rounds of talk, it is difficult to achieve a breakthrough from the impasse. The essence of the problem is the hostility and mutual mistrust of North Korea and the United States. Facing the containment policy of Washington, Pyongyang uses the nuclear issue as a means to bring the former into negotiation, and to deter the possibility of attacking by Washington. According to the Chinese strategic analysts, North Korea abolishing the nuclear programs and United States engagement of not attacking North Korea are the immediate objectives to solve the security crisis in the Korean Peninsula. Normalization of relationship between North Korea and United States with the final settlement of the Korean War through enacting international treaties is the ultimate goal in order to settle permanently the crisis.[23]

The dilemma for China is that what she could do is rather limited. She has made it very clear what she could not do. This includes basically applying pressure and sanctions. As all kinds of fundamental changes come from domestic factors, the pressure from the exterior is always short-lived. China cannot stand alone in solving the crisis, and a multilateral mechanism is crucially needed for the final settlement of the Peninsula crisis.[24] But what China could do is rather limited. Chinese analysts said that China should have a very clear judgement on her own national interests, and a definite and sensible policy. Since China can judge the matter from an objective position, she would be able to design a fair, reasonable and workable solution. She should be able to find a solution that could solve the matter in a limited period of time, with mutual similar and synchronized actions from both sides, and the whole process must be incremental.[25] All these words, though rational and reasonable, do not reflect how China is able to achieve a breakthrough in the current stalemate.

Chinese analysts stress that promoting peaceful negotiation among the parties concerned in the Korean Peninsula may be useful in elevating the international status of the nation. Yet, China should be more open in considering the possible solutions to the problem so as to walk out from the dilemma that Beijing has to face. For instance, in 1994, Ukraine, Kazakhstan and Belarus gave up nuclear weapons, in return for multilateral security guarantee from the five

---

[22] See *Ta Kung Pao*, 12 May 2004, p. A14, and 14 May 2004, p. A3.

[23] See Wu Baiyue, "Hot Points, Flash Points and Standing Points: Commenting on the International Situation in 2004", *Shijie Zhishi (World Affairs)*, No. 1, 2004, 1 January 2004, pp. 42-43.

[24] Ibid., p. 43.

[25] See Zhang Lianhuai, "A Test of Political Wisdom: the End of the Second Round of Six-party Talk concerning the Korean Nuclear Issue", p. 33.

members of the Nuclear Club. Moreover, they were offered a guarantee by the five powers "to refrain from economic coercion".[26] Can this "Ukraine" model be accepted by China as well?

CONCLUDING REMARKS

Although North Korea always insists that the so-called nuclear crisis is basically a bilateral problem between Pyongyang and Washington, the latter always stresses that the whole issue affects the regional security of Northeast Asia, so all the powers concerned should be involved in the resolution process. More particularly, China, long ally of North Korea, is considered as the key figure that could help to a great extent so solve the issue. Beijing of course aspires to become the chief mediator that help to pave the way towards peaceful conflict management. Beijing also emphasizes on neutrality and impartiality. Its impartial and objective position is regarded as instrumental in convincing the two major parties to arrive at a conclusion that benefits all. China seeks to change the behaviour of the two actors, aiming to achieve a formal settlement. However, despite the fact that China has succeeded of hosting three rounds of 6-party talk, up to now what China could do in changing the behaviour of both parties remains rather limited. She is not able to convince either North Korea or the United States to retreat from their original position.

All of the dilemma of China facing the North Korean regime play a part in affecting the effectiveness and efficiency of China as a successful mediator between the superpower and the last socialist country. By all means Chinese leaders cannot agree to the adventurous behaviour and brinkmanship activities provoked by the North Korean leaders, which serve the national interests of North Korea but detrimental to the interests of her neighbours. On the other hand, Chinese leaders cannot stand besides the United States in carrying out economic sanction or political coercion as a means to exchange for concessions from the intransigent Kim Jong Il. The traditional relationship between the two regimes and the similarities of the political institutions serve as a kind of umbilical cord that bind the two regimes together. The collapse of the Pyongyang regime is perceived as a setback in Chinese foreign policies, as the latter has been for a long time a kind of buffer in China's external behaviour vis-à-vis Japan and United States.

Yet, American analysts and officials are still enthusiastic in securing the help from China in pressing against North Korea. "Washington is seeking to convince China that North Korea is damaging its own interests and that it would be far better for Beijing to act to rein in Pyongyang than risk leaving it to Washington to do so........Behind the scenes, American should urge China to take more drastic action."[27] They think that a harder Chinese position against the North Korean regime would cause the latter to succumb to the pressure from the United States. In a report issued by the United States-China Economic and Security Review Commission to the American Congress in June 2004, the Commission urges the Bush administration to encourage the PRC to adopt a more ambitious attitude in forcing the DPRK to abolish completely its nuclear weapons. The Commission complains that China has not

[26] See Paul B. Stares & Banning Garrett, "Why North Korea might be ready for a deal", *International Herald Tribune*, 24 February 2004, p. 8.

[27] See Robyn Lim, "Persuading China to Rein in Pyongyang", *Asian Wall Street Journal*, 18 February 2004, p. A7.

tried her best to apply economic and political pressure on North Korea, forcing her to fully abandon her nuclear plan. It is stipulated that future development of United States-Chinese relations should be related to Beijing's ability to resolve the North Korean nuclear crisis.[28] Washington also wants China to support its Proliferation Security Initiative (PSI) so as to forbid the transfer of weapons of mass destruction and missiles. It envisages common efforts to "enhance law enforcement, judicial cooperation, and sharing of intelligence" in order to curb North Korea's activities in this regard.[29]

It is quite clear that both Pyongyang and Washington are not very enthusiastic in solving the issue in short-term. The former is hoping that President Bush would lose in the presidential election in November 2004, and that hopefully it would be easier to extract more benefits from the new Democratic government. The Bush administration is not willing to give up its stringent request for a complete destruction of the nuclear program of North Korea. In a study on international mediation, the foremost condition for a successful mediation is the existence of a "hurting stalemate" perceived by the parties concerned.

> "The parties reach a 'hurting stalemate' when their own efforts to manage the conflict are not going anywhere, and yet the costs, both human and economic, of pursuing the conflict continue to mount."[30]

It seems that for both North Korea and United States, they have not yet reached the "hurting stalemate". Thus, no solution of the problem is immediately available. But for China, it seems that she tends to align more with the South Korean government regarding the best policy towards the "misbehaviour" of North Korea. Engagement and encouragement rather than an intransigent attitude and threat of sanctions and coercion practiced by the Bush administration might be more fruitful in instigating incremental changes in North Korea. China believes that it is possible to solve the crisis in an incremental way but step-by-step substantial mutual actions are crucially needed. A less intransigent attitude of the United States might be helpful to China's role as the mediator, though she is still burdened with the series of dilemma, facing the unpredictable and irrational Kim Jong Il.

---

[28] See *Ta Kung Pao*, 17 June 2004, p. A2.

[29] Balbina Y. Hwang, "The Six-Party Talks: Keeping Diplomacy Alive", The DPRK briefing Book-Nautilus Institute, 23 February 2004.

[30] See Jacob Bercovitch, *Studies in International Mediation*, New York: Palgrave Macmillan, 2002, p. 19.

INDEX

A

B

C

D

E

F

G

H

I

J

K

L

P

Q

R

S

T